# A GENERAL VIEW

OF THE

## ORIGIN AND NATURE

OF THE

## Constitution and Government of the United States,

DEDUCED FROM THE

## POLITICAL HISTORY AND CONDITION

OF THE

## COLONIES AND STATES, FROM 1774 UNTIL 1788.

AND

## *The Decisions of the Supreme Court of the United States.*

TOGETHER WITH

Opinions in the Cases decided at January Term, 1837,

ARISING ON THE

**Restraints on the Powers of the States.**

———————

## BY HENRY BALDWIN,

One of the Associate Justices of the Supreme Court of the United States.

———————

## THE LAWBOOK EXCHANGE, LTD.
### Clark, New Jersey

ISBN 978-1-58477-098-5

Lawbook Exchange edition 2000, 2022

*The quality of this reprint is equivalent to the quality of the original work.*

## THE LAWBOOK EXCHANGE, LTD.

33 Terminal Avenue
Clark, New Jersey 07066-1321

*Please see our website for a selection of our other publications
and fine facsimile reprints of classic works of legal history:*
www.lawbookexchange.com

**Library of Congress Cataloging-in-Publication Data**

Baldwin, Henry, 1780-1844.
   A general view of the origin and nature of the Constitution and government of the
   United States : deduced from the political history and condition of the colonies and states
   .../by Henry Baldwin.
      p. cm.
   Originally published: Philadelphia : Printed by J.C. Clark, 1837.
   Includes bibliographical references and index.
   ISBN 1-58477-098-8 (Cloth : alk. paper)
   1. Constitutional history—United States.  I. Title.

KF4541 .B2 2000
342.73'029—dc21                                                                                        00-026728

*Printed in the United States of America on acid-free paper*

# A GENERAL VIEW

OF THE

## ORIGIN AND NATURE

OF THE

## Constitution and Government of the United States,

DEDUCED FROM THE

## POLITICAL HISTORY AND CONDITION

OF THE

## COLONIES AND STATES, FROM 1774 UNTIL 1788.

AND

## *The Decisions of the Supreme Court of the United States.*

TOGETHER WITH

## Opinions in the Cases decided at January Term, 1837,

ARISING ON THE

## Restraints on the Powers of the States.

———

## BY HENRY BALDWIN,

One of the Associate Justices of the Supreme Court of the United States.

———

## PHILADELPHIA:

PRINTED BY JOHN C. CLARK, 60 DOCK STREET.

1837.

## NOTE.

This volume was intended as a supplement to the eleventh volume of Peters' United States Supreme Court Reports. See page 113.

# INDEX

## THE PRINCIPAL MATTERS.

---

Adjudications in the courts in England since the revolution, their weight and effect, 3, 46.
Alliance between the states; nature and effect thereof, 59, 79, 186.
    Treaty of, with France; its nature and effect, 80, 86.
Allies in a war, rule as to acquisitions made by, 87.
Articles of confederation, nature and defects of, 11, 61, 66, 79, 105.

Bank notes and bank bills, distinction between, 119, 121.
Bills of credit, what are and what not, 114, 119, 122, 127.
Boundaries between provinces, how settled, 177.
    between states; agreements and compacts relating thereto, by the constitution, 170, 173, 174, 178.

Cessions of power and territory by states, 83.
Charters, violation of, a grievance of the colonies, 5, 139.
    protected by the constitution, 138, 140.
    to the colonies and proprietaries, 49.
Colonies, their connection with England, and political condition, till the declaration of independence, 26, 49, 61, 63, 70, 72.
Colonial governments, their nature and powers, 26, 50, 68, 141.
Commerce, extent of the power to regulate, 69, 181, 184, 185.
    its limitations, 182, 187.
Common law, the law of the colonies and states, 3.
    its rules in construing laws, grants, &c. 8.
Congress, how composed under the constitution, 32.
    powers of, within the states, 83, 95, 98, 183.
    powers of, within the territories, dock yards, &c. 85, 87, 98.
    proceedings of, before July 4, 1776, 4, 26, 59, 68.
    proceedings of, from 1776 till 1787, 77.
    consent of, to state laws, 172, 174.
Constitution of the United States, its nature and obligation, 11, 23, 29, 44, 66, 83, 101, 104, 137, 140
    how adopted, and by what people, 12, 17, 19, 24, 29, 32.
    rules for its construction, 3, 7, 9, 20, 43, 47, 99, 102, 104, 118, 129, 185.
    construction of particular parts thereof, 129, 185, 190.
    different constructions thereof, 2, 36, 100, 126.
    its practical effect and operation, 20.
    amendments thereto, 13, 18, 24, 45.
    exceptions, prohibitions, and reservations, 44, 64.
Constitutions of states, how formed, 18, 25, 29, 31, 32, 70, 75, 81.
Constitution of England, 4, 7, 51.
    compared with those of the United States, 53, 54.
Contracts, obligation of, inviolable by state law, 48, 128, 137, 140.
    what impairs and what not, 129, 131, 141, 176.

Corporations of government, 51, 82, 84, 138.
       private, rights of, 42, 136, 139, 140.
Conventions, of the states of England, 56.
       of the states of this Union, 12, 35, 59, 66.
Crown lands, to whom they belonged after the revolution, 49, 66, 75, 86.

Declaration of rights at the revolution in England, 43.
       of rights by the colonies and congress, 14, 26, 68.
       of independence, its effects on the political condition of the several states,
          28, 72, 75, 78.

Exceptions, in deeds and grants, how construed, 64, 171.

Ferries, right of, defined, and grants thereof, 150, 151, 153.
       nature, extent, and construction of, 156, 163, 168.
Franchise, corporate, what are, 136.
       of port markets, fairs, ferries, their extent, &c. 154, 157.

Government, federal law organized and administered, 20, 25, 33.
       its powers, nature and extent thereof, 22, 24, 66, 81, 183, 192.
       of states, their powers and restraints thereon, 14, 43, 88, 89, 186
       of territories, how organized, and powers, 85, 88, 91.
Grants, by prerogative or by government, how construed, 142, 143, 148, 164.
       to charitable or public use, 142, 143.
       for private benefit, 143, 144.
       of franchises on public highways and rivers, 142, 144, 146, 152.
       of franchises on private property, 146, 151.
       ancient, or charters, how construed, 43, 44.
       of franchises by prescription, on what founded, 164, 165.
       consideration of, and when void, 152, 155, 157, 161, 166.
       how proved, and their extent, 146, 149, 153, 154, 165.
       when exclusive, or may be concurrent, 157, 163, 165, 167.

Health laws, power of states to pass, 184.

Inspection laws, extent of the power of states to pass, 170, 184, 187.
       control of congress over, 189, 194.
Internal police of states, by whom to be regulated, 69, 182
       what is, 187, 194, 196.

Jurisdiction of states defined, and its extent, 88, 186.
       cession of, 66, 83, 87, 88, 93, 97.
       of federal and state governments, 183 to 196.

King, nature and extent of prerogative, 52, 53, 142, 165

Land in colonies, the absolute propriety thereof, 49.
Laws of states, when subject to revision and control by congress, 170, 189, 191
       when void and when valid, 185, 188.

Magna charta, the law of the colonies, 4, 6.
       its provisions, 77, 137, 139.

New states, how admitted into the Union, 22, 90, 92.

Ordinance of 1787, its provisions and effect, 5, 88, 90.

Paupers, power of a state to prevent their introduction, 185, 194.
People of the United States, the term defined, 31, 44.
       how they acted in adopting the constitution, 18, 31, 36
       by what people it was adopted, 30, 32, 82, 97
       how a people act in their " aggregate collective capacity," 32, 52, 60, 67
       how they acted before 1787, 81.
       how represented under the constitution, 33, 55.
Powers, prerogative of the states, 75, 143.
       reserved to the states by the constitution, 45, 171, 183

Powers, implied or constructive, their nature and effect, 38, 41, 102, 170*b*, 193.
       necessary and proper to carry into effect granted powers, 105, 182, 189.
       extent of enumerated powers of, granted to congress, 170*b*.
Population of the United States, how represented, 20, &c.
Preamble to the constitution, meaning and construction thereof, 30, 37, 61, 97.
Prerogative powers in the United States, how considered, 53, 55.
Prescription, grants by, defined, 165.
       to what estate they attach, 165.
Presumption in favour of the validity of state laws, 147, 162.
Prohibitions on states by the constitution, nature and effect thereof, 116, 170, 172, 187.

Reservation in a grant, nature and effect thereof, 45, 65.
       of powers in tenth amendment, to whom made, 64.
       its effect in the construction of the constitution, 19, 45, 64, 98, 103, 161, 192.

States, defined, 13, 16.
       confederation between, 16, 24.
       political situation of, during the revolution, the confederation, and under
         the constitution, 13, 14, 71, 83.
       boundaries and territory thereof, 87.
       how represented in congress, 33.

Territory, original right of, in whom vested, 66, 75, 86, 88, 93, 95.
       how it became vested in the United States, 87, 88, 91, 94, 97.
Treaty of peace with England, its operation and effect, 72, 86, 87.
       construction of treaties, 83, 172.

United States, the term defined, 13, 85.
       boundaries thereof, 86, 170*c*.

## ERRATA.

p. 7,  line 7 from top, for via tuta read *via trita*.
p. 7,  „  20 from bottom, for ex humo read ex *fumo*
p. 8,  „  5  „  for 1 Ser. read 1 *Lev.*
p. 8,  „  4  „  for 10 Ch 340, read 10 *Co.* 34. *b.*
p. 16, „  2  „  for or to make, read *as* to make.
p. 24, last line, for rates, read *ratio*.
p. 30, line 22 from top, for these United, read *the* United
p. 31,  „  7 from bottom, for ex risuribus, read ex *visceribus.*
p. 62, last line, for federar, read *fœdera.*
p. 64, line 5 from top, for vestion, read *question.*
p. 93,  „  11 from bottom, add, after devolution, *the rights of.*
p. 125,  „  3 from top, for 1770, read 1777.
p. 129,  „  3 from bottom, for exclusive, read *excessive.*
p. 130.  „  22 from top, for inefficient, read *efficient.*
p. 152,  „  17 from bottom, for toll throrough, read toll *thorough.*
p. 157, „  3  „  for 3 Ser. read 3 *Lev.*
p. 194,  „  15 from top, for such cause, read *just* cause.

# A GENERAL VIEW, &c.

---

If there are any cases, in which the judges of a Court of the last resort may, without apology, present the grounds of their judgment in detail, they are those which arise on an alleged repugnance between a law or act of a state, and the constitution of the United States. There are none which deserve such minute examination of fundamental principles, which bear on the grants and restrictions of powers, and when developed, impose their uniform applications under higher obligations, than those which rest upon this Court, and all its members. In such cases, it is peculiarly necessary to recur to safe principles, to sustain them, and when sustained, to make them the tests of the arguments to be examined; these principles are few and simple, and though somewhat obscured by too much refinement upon them, can be easily ascertained by the same mode in which we find the principles of other machines, a reference to the first moving power which gives the impulse to government.

As my opinions, on constitutional questions, are founded on a course of investigation different from that which is usually taken, I cannot in justice to myself, submit them to the profession without a full explanation of what may be deemed my peculiar views of the constitution. By taking it as the grant of the people of the several states, I find an easy solution of all questions arising under it; whereas, in taking it as the grant of the people of the United States in the aggregate, I am wholly unable to make its various provisions consistent with each other, or to find any safe rule of interpreting them separately. In a matter of such importance as this, I cannot *assume* a proposition on which all my opinions depend, but must establish it by all the authority that can be brought to support it, against opposing opinions of great weight, and which are those most commonly received. Without doing this, my premises would be at once declared unfounded, and my conclusions of course erroneous; it is therefore necessary for me to take this course, or withhold any publication of my opinions.

HENRY BALDWIN.

---

Briscoe and others v. The Commonwealth Bank of Kentucky.

Proprietors of Charles River Bridge v. Proprietors of Warren Bridge.

Poole and others v. Lessee of Fleeger and others.

The Mayor, &c. of New York v. Miln.

Though none of the judges who have concurred with the majority of the Court in their judgment in these cases, have delivered any separate opinion; and though, having been more anxious as to the result, than the course of reasoning, the illustrations or authority which led to it, it was my intention to have been content with a silent concurrence; yet reasons which have since occurred, have determined me to present my views in each case to the profession. In all of them the result has accorded with my opinions, formed when the cases were first presented for our decision at former terms, and my most deliberate judgment at the present; but in this respect my situation is peculiar, as none of the judges who sat during the former arguments, concur in all the present opinions of the majority. In the case of the Commonwealth Bank of Kentucky, I was in the minority; in the Charles River Bridge case, it now appears that I stood alone after the argument in 1831; the Tennessee Boundary Case hung in doubtful scales; and in the New York Case, I was one of a bare majority. By changes of judges and of opinions, there is now but one dissentient in three of the cases; and though my opinion still differs from that of three of my brethren, who sat in the fourth, six years ago, it is supported by the three who have since been appointed. Placed in a position as peculiar now as it was then and since, I feel called upon to defend it, and to explain the reasons why it was then assumed and is now retained.

In the fiftieth year after the frame of the constitution had been agreed on in convention, and submitted to the people for their ratification, this Court was called upon to decide four constitutional questions of deep interest; which had been long depending, and which neither counsel or judges deemed to have been settled by any authoritative exposition of those parts of the constitution that bore directly upon them, or came within any established principles and rules of construction of this Court which would govern them.

These questions were, 1st, What is a contract—its obligations, and what impairs it? 2d, What are bills of credit? 3d, What is commerce with foreign nations—what is not; and what is the internal police of a state? 4th, What is the effect of a compact of boundary, made between two states, with the consent of congress? On all of which there had long been, and continued to be, great diversity of opinion among the judges; which did not cease to exist after they were decided, and may exist in future, when the same or similar questions shall occur.

It had long been to me a subject of deep regret, that notwithstanding the numerous, consistent, most solemn, and, (with some few, and mostly late exceptions,) to my mind most satisfactory adjudications of this Court, in expounding the constitution, its meaning yet remains as unsettled, in political, professional, and judicial opinion, as it was immediately after its adoption. If one is to judge of the next, by the results of the past half century, there is but a slight assurance that that instrument will be better understood at the expiration, than it is at the beginning of the period. It is indeed to be feared, that unless some mode of interpretation, different from what has been usually pursued in argument, is adopted; the present uncertainty must become utter confusion. In reviewing the course of argument on both sides in these cases, the remark is fully justified, that we have been referred for the true interpretation of the constitution to books, essays, arguments, opinions, speeches, debates in conventions and legislative bodies, by jurists and statesmen, and by some who were neither; which would not be offered, or suffered to be read in any court, as entitled to respect in construing an ordinary act of legislation, or a contract between individuals. This reference has not been confined to expositions cotemporaneous or near to the time of the adoption of the constitution, the views of its framers, or those opinions to which courts of justice can consistently with their duty defer their own; but the range has been of the widest kind, embracing whatever has appeared in print on the various subjects involved, either here or abroad, and up to the present time, while these suits have been depending in this Court for re-argument. The history and spirit of the times, past and present, admonish us that new versions of the constitution will be promulgated, to meet the ever varying course of political events, or aspirations of power; and that if we suffer our judgments to be influenced by what has been pressed upon us as authority for present adjudication, we must pay the same respect to the same kind of authority, when future opinions shall be formed, and new expositions be announced. We have listened to the disquisitions of late writers on the constitution of England, to the decisions of their courts, nay, to the opinions of their judges given within the last year; as rules to guide us to the true intention of the framers of the constitution, in a most solemn instrument, carefully and most deliberately reduced to writing, in 1787. If we look to these as safe sources whence to now draw our knowledge of constitutional law, or respect them as a rule of present decision, they must be so taken in future; and though the *legislative* authority of Westminster-hall over us has been extinct for more than sixty years, this tribunal must continue to still look to its emanations, whether in treatises or judicial decrees, to ascertain the meaning of our own supreme law. I have long since been convinced that there are better and safer guides to professional and judicial inquiries after truth, on constitutional questions, than those which have been so often resorted to, without effecting the desired result; a clear and settled understanding of the terms and provisions of an instrument of writing, which operates with supreme authority wherever it applies. To me it seems that it can be made intelligible in all its parts, by applying to it those established rules and maxims of the common law, in the construction of statutes, and those accepted definitions of words, terms, and language, in which they had been used, and been received, as well known and understood, in their ordinary, or legal sense, according to the subject matter. In appealing to the common law, as the standard of exposition, in all doubts as to the meaning of written instruments; there is safety, certainty, and authority. The institutions of the colonies were based upon it; it was their system of jurisprudence, with only local exceptions, to suit the condition of the colonists, who claimed it as their birth-right and inheritance, 9 Cr. 333, in its largest sense, as including the whole system of English jurisprudence, 1 Gall. 493; the inexhaustible fountain from which we draw our laws, 9 S. & R. 330, 39, 58. So it continued after the colonies became states, in most of which the common law was adopted by acts of assembly, which gave it the force of a statute, from the time of such adoption, and as it was then; so that in the language of this Court—" At the adoption of the constitution, there were no states in this Union, the basis of whose jurisprudence was not essentially, that of the common law in its widest meaning; and probably no states were contemplated, in which it would not exist." 3 Pet. 446, 8. It is also the basis on which the federal system of jurisprudence was erected by the constitution, the judiciary and process acts, which refer to " *cases in law and in equity,*" " *suits at common law,*" " *the common law, the principles and usages of law,*" as they had at the time been defined and settled in England; 5 Cr. 222; 3 Wh. 221; 4 Wh. 115, 16; 7 Wh. 45; 10 Wh. 29, 32, 56, 8; 1 Pet. 613: and were adopted as then understood by the old states.

From the very beginning, till the consummation of the revolution, the people of the colonies and states, in all successive congresses, took their stand upon the common law and constitution of England, as the " heirs of freedom;" " English freemen, whose custom it is, derived from their ancestors, to make those tremble who dare to think of making them miserable." 1 Journ. Cong. 60, 65, 138. In the spirit and like the descendants of Britain, ib. 143, 9, who procured " the inestimable advantages of a free English constitution of government, which it is the privilege of all English subjects to enjoy." " Englishmen reared up this fabric," " of such strength as for ages to defy time, treachery, internal and foreign wars." " They gave the people of their colonies the form of their own government." " In this form, the first grand right is, that of the people having a share in their own government, by their representatives chose by themselves," &c. 1 Journ. 56. It is a bulwark defending their property, as trial by jury and the writ of habeas corpus defends their liberty; " as a part of our mild system of government, that sending its equitable energies through all classes and ranks of men; defends the poor from the rich, the weak from the powerful, the industrious from the rapacious, the peaceable from the violent, the tenants from the lords, and all from their superiors." " These are the rights without which a people cannot be free and happy, and under the protecting and encouraging influence of which, these colonies have hitherto so amazingly flourished and increased. These are the rights a profligate ministry are now striving by force of arms to ravish from us, and which we are, with one mind, resolved never to resign but with our lives." Ib. 56, 57. The very rights which placed the crown of Great Britain on the heads of the three princes of the house of Hanover, 170. Such was " the equitable system of English laws," ib. 30, 41, 50; " the inheritance left us by our forefathers," 66; " the great bulwark of our constitution," 148; " the first and best maxims of the constitution, venerable to Britons and to Americans," 163; " whose forefathers participated in the rights and liberties they boasted of, and conveyed the same fair inheritance to them. By that system the colonists claimed all the benefits secured to English subjects, whether they lived "3000, or 300 miles from the royal palace," 37; and the several colonies as *constituent members* of the British empire, rested for "the perfect security of their natural and civil rights, on the salutary and constitutional principles" it contained, 61. It was "the covenant chain" between the mother country and them; the charters of the king were their written civil constitutions of government, and the colonies would not part with, or loose their hold of this old covenant chain which united their fathers; 153, 4.

On this system, the congress, the people, and the colonies relied. They claimed as their indubitable right, the benefit of the common law of England, its constitution, and their several charters; in their Declaration of Rights, in 1774; 1 Journ. 77, &c.; in July, 1775; 1 Journ. 134, 176, 8; in December, 1775; ib. 263; and on the 4th July, 1776. Among the other grievances set forth in the Declaration of Independence, are the following: "He," (the king,) "has combined with others to subject us to a jurisdiction foreign to our constitution, and unacknowledged by our laws, giving his assent to their acts of pretended legislation," &c. &c.

"For abolishing the free system of English laws in a neighbouring province." Vide 1 Journ. 30, 58, 9, 64, 61, 174.

"For taking away our charters, abolishing our most valuable laws, and altering fundamentally the forms of our government." 1 Laws, 8, 9; 1 Journ. 125, 178.

The common law was not merely the basis of the revolution, in opposing the oppression of England, or deemed incompatible with the genius of the people after the revolution was effected, as a burthen imposed upon them; but the contrary. By the ordinance of 1787, it was declared to be "the basis whereon these republics, their laws, and constitutions, are *erected;* and which congress therein fixed and established, as the basis of all laws, constitutions, and governments, which forever hereafter shall be formed in the territory north-west of the Ohio. It was secured to them as a blessing whereby "to extend the fundamental principles of civil and religious liberty;" "that the inhabitants shall always be entitled to the benefits of," &c. and "of judicial proceedings according to the course of the common law." 1 Laws U. S. 479. That system, which had effected in England, what it was one of the declared objects of the present constitution to effect—"*to establish justice,*" and "secure the blessings of liberty to ourselves and our posterity, by the judicial power of the United States; which shall be vested in one supreme court, and in such inferior courts as the congress shall from time to time ordain and establish." To be administered in all cases in law or equity, as it had been, and then was in England, in all the states and territories of the United States: and the judges were directed, by the judiciary act, to take an oath "to do equal right to the poor and to the rich;" 1 Story, 56; as the judges in England had been enjoined by an ancient statute; 1 Ruff, 246.

In thus recurring to the source of those great principles, on which all our governments are founded, it is clear that they must be traced beyond the instrument which created them, to that great charter of English liberty, which embodied the common law; and from 1774, to 1787, was equally revered by the Britons of both continents. The great men of the revolution, in their first meeting in congress, on the 5th September, 1774, and in their proceedings till the 26th October, when "the congress then dissolved itself;" did not merely declare in their resolutions and letters, on what ground they stood in asserting the rights of the people and colonies, but pointed to it as their rallying point. To the journal published by their order, and verified by the autograph of their secretary, is prefixed, in the title page; a medallion of which the following is a fac simile.

The magna charta of England, was the pedestal on which the co-lumn and cap of liberty was raised, supported by the twelve colonies, assembled by their delegates; declaring that " on this we rely," " this we will defend."

In looking too to the names of the members of that congress,* six of whom, thirteen years afterwards, in a convention of twelve

---

* A number of the delegates, chosen and appointed by the several colonies and provinces in North America, to meet and hold a congress at Philadelphia, assembled at the Carpenters' Hall. Present, *From New Hampshire*, Major *John Sullivan*, Col. Nathaniel Fulsom, Esqs. *From Massachusetts-Bay*, Hon. Thomas Cushing, Samuel Adams, John Adams, Robert Treat Paine, Esqs. *From Rhode-Island and Providence Plantations*, Hon. Stephen Hopkins, Hon. Samuel Ward, Esqs. *From Connecticut*, Hon. Eliphalet Dyer, Silas Deane, Hon. *Roger Sherman*, Esqs. *From the City and County of New York, and other counties in the province of New York*, James Duane, John Jay, Philip Livingston, Isaac Low, Esqs. *From the county of Suffolk, in the province of New York*, Col. William Floyd, Esq. *From New Jersey*, James Kinsey, *William Livingston*, John Dehart, Stephen Crane, Richard Smith, Esqs. *From Pennsylvania*, Hon. Joseph Galloway, Samuel Rhoads, *Thomas Mifflin*, Charles Humphreys, John Morton, Edward Biddle, Esqs. *From New Castle, Kent, and Sussex, in Delaware*, Hon. Cæsar Rodney, Thomas M'Kean, *George Read*, Esqs. *From Maryland*, Robert Goldsborough, William Paca, Samuel Chase, Esqs. *From Virginia*, Hon. Peyton Randolph, *George Washington*, Patrick Henry, Richard Bland, Benjamin Harrison, Edmund Pendleton, Esqs. *From South Carolina*, Henry Middleton, *John Rutledge*, Christopher Gadsden, Thomas Lynch, Edward Rutledge, Esqs. 1 Journ. Cong. 35, 36.

of those colonies, then states, signed the proposed constitution; I
find a weight of political authority, which my mind cannot resist:
and so feel bound to trace the great work of the fathers of the revolution and the country, back to its source in the common law, the
magna charta, and constitution of England; the basis and pattern of
our own. In so doing, I feel well assured that in following their
*" via tuta,"* by which the constitution was established, and has consummated all its beneficent purposes, there will be found a *" via
tuta,"* to my judgment, on its true meaning in these parts that bear
on the cases which have been before us for adjudication. I shall do
it without the aid of any commentator, except this Court, as the
sworn interpreter, appointed by the constitution itself, not only to
expound the meaning of its provisions, but to pronounce final judgment on their results, on " all cases in law and equity arising under"
it. Nor shall I consult any other commentaries upon it than those
which are found in the opinions of the Court; delivered, with few exceptions, by the late venerated Chief Justice.

In thus adhering to the old maxim, *" Sed melius et tutius est,
petere fontes, quam sectare rivulos,"* I am well aware of departing
from the modern mode of construing our ancient charters, and grants
of governments; but if it should lead to their true interpretation, I
may be permitted to ask of those who may have the patience to read
and consider the general views of the constitution, herein presented
to explain the grounds of my concurring judgment in these cases,
*" Si quid novisti, rectius istis candide imperti, si non hic utere
mecum?"* In the full conviction, that by this mode of investigating
constitutional questions, there will be found standard rules by which
to measure the different parts of the supreme law, and extract its
true intentions, and that any other mode will be an abortive attempt,
*" ex humo dare lucem;"* I proceed to give my general views.
Taking it as already apparent, that in 1774, and 1776, *our* constitution was the *English constitution,* and the *free system of English
laws* was the *common law* then; and that system to yet be the law
of the land, by the authority of the states, the constitution, the acts
of congress, and the adjudications of this Court. It is in this law,
that we find the rules of interpretation of acts of assembly and of
congress; of public and private grants, charters, compacts, contracts;
and to which we resort, as the standard by which to make our decisions in all cases, where it has not been altered by established
usage, or legislative power. I know no other guide which is safer,
which better conducts the mind to certainty; nor do I feel at liberty
to follow any other than the principles of the common law, that are
well established and applicable to a case arising under the constitution, and which turns upon its interpretation; their adoption has been,
in my judgment, most clearly made by every authority which can
impose the obligation of obedience. My course then will be, to first
ascertain what are the settled rules and principles of the common
law, in the exposition of writings, public and private, in the definition of terms and language, used to denote the meaning and inten-

tion of those who made the instrument, and of the instrument itself, as the deliberate, written, agreed intention therein expressed. When thus ascertained, they will be applied to those parts of the constitution, which bear on the subject matters of these cases, as this Court has heretofore applied them: and believing that my opinion in each of these cases, is in perfect consistency with the former adjudications on kindred subjects, they will be referred to in their aid, with no other qualification than that the authority of those adjudications shall be deemed no farther binding than the Court itself has declared. "This opinion is confined to the case actually under consideration." 4 Wh. 207. "It is a maxim not to be disregarded, that general expressions in any opinion, are to be taken in connection with the case in which those expressions are used. If they go beyond the case, they may be respected, but ought not to control the judgment in a subsequent suit, when the very point is presented. The reason of this maxim is obvious. The question actually before the Court, is investigated with care and considered in its full extent. Other principles which may serve to illustrate it, are considered in their relation to the case decided; but their possible bearing on all other cases, is seldom completely investigated." 6 Wh. 399, 400. "Having such cases only in its view, the Court lays down a principle which is generally correct in terms, much broader than the decision, and not only much broader than the reasoning with which that decision is supported, but in some instances contradictory to its principle." Ib. 40; S. P. 12, Wh. 273, 333. Thus qualified, the judgments of this Court will be taken as the rule for mine, as to the principles and reasoning on which they are founded: but as to terms or names which are used for designation merely, I shall consider them as not affecting the substance of the subject matter referred to by the Court in using them, in a literal, or figurative sense.

The fundamental rule of construction, is to ascertain the intention of a law, a grant, charter, or contract in writing. "If the law expresses the sense of the legislature on the existing law, as plainly as a declaratory act, and expresses it in terms capable of effecting the object; the words ought to receive this construction. If this interpretation of the words should be too free for a judicial tribunal; yet if the legislature has made it, and explained its own meaning too unequivocally to be mistaken, courts may be justified in adopting that meaning." 12 Wh. 148 to 150. Laws and acts which tend to public utility, should receive the most liberal and benign interpretation to effect the object intended or declared, *est res majis valeat quam pereat;* 1 Bl. Com. 89; so as to make the *private* yield to the *public* interest, and in favour of public institutions, and all establishments of piety, charity, education, and public improvement; 11 Co. 70 to 78; Hob. 97, 122, 157; 1 Ser. 55; Dy. 255; 5 Co. 14, b.; 10 Co. 28, a; 9 Cr. 331; 3 Pet. 140, 481; 6 Pet. 436, 7; 10 Ch. 340. Courts will look to the provisions of a law to discover its objects, to meet its intention at the time it was made, which they will not suffer to be defeated; it will be sought in the cause and necessity of making the law, the meaning thus extracted, will be taken to be the law intended, as fully as if expressed in its letter; and a thing which is within the letter, but not within the intention of the law maker, is not within the statute. 1 Bl. Com. 60; 15 Johnson's Reports, 380; 14 Mass. 92, 3; 5 Wh. 94; 12 Wh. 151, 2; 6 Pet. 644.

" When the whole context demonstrates a particular intent in the legislature, to effect a certain object, some degree of implication may be called in to effect it." 6 Cr. 314; 1 Bl. Com. 92. The whole statute, and those on similar subjects, as the context, will be taken in aid, according to the apparent meaning of their provisions. 1 Bl. Com. 60; 1 Pick. 154, 5. The history and situation of the country will be referred to, to ascertain the reason and meaning of a provision, so as to enable the Court to apply the rule of construction. 1 Wh. 121; 4 Pet. 432. In doubtful cases, the title and preamble will be resorted to, to explain the law. 3 Wh. 631; 4 S. & R. 166. The old law, the mischief, and the remedy, will be examined, and the new law be so far expounded as to suppress the mischief, and advance the remedy. 11 Co. 72, &c.; 1 Bl. Com. 87; according to the subject matter. 1 Bl. Com. 229.

As the meaning and intention of the legislature when thus ascertained, is the law itself, the rule of action prescribed by legislative power, it follows necessarily, that such intention must be referred to the time of its enactment; and the terms and language used to express the intention, must be taken as then understood by those who so employed them, and not according to any subsequent definition or acceptation, varying from their then settled received meaning. 1 Bl. Com. 59, 60.

There is another source from which the intention of a law can be truly extracted, the condition of the country. 6 Wh. 416. Its usages and customs. 6 Pet. 714; 12 Wh. 437. The settled course of judicial or professional opinion. 5 Cr. 33; 2 Pet. 85; and legislative usage. 3 Dall. 398; 2 Pet. 656, 7; because these matters enter necessarily into the minds of the law makers, in any new provisions which can affect them. It is also an universal rule in this country, that, when an English statute, or any of its provisions or terms, have been adopted here, that its settled construction at the time of its adoption, is taken with it; but a contrary construction afterwards made, is not regarded. 5 Pet. 280, 1.

An adherence to these rules is called for, by the highest considerations in the construction of the constitution; if they are not followed, there are none others which a Court is at liberty to adopt, as the indiciæ of the intention of the members of the general convention which framed, and the state conventions who ratified it. Hence these rules have, by universal consent, been applied to the laws of all the states and of the Union, in their respective courts: and if not applied to that law, which is a rule of supreme authority over the legislatures and courts of both; human ingenuity, reasoning and learning, will only serve to make it the more unintelligible, as the period of its adoption becomes more distant; and time shall develope new theories or exigencies, which will make it still more obscure, by new readings, commentaries, and expositions. That those which have been hitherto applied to its construction, even those of this Court, have been insufficient to settle its meaning; is but too apparent in those questions now before us for adjudication, and those numerous ones which agitate and excite other tribunals and the country. Discarding all rules of interpretation, which are inconsistent with those which it has applied to the constitution, I shall follow in the path defined by this Court, and take that instrument, as it has declared it to have been intended by its framers, *to endure for ages to come;* 1 Wh. 326; 4 Wh. 415; *and designed to approach immortality,* as nearly as human institutions can approach it. 6 Wh. 387. A law of supreme obligation, made for the purposes it declares, Ib. 381; by enlightened patriots; men, whose intentions required no concealment, employing words which most directly and aptly expressed the idea *they* intended to convey, as well as *the people* who adopted it; must be understood to have employed words, *in their natural sense, and to have intended what they said.* "If any doubts exist, respecting the extent of any given power, it is a settled rule that the objects for which it is given, especially those which are expressed, should have great influence in the construction. The rule is given in the language of the instrument which confers the powers, taken in connection with its purposes." 9 Wh. 188, 9. "The words are to be taken in their natural and obvious sense, not in a sense unreasonably restricted or enlarged," 1 Wh. 326; "not that *enlarged* construction, which would extend words beyond their natural and obvious import; nor that *narrow* construction, which, in support of some theory, not to be found in the constitution, would cripple the government, and render it incompetent to the objects of its institution." 9. Wh. 188. "Its spirit is to be respected not less than its letter, yet the spirit is to be collected chiefly by the words." Where they conflict with each other, where different clauses bear upon each other, and would be inconsistent, unless the natural and common import of words be varied, construction becomes necessary; and a departure from the obvious meaning of words is justifiable. But if the plain meaning of a provision is to be disregarded, when not contradicted by any other provision in the same instrument, because we believe the framers could not have intended what they say; it must be one, in which the absurdity and injustice of applying the provision to the case, would be so monstrous, that all mankind would unite in rejecting the application. 4 Wh. 262, 3; 1 Bl. Com. 61. S. P.

It is proper to take a view of the literal meaning of the words to be expounded, of their connection with other words, and of the general objects to be accomplished by the prohibitory clause, or by the grant of power. 12 Wh. 437. The intention must prevail: it must be collected from the words of the instrument, which are to be understood in that sense in which they are generally used by those for whom the instrument was intended. Its provisions are not to be construed into insignificance, nor extended to objects not contemplated by its framers, or comprehended in it. 12 Wh. 332. It was not intended to use language, which would convey to the eye one idea, and, after deep reflection, impress on the mind another. 4 Wh. 420. Words must be taken in connection with those with which they are associated. 4. Wh. 418. The whole clause or sentence is to be taken together, and the intention collected from the whole. 12 Wh. 334. Every part of the article must be taken into view; and that construction adopted, which will consist with its words, and promote its general intention. The Court will not give affirmative words a negative operation, where it will defeat the intention, but may imply it, where the implication promotes the intention. 6 Wh. 398.

### THE CONSTITUTION IS A GRANT.

The circumstances under which the constitution was formed, the history of the times, the mischiefs of the confederation, and the motives which operated on the statesmen of the day, are also to be considered, in ascertaining the meaning of the constitution; which was intended to change a system, the full pressure of which was known and felt, by superseding the confederation, and substituting a new government, organized with substantive powers, to act directly on the subjects of their delegated powers, instead of through the instrumentality of state governments. 6 Wh. 308; 12 Wh. 438, 9; 1 Wh. 332.

This change was effected by the constitution, which, in the language of this Court, is a *grant*. "The grant does not convey power, which might be beneficial to the grantor, if retained by himself, or which can move solely to the benefit of the grantee; but is an *investment* of power for the general advantage, in the hands of *agents*, selected for that purpose, which power can never be exercised by the people themselves, but must be placed in the hands of *agents* or lie dormant," 9. Wh. 189. The language of the constitution is the same. "All *legislative powers* herein *granted*, shall be vested in a congress of the United States," &c. " *The executive power* shall be *vested* in a president of the United States of America." " *The judicial power* of the United States shall be *vested* in one Supreme Court."

Here then, there is something visible to the judicial eye, tangible by judicial minds, reasoning, illustration, and analogy; intelligible by judicial rules and maxims, which, through all time, have prescribed its nature, effect, and meaning. It is *a grant, by a grantor, to a grantee*, of the *things granted;* which are, *legislative, executive*, and *judicial power, vested by a constituent*, in *agents*, for the enumerated purposes and objects of the grant. It declares the grantor and constituent, to be " *the people of the United States*," who, for the purposes set forth, "ordained and established" it as a "constitution for the United States of America;" "the supreme law of the land;" creating what its framers unanimously named, " *the federal government of these states."* Its frame was "done in convention, by the unanimous consent of the states present." The 7th article whereof declared that, "the ratification of the conventions of nine states, shall be sufficient for the establishment of this constitution, between the states so ratifying the same." And, to leave no doubt of their intention, as to what should be deemed a convention of a state, the members thereof, by the unanimous order of the convention, laid it before congress, with their opinions, that it should be submitted to *a convention of delegates* chosen *in each state,* by *the people thereof,* under the recommendation of its legislatures, for their assent and ratification. 1 Vol. Laws U. S. 70, 71. No language can be more plain and clear, than the words of the constitution; nor can the in-tention of its framers more definitely appear, than by the unanimous order of the convention, submitting it to the old congress, under whose resolution the members had been appointed by the federal states. The intention of congress is equally manifest, in their unani-mous resolution, adopted after receiving "the report of the conven-tion, lately assembled in Philadelphia, in the words following: (the constitution) "That the said report, with the resolutions and letter accompanying the same, be transmitted to the several legislatures, in order to be submitted to a convention of delegates, chosen in *each state,* by *the people thereof,* in conformity to the resolves of the convention, made and provided in that case. 1 Laws, 59, 60. But this coincidence of the words of the constitution, with the expressed and unanimous declaration of the members of the convention, and the congress, is neither the only nor most satisfactory mode, by which to identify the *grantor,* who conveyed the powers invested by the grant; and the *constituent,* who appointed the appropriate agents for their execution by delegation.

There are other objects of the grant, besides the delegated powers of agency; the grant imposes conditions, limitations, prohibitions, and makes exceptions on the exercise of the powers of the states, and the people thereof; which form an all important part of that supreme law, which declares, that "the *judges in every state* shall be bound thereby, any thing in the *constitution* or *laws* of any state, to the contrary notwithstanding."

It is therefore, a law, paramount in authority over the people of the several states, who adopted it in their conventions; supreme, as well over their supreme law, ordained by their sovereign power, as those laws enacted in the ordinary course of legislation, by dele-gated power. The effect of which is, that the constitution, the crea-ture, prescribes rules to its creator, which expressly confine its action within defined limits, and annuls all acts which are prohibited or excepted. Nay, it goes further, it imposes as a condition, that states shall not act by their own law, or compact, or agreement, with another state, without the consent of congress; which is a creature created by the grant of the people of the states, in their separate conventions : from which it necessarily results, that *this grant, this constitution, and appointment of agents,* must emanate from some power, paramount over, or from the people of the several states themselves. We search the constitution in vain, to find the existence or recognition of such power paramount; there is no function which it can perform; it can control no action by the government, or any of its departments. The whole frame of the constitution can be deranged; the structure of government, with all its powers and prohibitions, may be prostrated by amendments, save that "no state shall, without its consent, be deprived of its equal suffrage in the senate," according to the provisions of the 5th article, which require the invocation of no power, paramount to that which can operate with such force.

The powers not delegated to the United States, or prohibited to the states, are, by the tenth amendment, "reserved to the states respectively, or to the people." These terms, "*states,*" "*states respectively,*" and "*the people,*" to whom this reservation is thus made, have been defined by this Court, too clearly, and too often to be mistaken, or to remain open for discussion, while its authority is respected.

THE TERM "STATE," AND "UNITED STATES," AND "THE PEOPLE," DEFINED AND EXPLAINED.

In Fletcher v. Peck, this term is applied to *a state*, as existing independently of any restraint; "*a single sovereign power;*" and to a state as one of *the United States,* under the federal connection between them, it is thus qualified.

"But Georgia cannot be viewed as a single *unconnected* sovereign power, on whose legislature no other restrictions are imposed than may be found in its own constitution. She is a part of a large empire. She is a member of the American Union, and that Union has *a constitution*, the supremacy of which all acknowledge, and which imposes limits to the legislatures of the several states, which none claim a right to pass." 6 Cr. 136.

The political situation of the United States, anterior to the formation of the constitution, and the change effected by its adoption, is better illustrated in the language of this Court than it can be in mine.

"It has been said, that they were sovereign, were completely independent, and were connected with each other only by a league. This is true. But when these allied sovereigns converted their league into a government, when they converted their congress of ambassadors, deputed to deliberate on their common concerns, and to recommend measures of general utility, into a legislature, empowered to enact laws on the most interesting subjects; the whole character in which the states appear, underwent a change, the extent of which must be determined by a fair consideration of the instrument by which that change was effected." 9 Wh. 187. Here, then, we have a power which was *single, sovereign, and unconnected;* with a legislature unrestricted, converting a *congress* into *a federal legislature*, which was fully competent to erect it. What were names and things, had been before taught by the same instructor. "This *term* United States, designates the whole American empire." It is the *name* given to *our great republic*, composed of states and territories; 5 Wh. 514; "constituent parts of one great empire;" 6 Wh. 414; who have formed a confederated government;" 12 Wh. 334; 2 Pet. 590, 1; by the act of *the people* of the "great empire," the "great republic," the "American empire," *the United States.* "The people of *America*," "the *American* people," "the people of the *United States*," are but terms and names, to designate the grantor of the *thing*, which was thus formed, by the people, of the constituent parts; the thing, the *power* which formed it, by a thing, *this constitution*, *established* by the ratifications of nine things, conventions of *nine states*, by the people of each as *a state.*

"These states are constituent parts of the United States. They are members of one great *empire*," ("members of the American *confederacy;*" 2 Pet. 312,) "for some purposes sovereign, for some purposes subordinate." 6 Wh. 414. The political character of the several states of this Union, in relation to each other, is this: "For all *national* purposes, the states and the citizens thereof, are one; united under the same sovereign authority, and governed by the same laws. In *all other* respects the states are necessarily *foreign* to and independent of each other. "They form a *confederated* government; yet the several states retain their individual sovereignties, and with respect to their municipal regulations, are to each other sovereign." 2 Pet. 590, 1; 10 Pet. 579. S. P.; 12 Wh. 334. "The national and state systems are to be regarded as *one whole.*" 6 Wh. 419. "In America, the powers of sovereignty are divided between the government of the Union, and those of the states. They are each sovereign with respect to the objects committed to it; and neither sovereign with respect to the objects committed to the other." 4 Wh. 410.

"The powers of the states depend on their own constitution; the people of every state had the right to modify and restrain them according to their own views of policy or principle; and they remain unaltered and unimpaired, except so far as they were granted to the government of the United States. These deductions have been positively recognised by the tenth amendment." 1 Wh. 325. "The powers retained by the states, proceed not from the people of America, but from the people of the several states, and remain after the adoption of the constitution what they were before, except so far as they may be abridged by that instrument." 4 Wh. 193. S. P.; 5 Wh. 17, 54; 9 Wh. 203, 9. "In our system, the legislature of a state is the supreme power; in all cases where its action is not restrained by the constitution of the United States." 12 Wh. 347. "Its jurisdiction is coextensive with its territory, coextensive with its legislative power," 3. Wh. 387;" and "subject to this grant of power, adheres to the territory as a portion of sovereignty not yet given away." The residuary powers of legislation are still in the state. Ib. 389 "The sovereignty of a state extends to every thing which exists by its own authority, or is introduced by its permission." 6 Wh. 429; 4 Pet. 564. "The jurisdiction of the nation within its own territory, is necessarily conclusive and absolute; it is susceptible of no limitation not imposed by itself. Any restriction upon it derived from an external source, would imply a diminution of its sovereignty, to the extent of the restriction, and an investment of that sovereignty to the same extent, in that power which could impose such restriction. All exceptions therefore, to the full and complete power of a nation within its own territories, must be traced up to the consent of the nation itself. They can flow from no other legitimate source." 7 Cr. 136.

In comparing these expressions of the Court with those of the old congress, it will be seen how perfectly they accord with each other in the use of terms. "The constituent members," 1 Journ. 61; the "state," from which we derive our origin, 66; "our fellow subjects in any part of the *empire*," 138. "Societies or governments, vested with perfect legislatures, were formed under charters from the crown, and an harmonious intercourse was established between the colonies, and the *kingdom* from which they derived their origin," 134, 141: "We mean not to dissolve that union, which has so long and so happily subsisted between us," and have no design "of separating from Great Britain, and establishing independent *states*," 138. "The union between our mother country and *these colonies*," &c.; "your loyal colonists," doubted not but that they should be admitted with the rest of the *empire*," &c., 140; "the *British* empire," 141; "the *whole* empire," 147, 8; "the *state* of Great Britain;" "North America," "wishes most ardently for a lasting connection with Great Britain," 149. "America is amazed," &c., 171; "The *several* colonies of it," &c., 27; "*these* colonies;" "the English colonies in North America;" "the *respective* colonies," 159, 60; "these his majesty's colonies," 289. "The *United* Colonies of North America," 134. The colonies of North America, 139. The *twelve United Colonies*, 142, 156, 7. Twelve *ancient* colonies, 149. Twelve united provinces, viz: &c., 152. The inhabitants and colonies of *America*, 153. The united colonies of North America, &c., 168. A congress, consisting of *twelve United Colonies*, assembled, 169. The *thirteen United Colonies* in North America, 263. All these are mere names, and the different terms of designation, which mean the same thing; so as to the name and term applied to the people of a state, kingdom, empire, or colony.

"The people of America," "the good people of the several colonies of North America," &c., 27; "the inhabitants of," &c., 28; "the people;" "English colonists;" Ib. "Americans," "the people of Great Britain," "the inhabitants of British America," 30, 36, 145. "Proprietors of the soil of America," 37; "*faithful subjects* of the colonies of North America," 63; "*your* faithful *people* in America;" "your whole people," 67; "the *good people* of these colonies, 137, 139; "your *loyal colonists*," 141, 147; "the *people* of twelve *ancient colonies*," 149; "*the people* throughout all these provinces and colonies," 170, 168, 264; " the people of these united colonies," 265.

These references suffice to show how names and terms are used by statesmen and judges, by congress, and this Court. It needs no reasoning to show, that the varied phraseology in the same political act, or judicial opinion, or in different ones, at different times, cannot change the thing referred to.

There is no difficulty in defining a state or nation. It is a body politic, a political community, formed by the people within certain boundaries; who, being separated from all others, adopt certain rules for their own government, with which no people without their limits can interfere. The power of each terminates at the line of separation; each is necessarily supreme within its own limits: of consequence, neither can have any jurisdiction within the limits of another, without its consent. The name given to such community, whether state, nation, power, people, or commonwealth, is only to denote its locality, as a self-governing body of men united for their own internal purposes, if two or more think proper to unite for common purposes, and to authorize the exertion of any power over themselves, by a body composed of delegates or ambassadors of each, they confederate. Each has the undoubted right of deciding, what portion of its own power, it will authorize to be exerted in a meeting, assembly, or congress, of all; what it will restrain, prohibit, or qualify. If this can be done by common consent, the terms of their union are defined, and according to their nature, they form a mere confederacy of states, or a federal government; the purposes and powers of which depend on the instrument agreed upon. If they cannot agree, then each state instructs its delegates according to its own will, and sends them to the body in which all the states are assembled by their deputies: each state is considered as present, and its will expressed by the vote of its delegates. The congress of states are left, in such case, to perform such duties as are enjoined, and execute such powers as are given to them, by their respective and varying instructions; the extent of which is testified in the credentials of the separate delegations, as before the confederation of 1781.

It is not necessary to give efficiency to the acts of the congress, that their power be derived from one state, nation, or people; if they are authorized by each to act within their boundaries, they can act within and on the whole; this action of congress does not make the states, or the people thereof one; they remain as distinct as before any confederacy; but congress, acting as the common legislature of each, for specified purposes, its laws operate in and over each state, as state laws do for state purposes. The power exercised is derived from the same people, who distribute it between the two governments, as they may think most conducive to the welfare of each and all; the machinery is simple, one moving perpetual power directs two machines, which will operate in harmony, by the lines of separation, drawn by the same hand. But if the line and rule are placed in one hand, guided by a master spirit, with controlling power over

thirteen subordinate ones; the one declares what are federal purposes, delegates federal powers, restricts states, and prohibits state
laws, by its single sovereign power; and as to its own will and
pleasure shall seem fit.  The lines of separation between the states
are effaced; the people of all are "compounded into one mass,"
having such supreme power as they may choose to assume; leaving
the states and people in their distinct capacities, only that portion of
sovereignty which remained in them, after the paramount power had
taken to itself all it wanted; and had denied to the governments of
the state the exercise of such powers, as the government of the
Union could not use; annulling or restraining them, according to
the supreme law, which was competent to effect whatever it ordained.

If such was the power which created the constitution, then our
federal system is like the solar; one sun, with as many planets as
there are "the several states, which may be included within this
Union:" with both systems alike created and put in motion, by an
invisible, incomprehensible, but almighty power, behind and beyond
them both, which can regulate and control the movements of all, at
its sovereign will.

Such a political creation may be a sublime conception; present
" the august spectacle of an assemblage of a whole people, by their
representatives in convention;" " conscious of the plenitude of their
own proper sovereignty, declaring with becoming dignity, We, the
people of the United States, do ordain and establish this constitution
for the United States of America."  Vide 12 Wh. 354; 2 Dall.
471.

There is no American, who, in looking to the blessings which the
establishment of the constitution has diffused over the whole Union,
can repress those feelings, which, like an inspiration, carry the mind
beyond the regions of fact, to those of fancy and imagination; and no
man more than the first, and the late Chief Justice of this Court, would
give way to the effusions of their patriotism, when contemplating the
glorious results of the happy consummation of a revolution, in which
one had devoted his time and labours to his country, and the other
pledged his life for her defence.  Yet, when we descend from fancy
to fact, look to the convention, in which the people did assemble,
how they acted, what they did, the work which came finished and
perfect from their hands, and the scenes of action; there is indeed a
moral grandeur and sublimity in the whole, which impresses itself on
the mind with irresistible force.

Cool reflection, however, corrects the impressions of enthusiasm,
reason and judgment concurring with more exciting impulses, convince us; that though the occasion and the act were of imposing grandeur and dignity, august in contemplation, and sublime in its beneficent
results; yet, like the constitution, and its best expositor, that these impressions are stamped on the mind, by the simplicity, rather than
the splendour of exhibition.

## THE ADOPTION OF THE CONSTITUTION.

Twelve states met in convention by their separate delegations, to digest, reduce to form, and submit to a congress of the states, a frame of government for such of the states, as should, in conventions of the state, ratify it as their act: the frame was made, it proposed the institution of a government between the states who should adopt it, nine of whom were declared competent. These separate conventions were not to be like the general convention, composed of members appointed by *state legislatures*, with power only to propose an act to them as *their* constituents, and through them to the *people* of the state. To the proposed act was prefaced a declaration, that it was to be the act of *the people*, and a *constitution* for a government, such as it delineated. So it was submitted to congress, and by them to each state legislature, who called conventions of delegates elected by *the people of each state;* nine of these conventions separately ratified the act, in the name of the people who had authorized it; and thus the proposed frame of government was established as a constitution for those nine states, who then composed "The United States of America;" and between themselves only. The declaration, in its front, therefore, necessarily refers, not to the time when it was proposed, but when it was ordained and established, by "the ratification of the conventions of nine states," as this was done by the people of those states; so the act declares, "We, the people of the United States, (which have ratified) do ordain (by our separate ratifications) this constitution," for (the states, and between the states so ratifying the same, who are thereby) "The United States of America."

Here is simplicity of movement, and plainness in delineating, *by whom, for whom* the act was done, and what *the act was* when ordained. All history proves, and all opinions agree that it was in this way that the great work was accomplished in fact, and if so, there was no other way in which it could have been done; no reasoning can reverse the fact, or ingenuity make the act of nine distinct bodies of people the act of one, in whom all the power exerted, was previously vested.

How it may be in theory, is not material; but taking the constitution as the creation of a competent power, existing and acting practically, and not one ideal and imaginary, operating only by theory; I find in the fifth article, and the tenth and eleventh amendments, express provisions, which point to the true source of power from which it emanated.

Every part of the constitution may be amended save one, without invoking the power of the whole people, or all the states; the amending power is in " the legislatures of three-fourths of the states," or by conventions of three-fourths thereof, "as the one or other mode may be proposed by congress." It depends on the number of the states, when each acts by its legislative power; and the majority of the delegates of the people in convention of each state, when it acts by its people, not a majority of the people of all.

The tenth amendment excepts from the constitution, and reserves "to the states respectively, or the people," all powers not delegated or prohibited. The eleventh amendment annuls a jurisdiction expressly granted to the judicial power, by the third article of the constitution; by prohibiting its exercise, in suits against a state, by individuals, it operates on suits pending, and makes void the exercise of any judicial power in such cases, either past, present, or future. 3 Dallas, 382, 3; 6 Wh. 405 to 409, S. P.; 9 Wh. 206, 16, 858; 12 Wh. 438; 6 Pet. 310, 741.

When, then, it is undeniable that there is behind the constitution a power which can, by amendments, erect a new structure of government; revoke the grant of any of the powers of congress; remove the restrictions on the states; make exceptions to the grant, and reservations out of it, of what would be otherwise included in it; and annul the judicial power, in cases on which they were actually exercising an undoubted constitutional jurisdiction; it has seemed to me, that the judicial eye could easily see, and the judicial mind fully understand, what, and where was that power, which forbade this Court to move; and which it felt bound to obey, when the constitution authorized them to proceed to judgment, as the right and law of the case should appear.

It is no imaginary power that can arrest the judicial arm, or a subordinate power that can, by its own authority, avoid the exercise of that judicial power over itself, which has been 'granted by a paramount power. Nor can "*the absolute* sovereignty of the nation, which when the constitution was adopted," was "in the people of *the nation;*" be controlled by the "*residuary* sovereignty" of *three-fourths* of the states, in the people thereof, when the amendments were made. That sovereignty which can control all others, must be absolute: that which is controlled must be subordinate. If it is said that the constitution authorized this amendment, we should impute little of wisdom, foresight, or common prudence, to those who framed or adopted it, by ascribing its creation to a power so indifferent to its preservation; or to make three-fourths of the states competent to throw off the shackles on their laws, which all the states, and the whole people thereof, had imposed. There cannot, therefore, be, in my opinion, a proposition more hostile to the provisions of the fifth article, and these amendments as understood by this Court, than that the constitution was a creation of the whole people of the United States, in their aggregate collective capacity; as the one people, of one nation or state, acting by the plenary sovereignty, and in the unity of absolute political power. In thus viewing this amendment, as to "the feature" which it thus expunged, I use it as this Court does. "This feature is no longer found in the constitution; but it aids in the construction of those clauses with which it was originally connected." 6 Cr. 139. Independently of these considerations, there is another which arises from the relative condition of the states as to extent and population; to which we must refer for the discovery of the intention of those who have left us a work "designed for immortality." 6 Wh. 387.

"We cannot look back to the history of the times, when, (12 Wh. 354,) the general convention assembled, without the conviction that the framers of the constitution would naturally examine the state of things existing at the time; and their work sufficiently attests that they did so." 6 Wh. 416. By a reference to this work, and the practical effects of its operation to the present time, we can, I think, ascertain from whose hands it has come to us to be expounded, by its objects and intentions.

THE PRACTICAL EFFECT AND OPERATION OF THE CONSTITUTION.

The apportionment of representation among the states, which was made by the constitution, was with a reference to the congress of the revolution, 1 Journ. 153, of the whole number 65; the six largest states had 43; the remaining 7, only 22; and the constitution could be adopted by nine states, having thirty-three representatives. When in 1789, the government was organized, there were only 11 states with 59 representatives: of which, 4 states had 32, and the other 7, only 27; yet they could elect a President, and had a majority of votes in the Senate: so that a *minority* of the people of the United States, had the operative power of two branches of the government; and could make the third, in which the majority was represented, either subservient to their will, or incapable of acting in opposition to it.

The president and sixteen senators, representing eight states, and a population entitled only to twenty-five representatives, could exercise the treaty-making power; and the President and twelve Senators, from states entitled only to nineteen representatives, could appoint all the executive, military, and judicial officers of the government; overruling five states entitled to thirty-nine representatives: whereby all offices could be filled, and treaties made the supreme law of the land, in defiance of the will of a majority of the people, and their representatives, estimating the population of 1789 by that of 1790.

Under the first census of 1790, the free white population of the thirteen states, was 3,100,000: of which, Massachusetts had 469,000; New York 314,000; Pennsylvania 424,000; and Virginia (and Kentucky) 503,000; making 1,710,000; leaving 1,390,000 to the other nine states. These four states had 56 members in the House of Representatives, the other states 47; they had 8 votes in the Senate, the other states 18; they had 64 votes for President, the other states 65. Nine states, with a white population of 1,390,000, could dissolve the old confederation, establish the new constitution, and throw out of the union, four states, containing 1,700,000, or could control them if they became parties to it.

Was this a government of a *majority* of the people of the United States, as *one people?* Did the *one people* "ordain and establish" this "Constitution for the United States of America?"

At the census of 1800, there were 16 states: the whole white population of which was 4,247,000; these 4 states, exclusive of Kentucky, (taken from Virginia) contained 2,226,000, the other 12 contained 2,021,000; these 4 states had 74 votes in the House, 8 in the Senate, and 82 for President; the other 12 states had 67 votes in the House, 24 in the Senate, and 91 for President; the minority, in effect, controlling every branch of the government, and competent to amend the constitution. What became then of the government of the *majority* of the free white population, composing the people of the United States?

At the census of 1810, there were 17 states, with a white population of 5,765,000: of which, these states contained 2,948,000, the other 13 contained 2,717,000; these 4 states had 93 votes in the House, 8 in the Senate, and 101 for President; the other 13 states had 88 votes in the House, 26 in the Senate, and 114 for President, the minority of the people still controlling.

At the census of 1820, there were 24 states, the white population 7,856,000; the 4 states, with Maine (taken from Massachusetts) and Kentucky, contained 4,199,000; the other 18 contained 3,657,000; the 6 states having 114 votes in the House, 12 in the Senate, and 126 for President; the other 18 states had 99 votes in the House, 36 in the Senate, and 135 for President—the minority still ascendant.

In 1830, the entire white population was 10,846,000, of which, these 6 states contained 5,535,000; the other 18 states, including the territories, 5,311,000; the 6 states have 124 votes in the House, 12 in the Senate, and 136 for President; the other 18 states, have 117 votes in the House, 36 in the Senate, and 153 for President.

It thus appears, that from the year 1790, till this time, the four states of Massachusetts, New York, Pennsylvania and Virginia, have contained within their original boundaries, a majority of the whole people of the United States: yet such is the structure of the government, that there is no one act which could be effected by such majority.

Adding to the free white population of these states, according to the last census, and their present boundaries, that of Ohio and Tennessee, the 6 states contain 6,090,000; the other 18 states 4,646,000, leaving a majority in the 6 states of 1,444,000; which may be found to be perfectly passive for all purposes, except representation, in the House of Representatives. There are 9 states, which contain in all, only 1,345,000 free inhabitants, which can defeat a treaty, impeachment, proposition to amend the constitution, or the passage of a law, without the approbation of the President, against the will of fifteen states, containing a majority of 8,146,000 of the people of the United States, in the aggregate. Thirteen states, with a population of 2,504,300, can elect a President in the last resort, in opposition to eleven states, with 8,232,000. Congress is bound to call a convention to amend the constitution, on the application of the legislatures of two-thirds of states, whose population is only 3,546,000, less than one-third of the aggregate of all the states: and amendments may be adopted by eighteen states, in opposition to an aggregate majority of 1,444,000; one of which amendments might give the smallest state, an *equality of suffrage* in the House of Representatives, and in voting for a President by electors. Seven states, with a white population of only 812,000, may defeat any constitutional amendment; though it might be called for by the residue of the people of the Union, amounting to 9,924,000 : so that a *minority* may force on a *majority* a *new government;* and less than one-thirteenth *of the people of the United States in the aggregate,* may continue the present without any change whatever, though the reasons which call for an alteration, may be most imperative for the good of the whole.

There are but two means of changing these results from the present organization of the government,—one is the division of the large, or the junction of small states into new ones; and the other, by giving them a representation in the senate, in proportion to their numbers. But the constitution has placed both beyond the power of any majority of the people, however preponderating; unless by a majority of the states in the one, and by all in the second case.

" New states may be admitted by the congress into this Union; but no new state shall be formed or erected, within the jurisdiction of any other state, nor any state be formed by the junction of two or more states or parts of states, without the consent of the legislature of the states concerned, as well as of the congress." 4 art. sec. 3, clause 1.

The senators of any thirteen states can prevent the admission of any new states, or the junction of old ones; this can be remedied only by an amendment, which seven states can prevent.

The fifth article, providing for amending the constitution, contains this proviso: " *and that no state without its consent shall be deprived of its equal suffrage in the senate.*" Thus the irrevocable, irrepealable supreme law of the land, has made Delaware, with an aggregate population of 77,000, the peer of New York in the senate, with her 2,000,000: and she may hold her rights in defiance of the constitutional power of twenty-three states, with an aggregate population of 12,789,000; equal to 166 to 1; in federal numbers, 165 to 1; and in free population, 147 to 1.

How contemptible are mere numbers, or majorities of the people, in comparison with the rights of states, by the standard of the constitution!!

The basis of representation, composed of people and property, mixed into the constituent body of federal members, leads irresistibly to the character of the government. The inevitable effect of making five slaves equal to three freemen, is, to take power from a majority of the people: so long as this apportionment of representation among the states continues; a *minority* of the *people of the United States* in the aggregate, may elect a *majority* of the members of the House of Representatives; and the conventions or legislatures of seven of the slave-holding states, can perpetuate this state of things.

The general result of the last census, including the District of Columbia and the territories, is: aggregate population, 12,856,000; slaves, 2,010,000; federal numbers, 12,052,000; free people, 10,846,000;

slaves represented, 1,206,000: thus, the representation of the states in which they are owned, is increased by the addition of twenty-seven members; is a representation of an actual minority of the free people; and though the minority, they may control even this branch of the government, by a majority equal to the slave representation.

These results are not the effect of accident; they must have been foreseen at the adoption of the constitution: unless it was anticipated that the population of the states would be in an inverse ratio to their territory.

In 1788, the whole territory of the thirteen states contained about 500,000 square miles; of which there was comprehended in the boundaries of Virginia and Kentucky, then one state, 103,000; in North Carolina, including Tennessee, 84,000; and in Georgia, including Mississippi and Alabama, 153,000: in the aggregate, 340,000. The other ten states, included only 167,000, adding the territory ceded by Virginia and New York, now composing the states of Ohio, Indiana, and Illinois, containing 134,000; all that was in possession of the confederacy or the states, was 640,000 square miles; of which, three states had more than one-half, while three others had no more than one-eighth part; two of which had only the one hundred and ninety-third, and one only the four hundreth part.

Yet this enormous disparity of territory has no more effect on the equality of a state with any other now, nor hereafter can have without its consent, than the disparity of population. Rhode Island, with 1,360 square miles of territory, is the peer of Virginia, with 64,000. Delaware is the equal of New York, though their population is most enormously disproportionate. The rights of these states are emphatically the rights of a *minority* of the *people;* and a government which can be organized, administered, and reorganized, by a *minority*, whose power is expressly guarantied against any *majority* of *states* or *people*, cannot be any other than a *"federal government of these states."*

There can be no political absurdity more palpable, than that which results from the theory that the people of the United States, as one people, have instituted a government of the people; a majority (of the people) government; or one which can be altered by the majority: for that majority has no one right, can do no one act under the constitution, or prevent such amendments as would expunge every semblance of a popular feature from it, by reducing *New York to an equality with Delaware,* in the House of Representatives, and in voting for President; these being the only particulars in which the people of the largest have any more right than those of the smallest states. Nor is there a political truth more apparent from the bills of rights in the constitutions of the several states; their unanimous declaration in congress, in October 1774, and July 1776; their alliance with France in 1778; with each other in 1781; and the supreme law of 1788, established by the people of each, between themselves, as each sovereign; than that the government which they have brought into existence, is a creature of the people of the several states, a government of a majority of the states; which may be in all its departments, and whole action, administered by the representatives of the minority of the people of the United States; and changed in its whole organization and distribution of powers, by such minority, in all respects save one; and that one is the provision which makes the right and power of the minority irresistible, by the equal suffrage in the Senate, forever secured to each state.

The thirteenth article of the confederacy contained a similar provision: the assent of each state was necessary to any alteration.

The principle, that a majority of states, of the people of the United States, or of either, in any unity of political character, could, in any stage of our history, *alter, abolish the old,* or *institute a new government,* is utterly without any sanction in the acts of the states or congress. States were *units,* who could impart or withdraw power at their pleasure, until they made an express delegation to congress by the league of 1781; each state had its option to become a party to the compact, constitution or grant, made in 1788, by nine states, or to remain a free, sovereign, independent state, nation or power, foreign to the new Union, after the old was dissolved.

By becoming separate parties, they did not divest themselves of their individual unity of character; they remain units as to representation, and *as units,* reserve all powers not delegated or prohibited: and the ultimate power of revoking all parts but one of the grant, with the concurrence of three-fourths of their associates, and modifying it at their pleasure.

This is the essence of supreme and sovereign power, which testifies that the ultimate absolute sovereignty, is in "the several states," and the people thereof; who can do by inherent right and power, any thing in relation to the constitution, or change of government, except depriving the smallest state of *its equal suffrage in the senate:* not in the United States, or the people thereof, as one nation, or one people, who in their unity of character or power, can do nothing either by inherent right, *or by representation,* as a majority.

The power which can rightfully exercise acts of supreme absolute sovereignty, is the sovereign power of a state; no body or power, which can neither move or act, can be sovereign: it exists constitutionally, but as matter incapable of either. The soil of the United States, is as much the source of political power, as its aggregate population. Until the power which can establish government is brought into action, and designates the one or the other as the basis of representation or taxation, each is a perfect dead body; and both are perfectly so by the constitution, in reference to the United States in the aggregate, or as one nation. But in reference to the states, both the land and the population, within their separate boundaries, are brought into operation; its *federal numbers* are made the stock from which representation arises, and become represented by the action of the qualified electors of the state; and the land in the state is assessed with taxation, by the same rates as its representation is apportioned;

by which land produces revenue, in the same proportion as population produces representation.

This rule is perfectly arbitrary, being the result of a compromise: the people of the states could base representation on property or people; they could select either, or a proportion of both, and the kind of either; and three-fourths of the states or people thereof, can now change the proportion, by excluding slaves altogether, enumerating them as each a freeman, or substituting any other species of property than slaves.

Representation by numbers is not by natural right: slaves have neither political rights or power; it is by compact, the will and pleasure of the states who have so ordained it, as separate sovereigns; and in doing so, have shown in whom the supreme power is vested, and yet remains to be exercised in the future, as it has been in the past.

The institution of the federal government is decisive of the question, it shows the creature and the creator; the power which has made and can unmake the machine it has set in motion, as the work of its own hands, moving within defined limits, operating only on specified subjects, by delegated authority, revocable at will.

The act of delegation is the exercise of sovereignty, and acting under it is a recognition of its supremacy: it may be without limitation in some cases, and until revoked it may be supreme; but it is so only as a delegated authority or agency,—the right to revoke, and render its exercise a nullity, is the test by which to ascertain in whom it is vested by original inherent right.

Men are not less free when they unite and form society out of its original elements, into a body politic for the mutual safety and happiness of the parts, by a government instituted for all.

Less or more bodies politic, may unite in their separate character for the same purposes; and agree that the power of each shall be administered by one or more bodies, whom they shall separately authorize to act in their name, and for their benefit, without a surrender or extinguishment of their sovereign character or attributes. When it is adopted voluntarily by each as an unit; the only effect is to create and erect a new body politic or corporation, by a charter or grant by the sovereign power of each. It may be declared revocable by each, by three-fourths, or require the assent of all, as by the confederation; yet as this is a matter of compact, it does not affect the nature of the ultimate sovereign power, which they separately reserve.

Thus, the constitution itself, gives an indelible stamp of character to the government it created. It is what all confederated or federal governments are, and from their nature must be; formed by the union of two or more states or nations, on an equal footing, by the act of federation; a league, alliance, or constitution, is the act of each constituent part; acting in the plenitude of its own separate sovereignty, it executes the act, which delegates to a body in which each is separately represented, such powers, as they thus agree, are necessary for their federative purposes; with such restraints on their

4

several powers, as will prevent the objects of the federation from being defeated.

### THE CONNECTION BETWEEN THE COLONIES AND ENGLAND—ITS DISSOLUTION, AND THE EFFECT THEREOF.

The statesmen of the colonies could not mistake the government under which they lived; the absolute sovereignty of the country was in the king and parliament; colonial and provincial governments were created by charters granted in virtue of royal prerogative, not by acts of parliament. "The British government, which was then our government," claimed the whole territory by right of discovery and conquest; 8 Wh. 588, (ante et post.); the right of the king to legislate over a conquered country, was never denied in Westminster hall, or questioned in parliament. Cowp. 204, 13; 9 Pet. 748. Hence, he may, by his grant by letters patent or charter, authorize the exercise of legislative power, by a government created in a colony, or the proprietary of a province; and letters patent will be presumed from prescription, when a territory has been long possessed, and the powers of government exercised with the assent and approbation of the crown, though none were in fact ever granted: as was the case of the three counties, now composing the state of Delaware. 1 Vez. Sr. 446. Penn v. Baltimore, Chalmers, 60, 40, 1.

No federal connection did or could exist between the mother country and the colonies, or between them, consistently with the constitution of England, whereby parliament was the controlling government over them by their own consent. The colonies could establish a federal government over themselves, when the power of Great Britain over them became extinct by the revolution; but neither they or the states entered into any act of federation, till 1781; neither their separate or unanimous declaration of independence, created or announced the existence of such political relation between them. They declared what was their then political situation, consequent upon the cessation of their allegiance to the king, and the dissolution of all connection between them and "the state of Great Britain," by the acts set forth, one of which was, "He has abdicated government here, by declaring us out of his protection, and waging war upon us. We must therefore acquiesce in the necessity which denounces our separation, and hold them as we do the rest of mankind, enemies in war, in peace friends."

A reference to the prior declarations of the congress, will elucidate this. In October, 1774, they declared among other rights, that they "were entitled to all privileges and immunities, granted by charter, or secured by their several codes of provincial laws;" "which cannot be taken from them, altered or abridged, without their own consent, by their representatives in their several provincial legislatures." 1 Journ. 28, 9.

In their petitions to the king, at the same time, they state their objects: "We ask but for peace, liberty and safety; we wish not a diminution of the prerogative, nor do we solicit the grant of any new right in our favour. Your royal authority over us, and our connection with Great Britain, we shall always carefully and zealously endeavour to support and maintain." 66.

In July, 1775, they declared, that "societies or governments, vested with perfect legislatures, were formed under charter from the crown," 134. After stating the causes which induced them to take up arms against the king, they proceed, "We mean not to dissolve that Union subsisting between us and our fellow subjects in the empire. Necessity has not driven us into that desperate measure, or induced us to excite any other nation to war against them. We have not raised armies with ambitious designs of separating from Great Britain, and establishing *independent states*," 138.

In their letter to the Six nations of Indians, they use a term peculiarly appropriate to a declaration of independence: "You, Indians, know how things are proportioned in a family—between the father and the son—the child carries a *little* pack. England, we regard as the father—this island may be compared to the son. The pack is increased; the boy sweats and staggers under the increased load, and asks that it may be lightened; asks if any of the fathers in any of their records, had described *such* a pack for a child; he is ready to fall every moment; but after all his cries and entreaties, the pack is redoubled; yet no voice from his father is heard. "He therefore gives one struggle and *throws off the pack;* and says he cannot take it up again." "This may serve to illustrate the present condition of the king's American subjects or children," 135. The language is plain, but very easily understood.

In December, 1775, they disavow any allegiance to parliament, but avow it to be due to the king; and deny that they have opposed any of the just prerogatives of the crown, or any legal exertion of those prerogatives, 263. Their petition to the king in 1774, taken in connection with this declaration, shows the precise ground assumed in 1774, and retained, till in the final struggle, *this pack* was thrown off by the boy. "We know of no laws binding on us, but such as have been transmitted to us by our ancestors; and such as have been consented to by ourselves, or our representatives, elected for that purpose. We, therefore, in the name of the people of these United Colonies, and by authority, according to the purest maxims of representation derived from them, declare, that whatever punishment," &c. 264, 265. Had the congress then declared, what they did afterwards, the only *pack* they ever acknowledged to have been constitutionally imposed on them, (the prerogative of the crown and consequent alleiance to the king,) would have been thrown off, and *the boy* becomeg a freeman. This was done in effect, on the 15th of May, 1776, when congress resolved, that "it is necessary that the exercise of *every kind of authority* under the said crown, should be *totally suppresed; and all the powers of government* exerted under the authority of the people of the colonies;" 2 Journ. 166. This resolution was a preamble to the resolution of the 10th, recommending to the *respective* assemblies and conventions of the United Colonies, to adopt governments for themselves, 158; taken with the original resolution, as agreed to on the 2d of July, as follows:

Resolved, " That these United Colonies are, and of right ought to be, free and independent states; that they are absolved from all allegiance to the British crown; and that all political connection between them and the state of Great Britain, is, and ought to be, totally dissolved." 2 Journ. 227. It may well be asked, in the words of congress, in December preceding, "Why all this ambiguity and obscurity, in what ought to be so plain and obvious, as that he who runs may read." "What allegiance is it that we forget? Allegiance to parliament? We never owed, we never owned it. Allegiance to our king? Our words have ever avowed it; our conduct has ever been consistent with it." 1 Journ. 263.

Now it is very immaterial what form of a declaration was adopted two days afterwards; when congress, for a fourth time, declared the rights and wrongs of the colonies, and their actual condition after an open annunciation of an existing war between the king and state of Great Britain and these United Colonies, then independent states.

### THE DECLARATION OF INDEPENDENCE.

It was announcing what had been done, and the causes for doing it; and must be taken to have been done, on the principles declared from the beginning of the complaints and struggles of the colonists, *to throw off the pack;* it declared *the pack removed,* and the *boys freemen.*

The result was obvious, and was so declared, "the thirteen colonies of Great Britain," thereby became "the thirteen United States of America;" connected in a war for their defence, but not confederated by a government, to make laws for, or to put a pack on them.

A comparison of this declaration, with the counter-declaration of parliament, as contained in 1 Bl. Com. 109, (a book then in quite as familiar use as now, and that was evidently under the eyes of congress at the time,) will show their meaning: " that *all* his majesty's *colonies* and plantations in America, *have been, are, and of right ought to be, subordinate* to, and *dependent* upon, the imperial crown and parliament of Great Britain." Congress declared that, " *these colonies are, and of right ought to be, free and independent states."* Not *all* his majesty's colonies in America, for Canada and Nova Scotia were no parties to the declaration; not that these colonies *had been* free, for they admitted they had been dependent, and the people had been the loyal and faithful subjects of the king; hence the words were appropriate. " *These* colonies, (now) *are,* and *of right ought to be,* not subordinate and dependent, but free and independent *states."* The same author defined what "the state of Great Britain" was. " A state, a realm, a nation, an empire; the supreme head whereof, is "the king; inferior to, accountable to, and dependent on no man upon earth;" " as sovereign and independent within these his dominions, as any emperor is in his empire," (the imperial dignity, 1 Journ. 65.) "and owes no subjection to any potentate upon earth," 1 Bl. Com. 242; or, in the language of this Court, "a single sovereign power," 6 Cr. 136. The transition was from this condition of a colony, to that of a state; from subordination to freedom; from dependence to independence. The declaration in its front was, by the thirteen states who had been colonies, were then what they were declared to be; and the name and style of each was separately affixed at the foot, as united by the style of the *United States* of America, as they had been since 1774, by that of the United *Colonies*, &c.

Their separate independence was proclaimed, and they remained towards each other as they were before, as colonies, and then as states; they did not alter their relations: the same *delegates* from the colonies acted as the *representatives of the states;* so declared themselves, and continued their session without new credentials. The appointing power being the same, the separate legislature of each state, as a state, nation, or empire; *the people*, the supreme head, as the king, the emperor, the sovereign.

*These* colonies were not declared to be free and independent states, by substituting congress in the place of king and parliament; nor by the people of the states, transferring *to the United States*, that allegiance they had owed to the crown; or making with *the state*, or *nation*, of the United States, a political connection, similar to that which had existed with *the state* of Great Britain.

A state, to be free, must be exempt from all external control; on a " separate and *equal station* with the other powers of the earth;" within whose territorial limits, no state or nation can have any jurisdiction: this is of the essence of *freedom*, and being *free*, in the grant and exercise of legislative power at their pleasure, a *state*, and *the people thereof*, must have the absolute sovereignty, illimitable, save by the people themselves. Such was the situation of the states and people, from 1776 till 1781, when the several state legislatures made an act of federation, as *allied sovereigns*, which was only a league or alliance; and being utterly defective, was substituted by a new act of federation; a constitution, ordained by *the people of the several states*, in their primary inherent right and power, existing in themselves; before any portion of its sovereignty had been impaired by any act of federation, or any severance from its territorial boundary.

## THE CONSTITUTION IS A GRANT BY THE PEOPLE OF THE SEVERAL STATES.

So taking the power which ordained the constitution, it can be traced in all its provisions and amendments, in perfect consistency with its preamble and mode of adoption; it is the same power which was exercised by the people of the colonies, when they abolished the royal governments, and established new ones by their own authority as states; and by which they abolished the confederation, and ordained the constitution. Viewed in all its bearings, as a grant, a charter, conveying and restricting the exercise of power, providing for its own amendments, and the amendments made pursuant thereto; the people of the several states are seen in all its movements; their acts are referrible to no other power; and the existence of any authority, not subordinate to theirs, deranges the whole system.

When it is so considered, without any theory but that which is developed in the English system of jurisprudence; which, in all its parts, is infused into all our institutions of government; there is no difficulty in finding out its intention by the settled rules of interpretation. We can understand the federal and state system in their origin, organization, and operation, as the work of the same hand; which, in the institution of one government for state purposes separately, and another for the federal purposes of thirteen united or confederated states, has acted in separate bodies; and can ascertain what it has granted, how far it has restrained itself, and measure the grant by its exceptions and reservations.

There never has been, or can be any difference of opinion as to the meaning of the ordaining parts of the constitution in the terms, " *the people of the several states;*" "*the several states which may be included in this union;*" "*each state;*" for they do not admit of two meanings. They refer to those states which, having ratified the constitution, are each a constituent part of the United States, composing, by their union, *the United States of America;* and to the people of each state, as *the people of these United States.* When terms are so definite in the body of an instrument, and one less definite is used in the preamble, which can be made equally definite by reference, the established maxim applies—"*id certum est quod certum reddi potest.*" Let then the term, *We, the people of the United States,* be referred to the second section of the first article, and compared with the terms, " *the people of the several states;*" " *the several states which may be included within this union;*" the sense of both is identical. So, when we refer the terms to the seventh article, prescribing the *manner* of ordaining and establishing the constitution, there is the same identity of meaning. No other variance exists between the terms in the preamble and body, than exists in other terms which are varied in form, but are the same in substance, and used in the same intention; as, " *each state;*" " *the several states;*" the several states " *which may be included within this union; the United States ;.* the United States *of America; a congress of the United States; the congress; congress,*" &c. When the various parts of an instrument can be made to harmonize, by referring the supposed doubtful words of one part to the certain words of another, without doing violence to their appropriate sense; every just rule of construction calls for such reference as will remove ambiguity: if the two terms cannot be reconciled, it is a settled rule, that the preamble is controlled by the enacting part. No case can arise to which these rules can be more applicable, and there is no discrepancy between the different terms ; one is less full and explicit than the others, the *name* given to the granting power is not its substance; the *thing* is the power; whenever that is clearly defined, the *name* will be made to suit it. If this term in the preamble was, by common consent, or the settled course of professional and judicial opinion, taken as a mere *name* given to a *thing* of an agreed determinate nature, it would be a waste of time to inquire whether the *name* was appropriate to the *thing;* or whether the reasoning, which makes the action of thirteen distinct bodies, at so many different times and places, produce the same result, as the action of one on the same object, and may be deemed in legal contemplation, the sole action of one body, was metaphysical or sound ; for it would be merely a discussion on *words*, which would not determine the sense of the constitution as to *substance* and *things*. That the states acted in the same distinct and separate capacity, in the creation of the government, as they did, and yet do in selecting their agents who administer its powers, is apparent in the seventh article, before quoted.

The mode of action was by the people of each state, in conventions of delegates chosen by themselves; the action of the separate conventions being, by their express authority, delegated for the special purpose, was the action of the people. The grant was theirs, of their powers; and thus made it was in perfect harmony with all the provisions in its body, and as declared in its front; that, " We, the people of the United States, do ordain and establish this constitution for the United States of America." The meaning is clear and plain, by a reference to the people of each of those states who ratified it in convention, and to the people of the several states who were to elect the representatives of the state, in a congress of the United States ; the *same people* performing different functions, the first in creating, the second in organizing the government of the states, which had been thus established between themselves.

In so taking the declaratory part of the instrument, it harmonizes throughout; no violence is done, or a strained construction put to any part; every word has its own meaning, when it is referred to its subject matter of application; power flows from its original and acknowledged fountains, and is distributed by each depository, among the appropriate agents for its execution. It is the same power which had been exerted in the institution of a government for each state ; was competent to do so for the states, which were united by an alliance of mere confederation, without any legislative power in their congress; by making any change which an organic power, absolute and unlimited, could effect, and which this Court has often declared it did effect in its exertion by separate bodies. If it was so taken as settled doctrine, it would be easy to expound the instrument in which this power was exerted, as a charter or grant, *ex visuribus suis*, the law at the time it was made, the common, the statute, and constitutional law of England, the history and state of the times then and before, the acts of the people, the states, and of congress, in their domestic and foreign relations, in some of which sources there would be found satisfactory means of its interpretation.

Three of these cases turn on those clauses of the constitution which restrain the states; the fourth depends, in my opinion, on those which are reserved by the tenth amendment: so that none can be decided, without identifying the power which made the grant, restrictions and reservations, by an original, inherent sovereign right, and which was competent for all these purposes. The preamble declares, that " We, the people of the United States, &c. do ordain and establish this constitution for the United States of America." That it was done by the power of the people, and not of the state legislatures is universally admitted; as also that they had the competent power to do it. The only question which is open is, whether this power was in the people of the separate states, as separate bodies politic, or in the whole people of the United States, as one.

THE OPINIONS OF THE COURT APPLIED TO THE PROVISIONS OF THE CONSTITUTION.

This Court, as the appropriate tribunal for expounding the constitution, has used various terms to express their sense of the term; as, *The people of the United States,* in 1 Wh. 324. The people of America, 4 Wh. 193. The American people, 4 Wh. 403. 6 Wh. 377, 381. It is deemed a term of "becoming dignity," suited to the solemnity of the occasion and instrument. 2 Dall. 471; 12 Wh. 354. But when they use the term, and describe how the people acted, and by what acts the instrument was adopted, they add this expression; which one would think was in language comprehensible and clear, excluding all construction, and admitting of no two-fold meaning or interpretation: "No political dreamer was ever wild enough to think of breaking down the lines which separate the states, and of compounding the American people into one common mass. Of consequence, when they act, they act in their states." 4 Wh. 403; M'Culloch v. Maryland.

Here is a declaration, that the organic power was not a *compound mass* of the people in their states. In a subsequent part of their opinion, they declare that the same power which *established,* is the same which is *represented* in, and exercised by congress, as well as what that power is, and in what body politic it was, is, and of right ought to be. " *The people of all the states,* have created the general government, and have conferred upon it the general power of taxation. *The people of all the states, and the states themselves, are represented in congress,* and by *their representatives* exercise this power." 4 Wh. 435. In the same case they had explained the difference between *the people of the states,* and *the states,* or *state sovereignties, state legislatures,* or, as they afterwards called it, *the supreme power;* all meaning the same thing, when referred to the power of the state, as exercised by the legislatures thereof. 12 Wh. 347. (Vide 1 Bl. Com. 147, p. 52.)

" To the formation of *a league,* such as was *the confederation,* the *state sovereignties* were certainly competent. But when in order to form a more perfect union, it was deemed necessary to change the alliance into an *effective government,* possessing *great and sover-*

*eign powers*, and acting *directly on the people*, the necessity of referring it to *the people*, and of *deriving its powers directly from them*, was felt and acknowledged by all;" 4 Wh. 404. In this language there is neither a mystical or an erudite meaning, in its clear and conclusive explanations of the two systems. The congress of the confederation, was a body which conducted the affairs of the league, under the authority of state legislatures only; and as the power could not rise higher than its source, congress could operate only by their secondary power; and reach the people only by requisitions on the states, to be enforced by state laws. The congress of the constitution, *representing both " the states,"* and *" the people of the several states,"* by a grant emanating directly from them, could operate on *the people of the state;* and carrying into effect their own laws, could, without the intervention of any intermediate power, execute them to the full extent of their granted powers.

Let these judicial expositions be applied to the constitution, to ascertain by its language, the meaning of the terms, *people, states, representation, congress:* taking them in the same order as the constitution does, in its ordaining part.

Art. 1. Sec. 1. " All legislative powers herein granted, shall be vested in *a congress of the United States*, which shall consist of a Senate and House of Representatives." This is a definition of the general term *congress*, and its constituent parts; which are composed as follows:

Sec. 2. " The House of Representatives shall be composed of members chosen every second year, by *the people of the several states;* and the electors *in each state*, shall have the qualifications requisite for the most numerous branch of the state legislature." This defines the parts of the one constituent body of the congress, and who shall elect them. The next clause prescribes the ratio of each state.

Clause 3. " Representatives and direct taxes, shall be apportioned among *the several states* which may be included within this Union, according to their *respective* numbers; which shall be determined, by adding to the whole number of free persons, including those bound to service for a term of years, and excluding Indians not taxed— three-fifths of all other persons." This defines the basis of representation to be, the *federal numbers* within the several states; not the *people* of the states only, who elect the representatives of each; they are included as free persons, each an unit; but all other persons are also included, five of whom make three units; the aggregate determines the number of members who shall be chosen by the people of the several states, to compose the House of Representatives.

" The number of representatives shall not exceed one for every thirty thousand; but each state shall have at least one representative: and until such enumeration shall be made, the *state* of New Hampshire shall have three," &c.

Thus, the members of the House of Representatives, elected by the *people of the several states*, according to an enumeration of the *re-*

5

*spective federal numbers* of the several states, are the representa-tives of *the several states.*

Clause 4. " When vacancies happen in *the representation from any state,* the executive authority thereof shall issue writs of elec-tion to fill such vacancy."

The *several* representatives of the *several states,* thus compose the *representation* from the *several states,* in the House of *Repre-sentatives,* as a constituent of *a Congress of the United States.*

Sec. 3. " The Senate of the United States shall be composed of two senators from each state, chosen by the legislature thereof, for six years; and each senator shall have one vote." Such senators are therefore the representatives of *each state,* in *the Senate,* who com-pose the other component part of a congress of the United States.

Sec. 4, clause 2. " The congress shall assemble at least once in every year." Here, then, we have a definition of the body in whom all legislative powers granted by the constitution, are vested: after their meeting it is, "*The United States in Congress assembled,*" the same as all preceding congresses had been termed. The mode in which the two constituent parts act in their legislative capacity, is by majorities, or two-thirds of the members, as the case may be; by the appropriate provision, applicable to all other legislative bodies. Though they are individually the representatives of the several states, and the members from each state are its representation in congress; yet that body being invested with legislative powers, au-thorized to act by majorities of votes, without any reference to states, as in the old congress, it follows, that as they may thus legislate to the full extent of their constitutional powers, their laws are binding throughout the territory of the states, who are within the Union. " They *serve* for all." Vide 1 Bl. Com. 159.

In creating the executive power of the government, the constitu-tion introduces a new principle, in directing how, and by whom, the person who is to hold the office of President, shall be elected; as it is neither by the people or the states, but by a third body, he is the representative of neither; but the officer designated in the mode pre-scribed, to perform the duties enjoined, and execute the powers con-ferred on him as an officer. The separate and distinct character of the states is, however, carried into his election.

Art. 2. Sec. 1. clause 2. " Each state shall appoint, in such man-ner as the legislature thereof may direct, a number of electors equal to the whole number of senators and representatives, to which the state may be entitled in the congress," &c.

Clause 3. " The electors shall meet in their respective states, and vote by ballot for a President." (Vide 12. Amendment.) " And if no person have a majority, then from the five highest on the list, the said House (of Representatives) shall in like manner choose the Pre-sident; but in choosing the President, the votes shall be taken by states, the representation from each state having one vote," &c., (as in the old congress of states and colonies. 1 Journ. 11: 1 Laws 14.)

These terms, " representation," " representation from each state,"

" having one vote," are peculiarly definite, and appropriate to the apportionment thereof, among the several states, who are separately represented in the House; another term, equally so to the Senate, as composed of two senators from each state, in a body in which the representation from the states, is the same in number, is used in the last clause of the fifth article of the constitution, relative to amendments : " And that no state, without its consent, shall be deprived of its *equal suffrage* in the Senate."

Thus far the constitution delineates the action of the people, the states, or state legislatures, and the electors, in organizing the legislative and executive departments of the government, which enables it to execute all its functions and powers: it remains only to be seen, how, and by what power, this organization of government, the distribution and administration of its powers, was authorized and directed.

Art. 7. " The ratifications of the conventions of nine states shall be sufficient for the establishment of this constitution, between the states so ratifying the same."

It is then, by the separate action of the states, in conventions of nine states, (not of a convention of nine states) that the grant was made; the act of eight produced no result; but when the ninth acted, the great work was effected as between the nine. Until the other four so acted, they were no part of the United States; nor were the people of the nonratifying states, any part of the people of the United States, who ordained and established it.

That the term, conventions of states, meant conventions of delegates, elected by the people of the several states, for the express purpose of assenting or dissenting, to their adoption of the proposed constitution, is admitted by all; as also, that no general convention of the whole people was ever convened for any purpose: and that the members of the convention which framed it, met, and acted as states, consented to, and signed it for and in behalf of the states, whom they respectively represented, appears on its face. It was proposed to the people of each state separately, and was so ratified; it existed only between those states, whose people had so accepted it. It would, therefore, most strangely contradict itself, throughout all its provisions, to so construe the preamble, as to make it a declaration, that it was ordained by any other power than that of the people of the several states, as distinct bodies politic, over whom no external power could be exerted, but by their own consent.

These are not only the necessary conclusions, which flow from the plain language and definite provisions of the constitution itself, but their settled interpretation by this Court. " From these conventions the constitution derives its whole authority. The government proceeds directly from the people, and is ordained and established in the name of the people." 4 Wh. 403.

If it is asked what people; the answer is at hand, " *A convention of delegates chosen in each state*, by *the people thereof, assembled in their several states.*" Ib. sup.

It was in this mode that " *the people of all the states created the government;*" it is in the mode pointed out by the constitution, that *the people of all the states* are *represented in the House of Representatives,* and *the states themselves* are represented in the Senate; and *both, by their representatives,* exercise the legislative powers which are granted to, and vested in a *congress of the United States.* The government is thus created by the people; organized by the people and states; its laws enacted by the representatives of both; and the executive power vested in a President, *elected by electors appointed by the states; each a distinct body.* The same people perform both functions; the one creative, the other elective; " *the people of the several states,*" the *states,* or state legislatures, each submitting the constitution to the convention of the people thereof; and when ratified, *choosing the senators,* and *directing the appointment of electors;* all done by the free action of the people and states, by their own internal power. When the creation and structure of the government are thus complete, by the separate action of people and states; its movements continue by the same action, and are renewed at the periods prescribed. The *people* of each state elect its representatives in the House; *each state* chooses two senators, and appoints its proper number of electors to elect a President. So it must act through all time as a government of states, put in motion by the power which acts, in altering old, and instituting new governments; which organizes, continues, and can amend, with such restraints, conditions, exceptions, and reservations, as were necessary to give efficiency to the latter, without " a vexatious interference with the internal concerns of the former;" 4 Wh. 628. By thus tracing both governments to the same fountain, and the power of both, emanating in separate grants, their bearing on both systems can be well understood, by referring any ambiguity in the grant, or any part thereof, to the same rules and standard of interpretation, by which we measure and expound other grants and charters, which convey property, delegate, restrain, or reserve power.

### THE DIFFERENT MODES OF CONSTRUING THE CONSTITUTION.

These considerations, however, have utterly failed to settle the true meaning of the term, " *We, the people of the United States,*" as the granting or constituent power of the federal government. So far from their being any general assent to that meaning, which, to my mind, is so apparent in the constitution, with its necessary practical results, which its framers and adopters must have known and foreseen to be inevitable; the reverse may be the common opinion.

It is but too apparent that there have been two classes of both statesmen and jurists, who, from the time of the convention of 1787 to the present time, have radically differed in their constitutional opinions. Those of one class, fearful of the recurrence of the evils of the confederation, adopt the most liberal rules of construction, in order to enlarge the granted powers of the federal government, and extend the restrictions on the states, and state laws, beyond their natural and obvious import. Those of the other class, more fearful of the gradual absorption of the powers of the states, by the assumption of powers tending to turn " a federal government of states" into a consolidated government of the Union; adopt the most narrow construction which can be put upon words, to contract the granted powers of the one, and the restrictions on the others, by which the reserved powers will be proportionably enlarged. There was a third class, of which there is yet a small remnant, who were willing to take the constitution with its amendments, as it is, and to expound it by the accepted rules of interpretation; whatever might be the result on the powers granted, restricted, excepted, or reserved; if it was the meaning and intention of the supreme law of the land, it was their rule of action. Each of the three classes, justly considering that political power operated like the screw in mechanism, gaining strength by every onward turn, losing the strength of its hold by a backward turn, and retaining its hold so far as it had turned. Each of the two first classes would, therefore, endeavour to find by construction, a lever by which to give it a power, stronger in one case, and weaker in the other; while the third would leave it at the precise point where the first moving power had fixed it; believing, that it ought to remain stationary, till the amending power should turn it forward or backward from its original position. Taking my position in the ranks of the third class, it has been my endeavour, in all stations, to find out the meaning of the constitution by its expressed intention, to be collected from all its parts by old settled rules; the history of the times which preceded, and the state of the times at its adoption. In so doing, I can give to the preamble, or to the declaratory part, no greater importance than to the other parts of the whole instrument; when they can all be reconciled, they must be made to do so; if they cannot be made consistent with each other, that which most clearly indicates the intention, must control; recital must yield to enactment; form to substance; the name to the thing. Those who use it as a lever, by which to press the screw more severely on the powers of the several states, must trace the power which first propelled it to some source of sovereignty, absolute and unlimited, in matters of government; else it cannot restrict the states.

If the preamble truly points to the majority of the whole people of the United States, in their aggregate collective capacity, as the original depository of this power; that power is competent for all purposes of consolidating, or distributing it, in one, or among many governments: but it necessarily excludes federation between the several states. They must come into it as equals in power, who can acknowledge no federal head, except the one created by the act of federation: no federal legislation can be exercised, but by a legislature which represents the constituent parts. If congress is the creation of the sovereign power of one state or nation, whose people have done the act in the unity of their political power, it is no federal government; there are no constituent parts by which to compose it.

The residuary sovereignty of the several states of this Union and the people thereof, cannot be the same as the absolute sovereignty of the one nation and people thereof; which by its own unaided power can institute a government over the whole thirteen states: the term *absolute*, admits no limitation as to power; *residuary*, can mean only that residuum which the absolute power has not pleased to exercise. The use of the terms absolute, and residuary sovereignty, thus applied, either in argument or illustration, is, of necessity, with a view to make the constitution operate by its grants and restriction; by an authority paramount to that of the people of the several states; and thus bear essentially on its exposition. Hence, the preamble has ever been the field selected by the first class, whereon to exert their strength, and on which they maintain their proposition; if they abandon that field, the constitution gives them no other defensible position. The object can be no other than by the potency of the preamble, to control the provisions of the constitution; so as to give to the term, " the people," the same meaning and reference wherever it is used.

The term is found only in three places; in the preamble it is " the people of the United States;" in the second section, first article, it is " the people of the several states;" and in the tenth amendment " the states respectively, or the people:" in all it is connected with " states;" but the phraseology is different as to both terms. It then becomes all important to examine, whether " the people of the United States," who established the constitution " of the several states;" who elect the " representation from each state;" and " the states respectively or the people," to whom all powers not granted or prohibited, are reserved; refer to the same or different bodies.

It cannot well be doubted, that if the general term in the preamble refers to the whole people in the aggregate, as " the people of the United States;" the still more general term in the tenth amendment must be taken in the same sense, " the people;" if they are so taken, then the intermediate term " the people of the several states," must receive the same interpretation, or there must be this consequence. That the granting, restraining, and the reserved powers, were, and are in the " one people," and the power of organizing and administering the government, is in the " several people of each state;" of course there can be no reserved power in them, and it must remain in that body which could grant, restrain, except and reserve, according to the doctrine of this Court. " Any restriction upon it, derived from an external source, would imply a diminution of its sovereignty to the extent of the restriction," &c. 7 Cr. 136. On the other hand, if the three terms mean the same thing, the one people, the words, " several states," " each state," are made to mean the states in the aggregate; by which the words " several" and " each" will be virtually expunged from the body of the instrument; and the words, " in the aggregate or collectively," inserted by construction. No one, then, can fail to perceive, that by adding these words, or taking out, or neutralizing the words " several" and " each," the whole constitution is made to speak in different language; and to express an intention wholly different from that which its words import, read as they are. I, therefore, wholly disclaim this mode of construing the constitution, by adding or altering a word; the tendency whereof is too well understood to be mistaken. It is to draw the attention from the body, the provisions, and the operations of the instrument, in the terms of which there is no ambiguity in defining the term people or states, and confine it to its caption or preamble, which in itself may admit of a reference to suit the object, if it is not compared with what is ordained and established in detail.

By adding to the term, " *We, the people of the United States,*" the word *severally*, all ambiguity is removed; (if any could exist after connecting it with the second section of the first article); the creating, organizing, and administering power is one. By adding the words, *in the aggregate*, or collectively, or any others of equivalent import, the two powers are necessarily separated, and must be incompatible, unless one can control the other in its appropriate function; so that if the constitution is to be construed by its preamble only, its meaning will depend on the interpolation of the word *severally*, or *collectively*. Now if there is any rule of interpretation, by which the word collectively may be added, so as to make the declaratory part refer to one people in the aggregate, and the ordaining part refer to " the people of the several states which may be included in this Union," and thus bring into action conflicting powers; *a fortiori*, the word *severally* may be added, to make the different terms correspond, and indicate the same power, in order to produce harmony between the parts, and make the instrument speak from its four corners, in the same language, and express the same intention. This, however, is not necessary for those who take the power to be several, inasmuch as the uncertainty of the one part is removed by reference to the certainty of the others; but as a matter of right in expounding writings, interpolation is not *an exclusive franchise;* the power is, in its nature, concurrent in both sides; the propriety of its exercise by either depends on the writing itself, or the nature of the interpolation, and its effect on its sense. Obliteration is next of kin to interpolation, and exercised by the same right; the one operates by addition, the other by subtraction, to change the sense of words or language, in order to put in or take out of the constitution, powers which one party is desirous of including within it, though not granted, and the other of excluding from it those which are granted; one striving to impose new, the other to remove existing restrictions, and thus to expand or contract it to suit their respective purposes. These are two of the modes by which the human intellect has, for fifty years, been exerted, to make a supreme law, by construction and implication, what it ought to have been in terms and declared intention, in the opinion of those who think that the federal government is too weak or too strong, and that of the states are under too little or too much restraint, if the words are taken in their natural and obvious, their ordinary or legally, defined sense. A third is, by supposing objects and purposes to have been intended by the particular provisions, which neither declare or refer to them; and making them the premises, draw from the words such conclusions as must follow from such premises, whether the words warrant them or not. Either mode effects the object; let words be added or taken out; let us assume certain objects and purposes, motives and intentions, not apparent in *express words*, or *necessary implication* resulting from those used; any one may make the constitution conform to his opinions, and meet his purposes: but it will not be the same as when it came from those who framed or adopted it, or as it should be read by the judicial eye. Whenever we depart from the established rules for expounding grants, and insert a new subject matter, on which power can be exerted by colour of the grant merely, and not by fair exposition, the power is absolute; for the constitution limits only those federal powers which it grants expressly in words; or in such terms as by their force and meaning necessarily imply it. So, when restrictions are imposed on states in definite cases, their extension in either mode, to other cases, is capable of no limitation; so when the same process is applied to narrow the powers of the one, or the restrictions on the other governments; or to expand or contract the exceptions on either powers, or the reservations of the amendments. The work of plain men must be explained by plain rules; those of subtlety and refinement tend to pervert its meaning and impair its effect: it cannot be a bond of perpetual union, by adding to, diminishing, or altering any term or clause which can change its sense in any way by mere implication: if it is made to speak in language different from its expressed or obvious meaning, it will defeat its own declared objects, and become the apple of discord, and the germ of disunion.

It tends little to the elucidation of truth from any writing, to dwell too much on mere phraseology, when it is evidently not the true index to its meaning: it tends to obscure it, when its substantial provisions are not closely examined by authoritative rules, and mere opinion substituted as the test of intention. The weighty matters of constitutional law are not in mere words and terms of designation: there are some legal instruments of which they may be the essence, or affect their operation; such as the technical terms of some art or science, which require research to find out their peculiar meanings, when they are used in a sense different from common import.

But when we approach an instrument so sacred as the constitution, discussions about words are dangerous, unless, when their meaning is admitted, and the intent is apparent; the contest is as to the phraseology or mode of expressing it, which is most appropriate or correct, according to its classical or other standard of definition, use or application. Without such admission, and when words are intended to be made substance, and terms things; there is great danger of an undue importance being attached to them, especially on those, upon which so much depends as those in the preamble. The great question is, what was the substantive *power*, the *acting thing*, which created the federal government, infused vitality and efficiency into its action; if we suffer our minds to be drawn from the great first moving power, to the mere terms which denote it, by engaging in a war of words, we shall pursue a phantom, a phrase. The *thing* sought will be first overlooked, next forgotten, and another be taken for it; and in the end we may repudiate that power,.that alone did or could act; and conclude, that what has been done, was by a power which never did, could, or can act, so as to effect the declared object, which it is admitted has been actually effected.

Apprehensions of this nature are not chimerical; they have been felt and expressed by this Court, after the experience of forty years; during which it had been seen, that discussions on words and terms had been made, with the endeavour to make the constitution refer to names not things. It had been carried so far, that the appropriate organ of the Court, thus expressed his and the sentiments of the majority, in the following language: in the exposition of a clause in the 10th section of the 1st article of the constitution, on which one of the causes now before us depends, viz: Briscoe et al v. The Commonwealth Bank of Kentucky. It is due, however, to the very able argument on both sides, to declare, that the remarks are not applicable to the course taken at this time, or intended to be so applied.

"And can this make any real difference? Is the proposition to be maintained, that the constitution meant to prohibit *names*, not *things?* That a very important act, big with great and ruinous mischief, which is expressly forbidden by words most appropriate for its description, may be performed by the substitution of a name? That the constitution, in one of its most important provisions, may be openly evaded by giving *a new name* to *an old thing?* We cannot think so. We think the *certificates* emitted under the authority of this act, are as entirely *bills* of credit, as if they had been so denominated in the act itself." 4 Pet. 433, Craig v. Missouri. In the entire correctness of these views, no one of that majority concurred more cordially than myself; and having so concurred, I may apply it, *mutatis mutandis*, to a term intended, not only to affect "*the most important provisions of the constitution;*" but to remove it, together with all its erections, from its foundation on the power of the people of the several states, to one resting on the power of one people of all the states; as the original power which exists, if at all, only in the preamble, and is unknown to any of its provisions. The same venerated organ of the Court had, in a great case and opinion, given his and their views on attempts to give to the constitution, "that enlarged construction, which would extend words beyond their natural and obvious import," by an express disclaimer, 9 Wh. 188: and in a subsequent part, thus expresses himself, in language equally appropriate to the two classes of statesmen and jurists. Those who desired to extend too widely, or contract too narrowly, the powers of the government, "in support of some theory not to be found in the constitution."

"Powerful and ingenious minds, taking as postulates, that the powers expressly granted to the government of the Union, are to be contracted by construction into the narrowest possible compass, and that the original powers of the states are retained, if any possible construction will retain them; may, by a course of well digested, but refined and metaphysical reasoning, founded on these premises, explain away the constitution of our country; and leave it a magnificent structure to look at, but totally unfit for use. They may so entangle and perplex the understanding, as to obscure principles which were before thought quite plain; and induce doubts, where, if the mind were to pursue its own course, none could be perceived. In such a case, it is peculiarly necessary to recur to safe and fundamental principles; to sustain those principles; and when sustained, to make them the tests of the arguments to be examined." 4 Wh. 222; Gibbons v. Ogden.

In this great opinion, concocted by a great mind, in which was stored the true principles of the constitutional law, as understood in the olden time, and as the illustrious father of federal jurisprudence expounded them in our own times; we find it concluding with sentiments, alike worthy of the great and good magistrate who expressed them; the tribunal whose judgment he pronounced; and the instrument as to which it was his first and last aspiration; *"esto perpetua."* As that case and opinion too, bears most essentially on one of the present ones, the Corporation of New York v. Miln; inclination and duty alike, induce me to follow in the path thus illumined, and with such a guide, refer to safe principles, sustain and make them the tests of the merits of all the cases before us. Assuming, that the principles of the constitution are "safe" and "fundamental;" that there can be no exposition of its words and meaning, so authoritative as that of this Court; I am not without the hope, that when the text and commentary are found to be in perfect harmony, there may be less discord concerning them, in judicial opinions, at least, if not in those of the profession, than there has been.

### THE CONSTITUTION OF ENGLAND, THE MODEL OF OURS.

No men were better acquainted with the jurisprudence of England, in all its branches, or had studied it more diligently, than the statesmen of the revolution, and those who framed the constitution; our institutions, our ideas of government, our principles of law, the rules of rights and property, were as perfectly English as our habits and language. The colonists based their course upon the constitution and laws of England; it was in them that they found out the nature of the government under which they lived; a definition of the rights and powers of the people; the duties of the government; and a line drawn between the asserted and legitimate powers of parliament and royal prerogative. Their appeals and remonstrances were founded on the principles of a constitution, understood and respected in both countries, as the standard, line, and rule of right and power, though it was unwritten; there were customs, charters of property and franchises, a magna charta, and acts of parliament, for their confirmation;

which secured the people in the enjoyment of their private and corporate rights, against violation by any law. *Grants, charters,* and *customs, confirmed* by parliament, had the *force of statutes;* and though they could be impaired or annulled by its supreme and transcendant power, in the mother country, where the people were represented; the colonists denied the power, unless they were also represented. They followed the examples of their ancestors, in making a declaration of their rights and wrongs at the commencement of their struggle; in which they claimed and complained as Englishmen, entitled to the benefit of English law. Taking their stand on its principles, they asserted them in all their public acts, which led to the revolution; and when they resolved on renouncing allegiance, and dissolving connection with the English government, congress did what parliament had done at the revolution of 1688. When they declared the throne vacant, and who should thenceforth occupy it, they also declared to whom allegiance was due, and prescribed the form of the oath; and when the change of government was effected in fact, announced it by a solemn declaration of the causes which led to it. Vide 3 Ruff. Statutes, 415, 440. The proceedings of parliament were a guide and the pattern of those of the states, and congress, from 1774, to July, 1776. The same principles pervaded the subsequent proceedings of both, till the present government was established; but their experience had taught them, that two great changes were indispensable, in order to avert, for the future, the perils and evils of the past. That the *supreme* power of government must not be vested in any legislative body, as it was in parliament; that the power of the people must be absolute and unlimited over all government; and that no power should be exercised, unless by their own authority. That the powers to be exercised by the legislature, as well as those prohibited, excepted, qualified, or reserved, should be defined by a written constitution of government; so that there might be more certainty and safety in ascertaining its meaning as a supreme law, than when it depended on usage, custom, and precedent. These changes were made by all the states but two, during the revolution.

### GRANTS TO BE CONSTRUED ACCORDING TO THE LAW, AS IT WAS WHEN THEY WERE MADE.

To understand the constitution then, we must trace its principles, terms and provisions, back through the leading acts of the people, states, and congress, to the great fountain of constitutional, statute, and common law, from which our statesmen traced our whole system of jurisprudence; and by a careful examination of the whole ground, endeavour to discover the intention of those who framed, who adopted the instrument, and its own expressed intention. That it is a charter of government, a grant of power, all admit: it is also an ancient charter, for the federal government rests upon it as a fundamental law; those of the states also, are regulated by it in its grants, as well as its restrictions; it ought therefore, to be expounded, as all such grants and charters are, according to what the law was at the time of making them. Co. Litt. 9, b; 94, b; 4 D. C. D. 546; and "according to ancient allowance," 2 Co. Inst. 282, a; "*Modern methods of conveyancing are not to be construed to affect ancient notions of equity.*" Amb. 288. by Lord Hardwicke. No subsequent judge can alter or vary from the law, according to his own private sentiments; he being sworn to determine, not according to his private sentiment, but according to the known laws and customs of the land; not delegated to pronounce a new law, but to maintain and expound the old one. 1 Bl. Com. 70. "The common law hath *no controller* in any part of it;" but by parliament; and if not "abrogated or altered," then it "remains still." "It appears in magna charta, and other ancient statutes." Co. Litt. 115, b.

This Court has declared, that they know no reason why "*a rule of interpretation to which all assent,*" should not be as applicable to the constitution as to other instruments," 12 Wh. 438; that the "interpretation of the terms," depends on "the language of the constitution itself, and the mischief to be prevented; which we know from the history of our country." 4 Pet. 431, 2.

Let whatever meaning be given to the constitution; whether a league, confederation, agreement, compact or treaty, "between the states so ratifying the same," as it expresses itself in the seventh article; its substance, essence, and nature, is a contract between states or nations, 2 Peters, 314; a grant, 9 Wheat. 189; speaking in the words of the grantor, in reference to the thing granted, and the thing reserved, 6 Pet. 741; with exceptions implying the pre-existence of the power excepted, 12 Wh. 438; 2 Pet. 313; 9 Wh. 200, 207; with prohibitions which restrict the grantor himself, 7 Cr. 136; and referring to the grantor all power not granted or prohibited, 1 Wh. 325; which remain in the grantor as before the grant, 4 Wh. 193; operating as an exclusion from the grant of what is excepted, reserved, or retained, 6 Pet. 312, 741. It is a settled rule, that grants by states, of things, to which the grantor has no right or title, are void, 9 Cr. 99; 5 Wh. 303; 6 Pet. 730: and that no external power can restrict a state, 7 Cr. 136.

### THE MEANING OF THE TERMS STATES AND PEOPLE.

It must then be ascertained, what is the constitutional meaning of *the people*, and *the states*. In the main position which I assumed, and have endeavoured to maintain, that each state was "a *single, supreme, sovereign, power,*" *exclusive,* and absolute, within its own boundaries; unless by its own grant by the constitution, and the restraints it has thereby imposed on itself; I can understand it in all its parts.

The *people* of a *state*, who had by their state constitution, granted the *power* of legislation to their *state* legislatures; had plenary power, to take from them such portions as they pleased, and by their grant vest them in a federal legislature.

The same people could, by the same power which made their constitution the supreme law of *the state*, make that of the United States, the supreme law of *the land*, embraced in the Union; by *each* declaring it so within their respective boundaries, and uniting all the constituent parts, by a deed, signed and executed by the people of each. They could grant and modify the powers they parted with, while the grant was in *fieri*; when consummated, they had no further power over it, for, by their own consent, a *case* arising under it could be decided only by the judicial power, as in a case arising under a grant of land by A. to B. So, when a state renounces all power to emit a bill of credit; to make a compact with another state, without the consent of congress; to impair the obligation of a contract, and declares its exercise to be prohibited; the consequence is plain. Limitations are imposed by itself, which it cannot pass; the act is declared by the people to be void, by being a violation of a supreme law, by which they have bound themselves. By this law, they order their judges to obey it; and by which, this Court must adjudge the act of the state to be void, for the want of power, in obedience to the command of that " single sovereign power," which could bind and had bound itself, to refer all cases arising under its own supreme law, to the judicial power of its own creation.

If a state has thereby became " shorn of its beams," and thenceforth shines with less than "its original brightness;" it is by its own act: and for the future, it must move within the circle by which it has confined its own action, until it shall be enlarged by another power, to which each state has bound itself to appeal. The amending power, existing in "the states, respectively, or the people," to be exercised pursuant to the fifth article of the constitution; which must be taken and construed as a clause of revocation, in a deed, grant, or charter, by an individual, the king, a proprietary, a colony, a state in its legislative capacity, or by the people as the sovereign thereof. It is a declaration by the grantor, that he reserves, and in the mode he has prescribed, will exercise his right to modify or revoke whatever he has granted; will remove any restrictions he has imposed on himself, whenever the requisite number of the separate parties concur, with such exceptions as are specified in the revoking clause. Subject to this power of revocation, the sixth article declares what the effect and obligation of the grant shall be; then the tenth amendment is added by way of a proviso, a condition and limitation, operating on the whole constitution; declaring that what is not granted or prohibited, is reserved to the organic power; " the states respectively, or the people," (respectively).

### THE RESPECT PAID TO THE OPINIONS OF THE SUPREME COURT OF THE UNITED STATES ON CONSTITUTIONAL QUESTIONS.

Such is the meaning of these terms, according to the language of the instrument in which they are used, the precedent acts of the people, the states, and the congress, the convention, and this Court, which, in any other cases than those arising under the constitution, would have been held to be conclusive, and closed all discussion.

There will not be found in judicial history, an instance of a question arising on the words or terms of a will, a deed, contract, law, or treaty, that would have been deemed an open one, after such a course of adjudication on their construction as has been already shown. Nor is there any other country, in which the decisions of its own supreme judicial tribunal would be overlooked, and the interpretation of its fundamental laws be sought in the opinions of foreign writers, or the adjudications of the inferior courts of foreign nations. In England, one judgment of the house of lords settles the law; and it is not suffered to be again discussed in an inferior court. Here too, the same effect is given to a final adjudication of this Court on any other question arising on a written instrument, save on the constitution. Yet their repeated definitions of the terms states, and people, of contracts, their obligations, cessions of territory, of jurisdiction, by deeds and laws of states, or treaties with foreign powers, have been unavailing. All profess to respect this Court, as competent to the high functions it exercises, as the constitutional arbiter of cases arising under the constitution: all profess to revere that instrument, as the best and most perfect emanation of human wisdom: but practically it would seem, that neither its framers or its constituted expositor, have expressed their intention in intelligible language. We find that every thing which has the semblance of judicial opinion, whether from the bench or bar of Westminster Hall, at this day; is pressed upon us as evidence of the meaning of a grant made fifty years since, without an inquiry how the law which bears upon it, was then. We are asked, in effect, to overlook its great feature as the supreme law of the land, speaking in the same language, from the time it was proposed to the present, and through the whole intervening period; and to make its construction accord with the fluctuations of judicial opinions in England, which we well know have been very great within the last fifty years.

### THE EFFECTS OF BEING INFLUENCED BY LATE DECISIONS IN ENGLAND.

If we follow this course in our opinions, and it should appear on investigation, that within this time the law has been reformed in England by judicial power, and we follow the example, one of two consequences are inevitable. The constitution will have one meaning in its application to the old states, and a different one as to the new ones; according to the law as laid down by some of the courts in England, a judge at nisi prius, or some elementary writer, at the different periods when each state became a party to it: or the law, as laid down at this day, must be incorporated into the constitution, as " *a fresh infusion;*" and it be made to speak retrospectively, in a language wholly unknown to its framers, and those who adopted it; nay, wholly different from what was understood, and universally accepted at the time, as declared by this Court in one uniform series of decisions for forty years. In either case, we give to these opinions of foreigners, which have no reference to our constitution, of men who know not its principles; not only a weight which they have not at home, but we virtually make this tribunal subject to the appellate power of foreign courts.

If, as an individual, I could be willing to waive the quantum of colonial dependence, which would be implied in thus recognising any judicial authority over us, as yet remaining in the land of our ancestors; I would expect at least, that it should be only that of a court of as high authority there as this Court has here; not of a court whose judgment may be reversed by the king's bench, exchequer chamber, and house of lords; the opinion of a single judge, which may be overruled in bank; or of a writer, whose lucubrations are read in neither court, or at nisi prius. As a judge, I am bound to take the law of a grant or charter as it was "at the time of making them, and their ancient allowance;" in the administration of the system of jurisprudence which pervades the land, I take it as it was when it was adopted, by the consent of the people, or their legislatures, by the constitution, congress, and this Court. As a constituent member of a court of the last resort, I feel bound by its solemn and deliberate expositions of the law, in cases involving the collisions of power between the state and federal governments; restraints on either, or the rights of individuals or of corporations, secured by either. The same rule must be the law in the thirteen old, and the thirteen new states, which have been admitted into the Union. If we suffer our minds to be influenced by other authority, we must expound our supreme law, our great bond of union, not by the rules and principles which were taken as settled law, at the time of its adoption, but as it now appears to be the doctrine of the day in foreign courts, which may be changed before the next term.

If the constitution is to be taken as a certain grant, an uniform line of power, one law, regulating old and new states alike, operating over the whole territory, whether within the original boundaries of the states, or late acquisitions by treaty; it must speak in the same language, and its terms have, in 1837, the same interpretation as they had in 1787, otherwise it must forever remain unsettled.

Judicial reformations of the existing law, are as much liable to be reformed, and the law restored to what it was, as present law is subject to future reforms; if we do not respect the opinions of our predecessors, it cannot be expected that our successors will respect ours. We must, therefore, look with a single eye to what the law was in 1787, as declared by this Court; and carry its settled principles into new cases as they arise: if we do not, it will become impossible to sustain the principles of the constitution against the assaults which will be made upon it. Our only safety is, in its being received as a standard rule of action and judgment, the same through all time, directing the government of the Union, and of the present and future states, as this Court say, "We cannot comprehend that train of reasoning which would maintain that the extent of power granted by the people is to be ascertained, not by the nature and terms of the grant, but by its date. Some state constitutions were formed before, some since, that of the United States. We cannot believe that their relation to each other is, in any degree, dependent upon this circumstance. Their respective powers must, we think, be precisely the same as if they had been formed at the same time." 4 Wh. 410.

If, then, the respective powers of the state and general governments are to be tested by the law, as it was, fifty years ago; I cannot regard its subsequent changes, when judicially examining the questions now before us. I cannot look to late adjudications in England as the rule by which to determine the effect of a grant of a ferry in 1640; a charter to a corporation for erecting a bridge in 1785; or what was the obligation of the contract granting them when it is made; but look only to the law as it then was. In so doing, I follow another principle settled by this Court, in Saunders v. Ogden; that though the obligation of a contract cannot be impaired by a law made subsequent to the contract, yet all contracts are subject to the regulations prescribed by laws, existing when the contract is made; 12 Wh. 368, 9. By a contrary course, the principle is completely reversed; we repudiate the law in force when the contract and grant was made; we apply to it the law as subsequently altered: so that while we are bound to declare a state law void, so far as it impairs the obligation of an existing contract, we give effect to an English decision, which may produce the same result. As an example, let the case of a grant of a ferry be taken to illustrate my position. In Saville, 11, 14, we have the definition of a ferry, given by the court of exchequer chamber, in 23 Eliz. 1581; which was then the highest court in the kingdom, as the house of lords had not then assumed their supreme appellate jurisdiction. It is admitted by the judges below, and counsel here, that the common law as to ferries is, and has ever been, the law of Massachusetts; notwithstanding which, an opinion given in 1835, by a lord chief baron of the exchequer, has been relied on in opposition to the case in Saville, to show the nature and extent of a ferry granted in 1640. Whether the latter or the former opinion may now be the received law in England, matters not; the colonists brought with them the law of ferries, as it was at the time of their emigration; this ancient grant of the colony must be construed accordingly. To be consistent, we must suspend a final judgment till the present court of exchequer chamber has reversed the principle established as the law for two hundred and fifty years. For it may so happen, that that court will not readily introduce any innovation into the common law on a subject so important, on the authority of a single judge; this Court certainly would not so far respect the opinion of one of its own members. That these views are peculiar, is evident from the course of argument and opinion: but their peculiarity is, in itself, no reason for abandoning them; if they are not erroneous, they are safe as a guide to a true interpretation of a grant of power, to be exercised by the several governments in the United States, whose basis was the constitution of England, and the common law; as the great system of jurisprudence, from which all our institutions arose.

THE POLITICAL CONDITION OF THE COLONIES OF GREAT BRITAIN.

I now proceed to trace the constituent power of government, in the several states, as the constituent power of the United States, of which the people are the head, the *"caput et finis;"*—the emperor, king, prince, potentate, sovereign, each of his own empire, realm, nation, or state; as the primary, original fountain of all legislative, executive, and judicial powers, granted or restrained, in and by the constitution, *to the colonies of Great Britain:* who became states of this Union, and were its constituents in 1788: according to my position, *each* in their own right, "absolute and unlimited in matters of *government, commerce and possessions;"* as held and enjoyed by them respectively, and not collectively, or in the aggregate, as one people, one state, or nation. The proposition is stated in these terms, as well to support it by the political and judicial authorities which bear favourably on it, as to negative the antagonist proposition; which having been laid down by authority of both descriptions, more weighty and influential, than mine can or ought to be; I must either make it the rule for my judgment, by submission to its results, or show by some paramount authority to which we all profess to submit, that it is not founded on historical facts, or the laws of the land.

"It is a fundamental maxim, and necessary principle of English tenures, that the king is the universal lord, and original proprietor of all the lands in his kingdom; and that no man doth or can possess any part of it, but what has mediately or immediately been derived as a gift from him, to be held upon feodal services." 2 Bl. Com. 51.

The feudal tenures were abolished under the commonwealth, and their abolition confirmed at the restoration, by the 12 Car. 2, ch. 24; and by the 4th section it was enacted, "that all tenures hereafter to be created by the king," &c., "shall be in free and common soccage, and shall be adjudged to be in free and common soccage only." 3 Ruff. 192. He is however the universal occupant, as all property is presumed to have been held by him. Co. Litt. 1; 4 Bac. 153; 7 D. C. D. 76; D. 63. By his charters, he gave both soil and jurisdiction to the proprietors of New Jersey, Pennsylvania, Maryland, and North Carolina; and one was *presumed* as to Delaware: by which these provinces were created principalities or seignories, in the nature of counties palatine in England, with the addition of general powers of legislation, subject to revision by the king in council. 1 Bl. Com. 108. In these provinces, the proprietary was deemed the count palatine, acting according to the law of the Roman and German empires, in the place, and by the deputed authority of the emperor. Seld. tit. Hon. 378, et seq. The imperator, or king of England, a sovereign equally independent in his dominions as any sovereign in his empire, 1 Bl. Com. 241, 2; retaining, therefore, only this ultimate power of revision in his privy council; the king, as an emperor, had created these provinces as counties palatine, which is the highest franchise known to the law of England, in

7

which the (proprietary or) count palatine, has *jura regalia* within his (province or) county, as fully as the king himself. 4 D. C. D. 454; Davis' Rep. 168; Selden. T. H. 384. *Proprietary governments*, granted to individuals, are subject to the express condition, that nothing shall be attempted which may derogate from the sovereignty of the mother country, 1 Bl. C. 108; as appears in their respective charters, fealty is reserved. Vid. Pat. Laws N. J. app. 1; 5 Smith Pa. L. 406; L. of Maryland, 1; N. C. Laws, 1.

No lands in these provinces therefore, could be granted, or jurisdiction exercised over them, unless by the proprietary; in whom the absolute propriety and dominion thereof was vested. "In the *royal colonies* the king made no grant of lands to them. In the creation of *provincial establishments*, the constitutions of which depended on the respective commissions issued by the crown to the governors, and the instructions which usually accompany those commissions; under the authority of which, provincial assemblies are constituted with the power of making local ordinances, not repugnant to the laws of England." 1 Bl. Com. 108. A third class were, '*charter governments*,' in the nature of civil corporations, with the power of making by-laws for their own internal regulation, not contrary to the laws of England; and with such rights and authorities, as are *specially* given them in their several charters of incorporation. The form of government in most of them, is borrowed from that of England. They have a governor, named by the king, (or in some proprietary provinces by the proprietary,) who is his representative or deputy. They have courts of justice of their own, from whose decisions an appeal lies to the king and council here, in England. Their general assemblies, which are their house of commons, together with their council of state, being their upper house, with the concurrence of the king or his representative, the governor, make laws suited to their emergencies." But it is declared by statute, 7 and 8 W. and M. ch. 22; 3 Ruff, 609; "that *all the colonies* are subordinate to, and *dependent* upon the imperial crown and parliament of Great Britain, who have full power and authority to make laws and statutes of sufficient validity to bind *the people of America, subjects* of the crown of Great Britain, in all cases whatsoever." 1 Bl. Com. 109. This was the English view of our colonial condition. The American view is presented in the *declaration of rights* by the colonies, in the congress, on the 14th of October, 1774, as theirs; and also, (which will be referred to hereafter) showing the grounds assumed by the mother country. But the *association* drawn up on the 20th of the same month, shows, that they agreed on the condition of the *people* of the colonies, who in *a full* and *free representation thereof*; thus headed their association : " *We, his majesty's most loyal subjects*," &c.; so they then were, and so they remained, till they become bound to the colonies or states, by the allegiance due to the king, which devolved on them when they ceased to be *dependent* on him. Vide, 1 Journ. Cong. 31, 62, 28, 66, 134, 263, and ante, 25, 26.

Thus the colonies were considered by the mother country and themselves, and such were their respective relations by the constitution and laws of England, which were theirs. " The British government, which was then *our* government, and whose rights have passed to the United States," 8 Wh. 588, as instituted and organized; must then be examined in its great outlines, as the pattern of the *colonial state* and *federal* governments, which have superseded it, but which are all founded on the same fundamental principles. All resting on the supreme power of *the people* of *the state*, as *one state;* but consisting of the people of three distinct *estates* in England; *each* acting separately in constituting the government of the nation, the state, empire, realm, or kingdom; and in its administration, as the power which created and continues it, is in those separate estates, as the *constituent parts.* The colonies were mere *dependencies* of the state, a part of its dominion, but not of itself; for from the preceding view taken by *Mr. Justice Blackstone*, it is evident that they were not *states* or *estates* of the kingdom, as they are defined in p. 50, 51. " The legislature of the kingdom is entrusted to three distinct powers, entirely independent of each other: the king, the lords spiritual and temporal, which is an aristocratical assembly of persons, selected for their piety, their birth, their wisdom, their valour, or their property;" and " the house of commons, freely chosen by the people from among themselves, which makes it a kind of democracy: this aggregate body, actuated by different springs, and attentive to different interests, composes the British parliament, and has the supreme disposal of every thing;" 51; as the power of making laws constitutes the supreme authority; so, wherever the supreme authority in any state resides, it is the right of that authority to make laws; 52. (Vide 12 Wh. 347.) " With us, therefore, in England, this supreme power is divided into two branches; the one legislative, to wit: the parliament, consisting of king, lords and commons; the other executive, consisting of the king alone; the British parliament in which the legislative power and, of course, the supreme and absolute authority of *the state* is vested by our constitution; 1 Bl. Com. 147. Parliaments are " general councils," 149; " an assembly that met and conferred together;" "*general assemblies* of the *states*," 147; " great council;" " the meeting of wise men;" "*conventus magnatum*," &c., 148; to make new laws; *novis injuriis emersis, nova constituere* remedia, &c. (*Congress*, to " *consilio*," *convention, constituere.*) A legislative assembly, 1 Bl. Com. 189.

The constituent parts (Vide 6 Wh. 414) of a parliament are, " *the king* in his political capacity, and *the three estates* of *the realm*, the *lords spiritual*, the lords *temporal*, (who sit together with the king in one house,) and *the commons*, who sit by themselves in another." And the king and these three estates together, form " *the great corporation* or *body politic* of the kingdom, of which the king is said to be *caput principium et finis.*" 1 Bl. Com. 153. These are " the constituent parts of the sovereign power," 156. Both classes of lords, however, though in the eye of the law, the lords spiritual are a distinct estate from the lords temporal, and are so distinguished in most of our acts of parliament, yet in practice they " are usually blended together under the one name, *the lords;* they intermix in their votes, and the majority of such intermixture joins both estates," 156. The lords spiritual being archbishops and bishops, and formerly abbots and priors, who hold, or are supposed to hold, ancient baronies under the king, in right whereof they were allowed their seats in the house of lords, 155. The *lords temporal* consist of all the peers of the realm, 156; as a body of nobles having a distinct assembly, deliberation, and powers from the commons, in order to support the rights of the crown and the *people*, by forming a barrier to withstand the encroachments of both, 158; representing themselves and the landed property of the kingdom, they hold or are supposed to hold.

The commons consist of all such men of property in the kingdom, as have not seats in the house of lords, every one of which has a voice in parliament, either personally, or by his representatives. In a free state, every man who is supposed a free agent, ought to be in some measure his own governor; vide 1 Journ. Cong. 59; therefore, a branch, at least, of the legislative power should reside in the whole body of the people. " And this power, when the territories of the state are *small*, and its citizens *easily known*, should be exercised by the people in their *aggregate or collective capacity*, as was wisely ordained in the *petty* republics of Greece, and the *first rudiments* of the Roman *state*," 158; vide 2 Dall. 470. (This is the principle which is now applied to the people of an *empire*, extending from the *Atlantic to the Pacific Ocean!*) " In a *large state*, the people should do that *by their representatives*, which is impracticable to perform in *person;* and have them chosen by a number of minute and *separate* districts, wherein all the voters are or may be safely distinguished." The *counties* are therefore represented by knights, elected by the proprietors of land; the *cities* and *boroughs* by citizens and burgesses, chosen by the mercantile or supposed trading interest of the *nation.* "And every member, though chosen by one particular district, when elected and returned, serves for the *whole realm.* For the end of his coming thither, is not particular, but general, not barely to advantage *his constituents*, but the commonwealth; and therefore he is not bound, like *a deputy* in the *United Provinces*, to *consult* with, or take the advice of *his constituents*, upon any particular point; unless he himself thinks it proper or prudent to do so."

"These are the constituent parts of a parliament," *parts* of which *each* is so necessary, that the consent of *all three* is required to make any new law, that shall bind the subject; "these parts are *parliament*, thus united together, and considered as *one aggregate body;*" 159, 160, 149. The king, lords and commons *in parliament assembled*, 196.

The king is a *constituent part* of the supreme legislative power, 261; *the executive power*, a *branch* thereof, whose "share of legislation" is "in the power of *rejecting*, rather than *resolving*," this being sufficient to answer the end proposed, 154; the lords, in *law*, two estates, in *practice*, one, representing their own rights and landed property, or supposed so; the commons, composed of the knights of shires, as the *representatives* of the landholders, or landed estates of the kingdom, 172; citizens and burghers supposed to be elected by the trading interest, as the *representatives* of the most flourishing towns, who, as they increased in trade and population, were admitted to a share in the legislature, and yet retain it, though they had decayed; and the *representatives* of the two universities, to protect in the legislature the rights of the *republic of letters*, 174; so of the cinque ports. Herein we have the legislative power of the colonies and states, by substituting the term *general assembly* in their charters and constitutions, in lieu of *parliament;* excepting only the restrictions and qualifications by them respectively imposed. We have also the merely *resolving* power of "*the United States of America in Congress assembled*," before the confederation; and the power to *make requisitions* on *the states* under it, which was but a shadow of a parliament. But we have the substance of "all *legislative powers* herein granted, (which) shall be vested in a *congress* of the *United States;*" the American parliament, composed of the President, Senate, and House of Representatives, the caption of whose laws is, " Be it enacted by the Senate and House of Representatives, &c., in Congress assembled;" as in England, by the *lords spiritual and temporal*, and *commons*, in *parliament assembled.* The great difference between the two constitutions is, the one *defines* the "legislative power, and limits it by enumerating the subjects of its exercise;" 4 Wh. 405; 9 Wh. 188, 9, 195; the other does not; of consequence, it is *supreme and absolute;* but *both* define the executive power, when it acts otherwise than its appropriate part in legislation. In England, it is by the *prerogative* power, inherent in the *person* who fills the throne, as *king* or *queen;* here it is like legislative power, which is only what is granted by express words, or necessary implication, resulting therefrom; 1 Wh. 326. The president is invested with certain important political powers; 1 Cr. 166; which, if he or any officer acting by his orders, exceeds, the act is void, and the officer suable, 171; as a legislative act, repugnant to the constitution, is void, 177, so must an executive act be. But when the executive acts within the powers delegated, his acts have the power of the constitution, in the same extent as acts of congress; 1 Cr. 164, 172.

The *royal* prerogative can no more be exercised by the *executive power* here, than the transcendent *absolute power* of parliament can be by *congress*. Both powers are exerted by constitutionally delegated powers, and are void else.

In England, the king's prerogative is *limited* by certain bounds; it extends to all things not injurious to his subjects; 1 Bl. Com. 239. (The exemptions need not be stated here, as they will be more appropriately referred to in one of the cases.) The executive power is placed in the king, for the sake of unanimity, strength, and despatch; he is the chief magistrate of *the nation;* 250. He may reject what bills; make what treaties; may coin what money; may create what peers, and pardon what offences he pleases; unless when the constitution hath expressly, or by evident consequence, laid down some exception or boundary, declaring, that thus far the prerogative shall go, and no farther; 250.

" With regard to foreign concerns, the king is the delegate or representative of his people, in whom, as in a centre, all the rays of his people are united;" 252. " As their representative, he has the sole power of sending and receiving ambassadors;" 253. " The sole prerogative of making war and peace;" 257. " The first in military command in the kingdom;" 262. " It is partly upon the same, and partly upon a fiscal foundation, to secure his marine revenue, that the king has the prerogative of appointing ports and havens." " The navigable rivers and havens were computed among the regalia, and were subject to the sovereign of the state; the king is their guardian, and lord of the whole shore." " But though the king had a power of granting the franchise of havens and ports, yet he had not the power of resumption, or of narrowing, or confining their limits, when once established;" 264. " He is the fountain of justice, and general conservator of the peace;" 266; " though he has delegated his whole judicial power to his judges;" 267. " From the same original, of the kings being the fountains of justice, we may also deduce the prerogative of issuing proclamations, which is vested in the king alone;" 270; " of conferring privileges;" 272. " He is, with regard to domestic concerns, the arbiter of commerce;" 273; " and, as such, has the regulation of weights and measures;" 274; " and as money is the medium of commerce, it is the king's prerogative, as the arbiter of domestic commerce, to give it authority or to make it current;" 276. " The denomination or value for which the coin is to pass current, is likewise in the breast of the king; he may legitimate foreign coin, declaring at what value it may be taken in payment;" 278. " The king may, also, at any time, decry or run down any coin of the kingdom, and make it no longer current." 279.

### THE FEATURES OF THE BRITISH AND FEDERAL GOVERNMENTS COMPARED.

In this outline of *our* old constitution of government, we see the pattern of our *new* one, though with a different distribution of powers; the most important of those which are in the king, by prerogative, in England, are granted to congress; the judicial power is vested in the courts of the United States, exclusively; and the executive power is as much defined by enumeration, as the legislative and judicial powers of the constitution are. Herein consists one great difference between the two governments; and from this there arises another, which is all important. The powers not delegated, or prohibited, being reserved to the states respectively, or the people; none can exist by prerogative, or inherent power, in any branch of the government. Hence the effect of a specification of the powers granted and prohibited, and the express reservation of all others, leaves to the states all the prerogative powers of the king over those subjects which are involved in these four cases, either directly or collaterally; on none of which are any "powers granted to the United States by this constitution." The only questions involved are, whether the laws and acts of the states come within the prohibition; if they do not, they are valid, as the exercise of their reserved powers: to regulate their internal polity, police, and commerce; to grant charters of incorporation, for enjoying franchises over public rivers and arms of the sea, within a state; for the establishing the boundaries between states; and creating a bank corporation to deal with the funds of a state, according to the terms of the charter.

There is another difference between the executive power here and in England. The king is a natural person, on whom the crown descends by hereditary right, as real estate does; and in whom the executive power vests, by birth, on the demise of the crown, so that the crown is never without an heir; 1 Bl. Com. 190. Here the executive power is vested in a president; who is an officer created by the constitution, to perform the designated functions of an office, which is filled by an election in the first place; on the demise of the incumbent, the office devolves on certain other officers, named in the constitution, and act of congress. Of consequence, whether the office is filled by the person elected thereto, by "the electors from each state," or by "the representation from each state, in the house of representatives," by "each state having one vote;" or by devolution on the officer designated to fill it; the executive power is equally vested in him, as the president of the United States. The office is filled, the officer filling it, whether the vice president, on whom it devolves by the constitution, the president pro tempore of the senate, or the speaker of the house of representatives, on whom the office devolves in succession by law; the character of the office, the nature and power of the office is the same. It is precisely what the constitution has declared; neither more nor less; his legislative functions are like the king's, except that his veto is not absolute: but in his executive capacity he is, and can be no more than an officer; the chief executive magistrate, as the chief justice, is the chief judicial magistrate of the United States.

The name, or style given, imports no power; before and under the confederation, congress elected a president, who was ex officio, and from the nature and character of the body over which he presided, "President of the United States of America in Congress assembled;" 1 Laws, 481. But the title was a mere name, till the constitution made it a *thing*—"the executive power," on some subjects supreme; on others subordinate; according to its provisions, in designating the respective powers confided to him as an agency, as all the grants of power to the other branches of the government are declared to be by this Court. He has, therefore, no representative character; has no representative function to perform; and neither by his representation of the states, or the people, can exercise any powers reserved to them; though they are the very powers vested in the king by pre-rogative, as the delegate or representative of the people of his king-dom or empire.

In other respects, the great features of both governments are the same; both established by the people of the estates of one, the states of the other; each state or estate represented by their representatives in distinct bodies, forming independent branches of the legislature, chosen or appointed in a different manner; but each representing their several and respective estates or states; though, when elected and returned, "serving for the whole realm;" the whole United States. "The estates of the realm," in parliament; "the United States, which may be included within this Union" in congress, acting by "the representation from each state," in the house of commons, or representatives, and in the house of lords or senate, by persons entitled by birth, office, tenure, or appointment by the king, or "chosen from each state, by the legislature thereof;" and both lords and senate constituting the middle power, between the executive and the people.

There is another feature common to both governments. In Eng-land the king has his constitutional counsellors and councils. The *peers of the realm* are, by their birth, hereditary counsellors of the crown; and may be called together by the king to impart their ad-vice, 227. *The judges* are a council for law matters, 229. But the principal council is *the privy council,* and by way of eminence is called the *council,* 229. So the president has his *councils.* "He may require the opinion in writing of the principal officer at the head of each of the executive departments," &c. 2 Sec. 2 Art, Clause 2, Const. This is called a *cabinet council;* it is a *privy council,* in which the president is present, as the king is in person in his. 4 Bl. Com. 231. The *senate* is the *council* in making trea-ties, in *advising* and *consenting* to appointments to office. *Sena-tors* are not, ex officio, counsellors individually; but the president "may convene both houses, *or either* of them."

CONVENTIONS OF THE ESTATES OF THE KINGDOM OF ENGLAND, COM-PARED WITH CONVENTIONS OF THE STATES OF THE AMERICAN UNION. THE ENGLISH DECLARATION OF RIGHTS AND WRONGS IN 1688; THE PATTERN OF THE AMERICAN DECLARATION OF 1774, 1775, AND 1776. THE ABJURATION OF ALLEGIANCE TO JAMES THE 2D, AND GEORGE THE 3D, COMPARED.

Another striking feature of affinity in the great political institu-tions of both countries, is in the *convention* of the *estates* of the one, and the *states* of the other, as its organic power: they pass *ordi-nances* rather than *acts of parliament.* 1 Bl. 156. In England it is called a "*convention* parliament," 151; because the two houses meet, as the *representatives* of their *several estates;* each sitting and acting separately, as in their legislative capacity, but acting as *a constituent convention.* There can be no constitutional parliament without a king: the houses meet in convention, and declare the rightful heir to the throne to be the king, as at the restoration, 151; or as at the revolution of 1688, when the houses as conventions, declared *the throne vacant,* by the king having abdicated the crown; *name the person to fill it,* and fix *the succession in* future: but in both cases acts of parliament were passed, when all the constituent parts were assembled, to confirm and validate the acts of the conventions. 3 Ruff. 145, 415; 1 Bl. Com. 211, &c.

In one of the acts of confirmation, the conventions of 1688 are thus noticed; "whereas *the lords,* spiritual and temporal, and commons, assembled," &c., *lawfully, fully,* and *freely, representing all the estates of "the people of this realm,* did," &c. 3 Ruff. 440. *How* they assembled, appears from the journals of the two houses. The lords met separately in convention, and received a letter from the prince of Orange, addressed *to the lords, spiritual and temporal, assembled in convention,* 14 Journ. Lords, 101, 2; and proceeded as a convention, till they agreed upon certain resolutions of the convention of the commons, declaring, "that the king had abdicated the government, and the throne being thereby vacant." Ib. 125.

Those persons who had been members of the house of commons in the last parliament, met, pursuant to a letter addressed to them from the prince of Orange, and passed some resolutions, 10 Journ. Comm. 5, 6; proposing a convention, to consist of as many members from each county, &c., as are of right to be sent to parliament, to be elected to represent them, and entered into *an association,* "engaging *to Almighty God, the prince of Orange,* and *to one another,* in defence of it, never to depart from it, until our religion, *our laws,* and *our liberties,* are secured," &c. p. 6, a. b. Writs of election were issued for the election of members of the convention, "*of such a number of persons to represent them, as from every such place is or are of right to be sent to parliament.*" 7, b, 8, a. Members having been elected, met and chose a chairman, and called themselves the "*commons,*" 9, a. 11, a. 12, a. "*the house;*" and "*the present convention,*" 13, a. In their proceedings they "*resolved, nemine contradicente,*" 16, a.; drew up the heads of what they desired, 17, a.; and agreed upon a joint declaration by the two conventions, 23, a.; which, after being amended, was headed, "Die Martis, 12 Februaris, 1688."

"The declaration of the lords spiritual and temporal, and commons, assembled at Westminster." Vide 1 vol. Laws, U. S. 7.; 1 Journ. Cong. 27, 8, 312.

"Whereas the late king, James the second," &c., (enumerating specially the wrongs and grievances,) "*having abdicated the government, and the throne being thereby vacant,*" (after stating the election of the members, *pursuant to the letters* of the prince of Orange, proceeds.) "And thereupon the said *lords, spiritual and temporal, and commons,* pursuant to *their respective* letters, and elections, being now assembled in a full and free *representation of*

8

*this nation,* taking into their most serious consideration, the best means for attaining the ends aforesaid, do in the first place, (as their ancestors in like cases have usually done,) for the vindicating and asserting their ancient rights and liberties, *declare,"* &c. "And they do claim, demand, and insist, upon all and singular, the premises, as their undoubted rights and liberties, and that no declarations, judgments, doings and proceedings, to the prejudice of *the people* in any of the said premises, ought in any wise to be drawn hereafter, into consequence or example." William and Mary are then declared king and queen of England, &c. "And that the oaths hereafter mentioned, be taken by all persons of whom the oaths of allegiance and supremacy might be required by law instead of them; and that the said oaths of allegiance and supremacy *be abrogated."* The new oath of *allegiance* was to king William and queen Mary. In the oath of *supremacy* is this clause. "And I do declare, that no foreign prince, prelate, state, or potentate, hath or ought to have, any jurisdiction, power, superiority, pre*h*eminence, or authority, ecclesiastical or spiritual, *within this realm."* 10 Journ. Comm. 289; 14 Journ. Lords, 124, 5; 3 Ruff. 440, 42.

This declaration has never been misunderstood in England; no lawyer or judge has ever held, that the *two conventions* were *one,* that *the people* they represented were *one;* but the contrary; the declaration has, by the assent of all, been taken to be what it says it is in the heading, the act of the *lords* and *commons,* assembled *pursuant* to *their respective* letters, which were addressed by the prince to the *house of lords,* separately, from the one to *individuals* merely. By the fundamental law of the kingdom both could not form one body. *The lords* represented the *two estates* of the *nobility* and *clergy; once lords,* they remained so though the throne was vacant. They sat in their own right, representing *themselves* and *property,* as *two* estates or states of the nation or realm, wholly distinct from the *third* estate or state; that *estate* was the *whole* body *of the people,* represented in the convention of the commons. As there was no king, there could be no parliament, or house of commons in any other capacity than in a convention; those persons who *had been* members of parliament were no longer so, hence the letter addressed to them was not to assemble *as a constituent part* of a parliament, but to call *a conventio,,* to be composed of *representatives* of *the people* of the counties, &c. *to be elected* by the same electors of the several places who voted for members of the house of commons, and for the same number. Thus the estates of the kingdom remained distinct as before, when there existed a parliament in all its parts; the two conventions acting separately and concurring in opinion, made *one declaration,* to which they had separately agreed, as separate conventions, who were a full *representation* of the *nation,* of the *three estates* thereof, lords *spiritual, temporal,* and *commons.* They did not represent *the head* of the *state, the king,* because there was none; hence they used the term *nation,* not *kingdom,* as there could be none without a head, nor estates of *the kingdom,* when for the want of the executive power there was no government in existence. But those three estates embraced the whole nation, in all its component parts, though not *the state* in its supreme corporate capacity; 1 Bl. Com. 147; yet parts of the *nation,* empire, or the realm; 1 Bl. Com. 242; consisting of the clergy and nobility, or *lords,* and the people, or *commons,* who were the nation. Now it is most strange, that when we compare these proceedings with those which commenced in *the colonies,* in 1774, from the first assembling of congress, till they made "*a declaration*" of rights and wrongs, and entered into "*an association,*" preparatory to a revolution; and from that time to July, 1776, when the revolution being effected, and the colonies had in fact became *states,* and made "*the unanimous declaration of the thirteen United States of America,*" announcing that fact to the world; that both declarations *patterned* from the declaration of 1688, throughout, and in many parts *copied,* should be taken to be the declarations of *one people,* in *a congress,* representing *one nation,* instituting a *national government* thereof; and not as thirteen colonies or states *una animo,* declaring each to be a free and independent state, when the name of each was affixed, signed by their separate agents, calling themselves their representatives. It is equally strange, when in 1781, the same states by "articles of confederation and perpetual union" between them, naming each, entered into a confederacy or league of alliance, the style of which was "the United States of America," the second article whereof declared, "each state retains its freedom, sovereignty, and independence, and every power, jurisdiction and right which is not by this confederation expressly delegated to the United States in congress assembled;" and by the third article, "the said states hereby severally enter into a firm league of friendship with each other," &c.; that there then existed an unity of political power, in the people and government of one state or nation, compounding the people, and power of all the states, into one, from 1776; so that no particular state had any power, right, or jurisdiction to retain to itself, or delegate to the United States. It is stranger still that it should be asserted, that congress acted as the representatives of one people, state, or nation; when it is an admitted fact, that the first rule adopted by the congress of 1774, was, "*Resolved,* That, in determining questions in this congress, each colony or province shall have one vote." 1 Journ. 11. So it continued till the confederation which declared, "each state shall have one vote;" 1 Laws U. S. 14; and so it remained till the old congress was dissolved, in 1788, by the adoption of the constitution by nine states, each having one vote in a convention of the people thereof.

If there can be a political truth, it would seem to be this, that where, in a body composed of sixty-five members, there could be only thirteen votes, if all the states were present, and there must be one vote less for each state that was absent; that the body did not, and could not represent, and act for all the states and the whole people, as a national legislature, "serving for the whole realm," nation, or state. They were a mere congress of states, colonies, or provinces; the legislature of each of which was the separate constituent of its own deputies, or "ambassadors," who gave the vote of their "sovereign," and not their own; and, therefore, could by no political possibility, be a legislature in any political sense, as the representatives of a people in their aggregate collective capacity.

### THE PERVERSION OF THE TERM "THE PEOPLE IN THEIR AGGREGATE OR COLLECTIVE CAPACITY."

If any thing connected with the construction of the constitution can be deemed a bold and unwarranted theory, or extravagant doctrine, it is in the application of the remarks of Mr. Justice Blackstone, in 1 Bl. Com. 158, 9, before quoted, as to the people of a small state, such as "the petty republics of Greece, and the first rudiments of the Roman state." There, he says, the people legislated "in *their aggregate or collective capacity;*" which term he uses in contrast with legislative powers exercised by representation of the people in a large state: the power is the same in the people of a large or small state; the only difference is in the mode of its exercise: in the latter case it is in their primary assemblies, in the former by representatives, elected to act as their agents by their authority. Now, when we find a term used in reference to a petty state, whose whole territory was not as large as a county in one of the states, or its population equal to many towns or cities, applied to the establishment of a government of this Union, of an almost boundless extent; the utter fallacy of any proposition founded upon it, is self-evident. It never has been true, in fact, that the people of any of the states assembled to make laws, in any other way than by representation; the people of Athens would meet at the Areopagus, and of Rome at the Capitol, to make laws or decrees; but the people of England or the United States never so met. When their action is in their primary assemblies, as an aggregate or collective body, it is, and always has been, either to express their opinion, or exercise the elective franchise in choosing their representatives; this is done, as Blackstone says, in designated districts; for, in a large state, the people must do that by representatives, which they cannot do in person; that is, legislate by their duly selected agents, and not personally. No lawyer in Westminster Hall would venture to assert, that the ordinances of the convention of 1688, were the acts of the people of the kingdom, in their "aggregate or collective capacity;" as the people of Athens or Rome, when in an assembly, they would put down one ruler and appoint another, or change their form of government. No commentator on the constitution of England, has ever confounded the action of the people of a county or city, in the election of the members of a convention, with the action of the convention by its ordinances; and no theorist has been hardy enough to take the position, that when the people act in a convention of their representatives, they act at the same time in their individual capacity. In England, at least, there is an agreed distinction between the con-

stituent and the agent; between a body composed wholly of constituents, and another body of mere agents; between electing the
agents for ordaining a fundamental law, and its enaction by those
agents under their delegated authority. There, too, the nature of a
representative government appears, in the opinion of their jurists
and statesmen, as it does in its practical operations; fact, principle,
and theory, point to the same original source of power; and "no
political dreamer" thinks of compounding the people or the estates
of the kingdom, into one mass, or one estate. Their unwritten constitution is clearly understood; the powers of all corporations or
bodies politic are accurately defined, whether they relate to government or other matters; and voluminous as the reports of their judicial
proceedings are, we seldom see one which involves a question of
constitutional power, in any department or office of government.

How different the case is here needs no further explanation than
what is afforded by our judicial and political history; we have not
yet attained a knowledge of the power on which the federal government rests; the meaning of the preamble of the constitution is unsettled; and as we trace it to the bodies which adopted it, the difficulty thickens. A great question is at the threshold, and must be
removed, before we can examine the interior of the structure. All
admit, that in fact, the constitution was established by the ratification of the people of the several states, in separate conventions or
representatives, whom they elected in the respective counties: yet
the preponderance of political and professional authority, is in favour
of the proposition, that it was the act of the people in their collective capacity. When this shall become settled doctrine, it will be
seen how much better the nature and science of government is now
understood, than it has been in England; and was understood by the
congresses and conventions of these states, from 1774 till 1787. It
will also illustrate the *happy* effects which flow from the great fundamental principle of the American system of government—the *certainty* of a written constitution.

The congress of the revolution, and the convention of 1787, were
ignorant of *any other legislative power than that of the separate
states.* It is attributing to the members of congress in 1777, the
most utter and profound ignorance of the nature and powers of the
government of the revolution, which they themselves administered
for five years, if it was such an one as commentators now hold it to
have been. In the letter recommending it to the states to adopt the
articles of the confederation, they say, " Every motive calls upon us
to hasten its conclusion;" "it will add weight and respect to our
councils at home, and to our treaties abroad." " In short, this salutary measure can be no longer deferred. It seems essential to our
very existence as a free people, and without it we may soon be con-
strained to bid adieu to independence, to liberty, and to safety," &c.
1 Laws U. S. 13. The remedy was far worse than the disease, according to modern theory; but the practical statesmen and jurists of
the day, deemed it of vital importance to have a government in form,

though utterly defective in substance and execution. Bad as it was, it was better than none; a line of *duty* was prescribed to the states; if they did not follow it, it was not because it was not plain; whereas, before, the only line was drawn by the states themselves, in their separate instructions to their delegates, or in acting on their recommendation. When too it is recollected, that congress asked for the delegation of the shadow of power by *states,* when, according to the commentary, they had the substance already, by delegation from the *people;* the men of the revolution were either ignorant in what a government consisted, or the expositors of their acts have made one which never existed but in their own fancy.

The same remarks will apply to the members of the convention of 1787, if we so take the words of the preamble of the proposed constitution, as to be a declaration that the political existence, and organic power of the several states and people, had become so amalgamated into one body of supreme power, as to make it the sole grantor of the powers of the federal government, and competent to restrict the states, and control existing state constitutions. Their letter to congress, and of the latter to the several state legislatures, asking separate conventions of the people in each to ratify it; was an act indicating political fatuity, if the instrument contained, and was intended to be a declaration, that when ratified by such conventions of nine states, and thus established, it was not " by the people of the several states," but of all collectively.

THE VIEWS OF THE GENERAL CONVENTION OF 1787, AND THE STATES.

It would also be an imputation of political treachery to the states, who were the constituents of that convention, to draw up a frame of government, which in all its provisions explicitly declared the separate existence and action of " the people of the several states, and of each state," in all the movements of the government, in all time, in language admitting of no twofold interpretation; And then prefixing to it a declaration, by which the states, in their most sovereign capacity, in separate conventions of the people, are made to admit and acknowledge, that " the absolute sovereignty" in matters of government, was not, and from July, 1776, had not been invested in the people of the separate states; and that they had, at the adoption of the constitution, only such " residuary sovereignty," as remained after a paramount power had made a supreme law over them. Had the convention so announced it to the congress, the legislatures, or the people of the states, in proposing its ratification; there would have been a fifth unanimous declaration of the rights of the states and people; not only of rights, but of wrongs and grievances, more aggravated than those which led to the revolution, because they were attempted by their own representatives, in violation of their instructions. No state convention would have convened; congress would have at once rejected the proposition, and in the name of each state declared, *non in hæc federar venemur;* they would have pointed to their four declarations in October, 1774, July and December, 1775, and July, 1776; to the articles of confederation, and their state constitutions; as so many denials in the most solemn forms, of the proposition submitted. It is not credible, that when the power of parliament to legislate for *colonies* who avowed allegiance to the king, was utterly denied, even under the British constitution, the authority of which was universally admitted; the free and independent *states*, who had eleven years before renounced their allegiance to the crown, and abolished their old constitution, would have adopted a new one which left them less free in legislation, than they were in their colonial condition. After throwing off the *pack* put on their backs, while *boys* and *children*, as parts of the family of one common father, by an usurped power of legislation; they would not, as *men*, and as *freemen*, emancipated by their own acts, take up another pack, still heavier and more grievous.

THE SUPREMACY OF THE CONSTITUTION OVER STATES, GREATER THAN PARLIAMENT OVER THE COLONIES.

Parliament never asserted by the plenitude of its omnipotence, such powers of legislation over the colonies, or attempted to impose such restrictions on colonial or provincial legislatures, as are exerted by the constitution; and if it is a supreme law, overriding state constitutions, by any other authority than that of the people of each, without and against their consent, it is one more sovereign over them than that which they threw off by the revolution. Every principle by which it was conducted, every object sought to be attained, was reversed and frustrated; if, in 1787, the states were not in that "separate and equal station among the powers of the earth," which they assumed in 1776, and did not then each retain all powers which they had not expressly delegated to the congress in 1781. Every state constitution asserted palpable falsehoods; and the people thereof exercised usurped powers, if the sole right of instituting any government over them was not in themselves alone. And thus, every solemn act, and written document of the congress, and the states, for thirteen years, will become utterly falsified; if the "power, right, and jurisdiction" of the federal government, and the authority of the constitution is not by grant from each state, of what all had so often declared to be inherent in the people thereof, by original right, and which it had hitherto retained. If these powers were in the whole people of the United States, as one " single sovereign power," from 1774, till 1787, that power still exists in its original plenitude; and the judges of this, and all state courts, are bound to obey and expound it as the grant of that power, speaking in its words, and expressing thereby its intention, as the grantor in whom there was full and absolute right to do whatever it has ordained.

## THE EFFECT OF TAKING THE CONSTITUTION AS A GRANT BY ONE PEOPLE.

If the constitution was only a grant of power, it would be of little importance to inquire whether it was to be considered as made by the one, or the separate people of the states who adopted it; for its obligation on those states would be unquestioned. But the importance of the vestion arises on the restrictions and amendments; whether a state restricts itself, or is restricted by an external power; whether the reservations are to the people collectively, or the people of each state. And it must be remembered, that the terms of reservation in the 10th amendment, make no change in the constitution, in virtue of the amending power in the 5th article; it is a declaration by the grantor, of the meaning and effect of the grant and prohibition, which none but the granting power was competent to make. Hence, it is necessary that there should be: first, a competent power to grant the thing granted; and next, the grantor must have competent power to prohibit and restrain states and state laws; to make exceptions to the grants and restrictions, and to reserve to itself all other powers not exercised by the grant: and as B can make no exception or reservation out of a grant made by A, all these powers must be original in the one who was competent to make the grant. If it is in A, the grant throughout being his act, is easily construed as one deed, with its various clauses; which, when referred to one person, whose intention it expresses, is taken as a simple, plain writing, the one part whereof explains the other, by reference and established rules. But if the grant is taken to be the act of A, in granting certain things to C, restraining a previous or subsequent grant by B to D; declaring what B or D may or may not do; and there is attached to the grant a proviso or defeasance by B, that what is not granted to C, or prohibited to B and D, shall be reserved to B or D, the whole is unintelligible. The exceptions and reservations being of original right and title, which is vested in A, are void and inoperative, if not made by A himself; they remain in him, and cannot pass to B or D without direct grant: of consequence, the grant becomes disencumbered of any exception or reservation; and must be taken, by all the rules of law, as if it contained none in terms. Taking, then, the constitution as the grant of the one people to congress, imposing restrictions on the states acting in the legislatures thereof, and the people acting in convention; and the tenth amendment operating as a proviso or defeasance on every part thereof, not as an actual or intended alteration of any of its provisions; it must follow: That as it was made by a power subordinate to that which ordained the constitution, it was incompetent to except or reserve any thing out of, or from it, to the people of the several states, if they are not the grantor; or to the states respectively, if each was not a grantor. Not being parties to the grant, they are strangers to it; and no principle of law is better settled, than that an exception or reservation to a stranger, is void: it must be to the lessor, donor, or feoffor, and his heirs, who are privy in blood, and not to any who is privy in estate, as to him in possession, remainder, reversion, &c; 8 Co. 70, b, 71, a; Shep. Touch. 77, 80; 4 D. C. D. 288, 9; Fait. E. 5, 6; 9 Joh. R. 75. An exception is of something out of that which the grantor had granted before by the deed, Shep. Touch. 77; a reservation doth always reserve that which was not before, or abridge the tenure of that which was before, ib. 80; and sometimes it has the force of a saving, or exception, to reserve a new thing, or except part of the thing granted; Co. Litt. 143, a. It is therefore evident, that to give any effect to the reservation, it must be taken as the act and words of the grantor, 10 Co. 106, b; 4 D. C. D. 290; and that whatever meaning is given to the term in the preamble, must be carried into the exceptions and reservations; so as to make the reserved powers a part of what was in the people before the grant, or something excepted from it.

### THE EFFECT OF AN EXCEPTION OR RESERVATION IN A GRANT.

No jurist has ever questioned the universal application of the maxim, "*poterit enim quis rem dare et partem rei retinere, vel partem de pertinentibus; et illa pars quam retinet semper cum eo est et semper fuit.*" Co. Litt. 47, a. Whether the words operate as an exception or reservation, the effect is the same; the part or thing excepted or reserved, always is in the grantor, and always was; and the maxim has been adopted by this Court in its common law meaning, by the words of the grantor, denoting his intentions, and to be construed accordingly. 6 Pet. 310, 741; 4 D. C. D. 290; Fait. E. 8.

It is then a necessary consequence of these rules, that the people of the several states, have now no reserved powers, or that they are the granting power of the constitution; and as grantors, could make exceptions to the powers of congress, to their own reserved powers, and reserve what was not so granted or excepted. Another rule results from the preceding ones, which this Court lays down as one " to which all assent," that an exception to any power proves, that in the opinion of the lawgiver, the power was in existence had there been no exception. 12 Wh. 438, 9; 9 Wh. 206, 7, 16. The exception marks the extent of the power, 9 Wh. 191; the thing granted, is ascertained by what is excepted or reserved, 6 Pet. 310, 741; an exception will not be inserted by construction, 4 Pet. 462, 3; but shall be taken strictly against the grantor, 4 D. C. D. 290; and "an exception out of an exception, leaves the thing unexcepted." Ib. Fait. E. 7.

By keeping in view these unquestioned rules, it is easy to understand the constitution in all its parts as a grant; and by so considering it, we can trace the true grantor in its provisions, its history, and the political situation of the states at the time of its adoption, and back to their colonial condition. If by so doing certainty can be attained, no labour can be too great; nor can time be deemed uselessly employed, if it leads to satisfactory conclusions on a subject so important.

9

THE NATURE AND ORIGIN OF THE FEDERAL GOVERNMENT, AS DE-
CLARED BY THE CONVENTION OF 1787, AND BY THIS COURT.

The political history of our country presents a narrative of one
continued struggle between the states and the confederacy, either for
territory or political power.

At an early period of the war of the revolution, the question
whether the vacant lands which lay within the boundaries of particular states, belonged to them exclusively, or become the joint
property of all the states; was a momentous one which convulsed
our confederacy, and threatened its existence; but it has been com-
promised, and is not now to be disturbed. 6 Cr. 142; 5 Wh. 376.
It was settled by cessions by particular states, and the adoption of
the articles of confederation. Vide post. When that was done, the
question of power arose out of the incompetency of congress to
effectuate the objects of its adoption; the collision of opinion was
not what were the relative powers of the several states and of congress; for it was *then* admitted that what was not expressly delegated, was retained by and remained in each state. That a new
government was necessary was the universal opinion; but the difficulty was, in agreeing what additional powers should be given to
congress by the surrender of the states; no statesman or jurist pretended that this could be done in any other way than by the voluntary act of the separate states; in their sovereign capacity, by the
people in conventions.

This difficulty did not cease by the unanimous act proposed by the
general convention. In their letter submitting it to congress, we find
them stating the same reasons which embarrassed their action, and
long delayed its ratification by the states. "It is obviously impracticable in *the federal government of these states,* to secure all rights
of independent sovereignty to each, and yet provide for the interest
and safety of all." "It is at all times difficult to draw with precision the line between those rights which must be surrendered, and
those which may be reserved; and on the present occasion, this difficulty was increased by a difference of opinion among the several
states, as to their situation, extent, habits, and particular interests:"
"and thus the constitution which we present, is the result of a spirit
of amity, and of that mutual deference and concession, which the
peculiarity of our political situation rendered indispensable." 1
Laws U. S. 71.

There can be no misunderstanding of the meaning of this letter,
that the convention had proposed the frame of a "federal government of these states," to be created by a surrender of the necessary
powers by the several states, to be made by the people in separate
conventions; so as to make the constitution paramount to those of the
states, and not leave the powers of congress dependent on a grant by
the legislature, which the people could revoke or change. So it has
been considered by this Court, in a most elaborate opinion. "This
mode of proceeding was adopted; and by the convention, by con-

gress, and by the state legislatures, the instrument was submitted to the people." " They acted upon it in the only manner in which they can act, safely, effectively, and wisely, on such a subject, by assembling in convention; it is true they assembled in their several states, and where else should they have assembled? No political dreamer was ever wild enough to think of breaking down the lines which separate the states, and of compounding the American people into one common mass. Of consequence, when they act, they act in their states. But the measures they adopt, do not, on that account, cease to be the measures of the people themselves, or become the measures of the state governments. From these conventions the constitution derives its whole authority. The assent of the states, in their sovereign capacity, is implied in calling a convention; and thus submitting that instrument to the people. But the people were at perfect liberty to accept or reject it, and their act was final. It required not the affirmance, and could not be negatived by the state governments. The constitution, when thus adopted, was of complete obligation; bound the state sovereignties; and the government proceeded directly from the people." 4 Wh. 403, 4.

Neither in this, or any other opinion of the late Chief Justice, will there be found an expression like that of " the people in their aggregate or collective capacity," being the constituent power of the government; it will not be found in any act of any state legislature, convention, or congress; while every declaration by either asserts all power to be, and to have been, in the people of the several colonies or states. Every fundamental principle of that government, from which all ours have been mainly patterned; every movement of the people of both countries, in convention of their representatives; explodes the doctrine. So, too, the concurring declarations of this Court, sufficiently numerous to establish a code on any other subject, have indicated and made visible to the most ordinary capacity, the organic power which created, and was alone competent to create government. In one of their opinions, delivered twenty-five years since, they little imagined the present clouds which hang over the knowledge of those bodies, in which that power was vested. " The course of reasoning which leads to this conclusion, is simple, obvious, and admits of but little illustration. The powers of the general government are made up of concessions from the several states; whatever is not expressly given to the former, the latter expressly reserves;" 7 Cr. 33; United States v. Hudson and Goodwin.

It is but reasonable, that this coincidence between the terms of the instrument, the cotemporaneous declaration of those who framed it, the action upon it by congress, state legislatures and conventions, and the exposition of all that was done, as given by this Court; would have led to the universal conviction, that the words and terms used were intended and must be taken in their declared sense. But as it has not sufficed to produce this effect, it becomes indispensable to recur to those acts of the colonies, the states, and congress; from which the conclusion has been drawn, that the grantor of the constitution, was not the people of the several states.

THE PROCEEDINGS OF THE CONGRESS OF 1774. THE DECLARATION OF THE RIGHTS OF THE COLONIES AND COLONISTS.

From the preceding view of the colonies prior to 1774, and while the ancient relations between them and the mother country continued, it is most manifest that they were as separate from each other, in all matters of internal government, as they now are. Their only political connection was by their union under one common sovereign, as it is now under the constitution; their governments were in virtue of separate charters then, as they are now under their several constitutions; and no one, or any number of colonies, had any more power within their limits, than the states have now. No other controlling power did, or could exist then, under the old constitution of the kingdom, than does now under that of the Union, save such as it imposed.

Though they had assembled in congress to consult on their common concerns, they had never made a government over themselves; and when they met in 1774, their proceedings showed in what capacity they acted. They first resolved, that *each colony* should have *one vote*, which was an explicit declaration, that they acted separately in all they did; their declaration of rights and resolutions are also too unequivocal for any double or doubtful meaning to be attached to them.

After reciting the grievances suffered in consequence of certain acts of parliament, and of the crown, they declare the character and authority under which they act. " The good people of the *several* colonies of New Hampshire, Massachusetts Bay, Rhode Island and Providence Plantations, Connecticut, New York, New Jersey, Pennsylvania, New Castle, Kent, and Sussex on the Delaware, Maryland, Virginia, North Carolina, and South Carolina, justly alarmed at these arbitrary proceedings of parliament and administration, have *severally* elected, constituted, and appointed *deputies*, to meet and sit in the city of Philadelphia, in order to obtain such establishment as that their religion, laws, and liberties, may not be subverted."

" Whereupon, the deputies, so appointed, *being now assembled, in a full and free representation of these colonies*, taking into their most serious consideration the best means of attaining the ends aforesaid; do, in the first place, as Englishmen, *their ancestors, in like cases have usually done, for asserting and vindicating their rights and liberties, declare*," (Vide ante, p. 44.)

" That all the inhabitants of the English colonies in North America by the immutable laws of nature, the principles of the English constitution, and their *several charters and compacts*, have the following *rights:*"

" *Resolved, N. C. D.* 1. That they are entitled to life, liberty and property; and they have never ceded to any foreign power whatever, a right to dispose of either without their consent."

"*Resolved, N. C. D.* 2. That our ancestors, who first settled these colonies, were, at the time of their emigration from the mother country, entitled to all the rights, liberties, and immunities of free and natural born subjects within the *realm* of England."

"*Resolved, N. C. D.* 3. That by such emigration they by no means forfeited, or surrendered, or lost any of these rights; but that they were, and their dependents now are, entitled to the exercise and enjoyment of all such of them, as their *local* and other circumstances enable them to exercise and enjoy."

"*Resolved, N. C. D.* 4. That the foundation of English liberty, and of all free government, is a right in the people to participate in their legislative council; and as the English colonies are not represented, and from their local and other circumstances cannot properly be represented in the British parliament, they are entitled to a *free and exclusive power of legislation in their several provincial legislatures,* where their right of representation can alone be preserved, in all cases of taxation and internal polity, *subject only* to the *negative* of *their sovereign,* in such manner as has been heretofore used and accustomed. But from the necessity of the case, and a regard to the mutual interest of both countries, we cheerfully consent to the operation of such acts of the British parliament, as are bona fide restrained to the regulation of *our external commerce;* for the purpose of securing the commercial advantages of the whole empire to the mother country, and the commercial benefits of *its respective members,* excluding every idea of taxation, internal or external, for raising a revenue on the subjects in America without their consent."

"*Resolved, N. C. D.* 7. That these his majesty's colonies are likewise entitled to all the immunities and privileges granted and confirmed to them *by royal charters, or secured by their several codes of provincial laws.*"

"*All and each of which* the aforesaid deputies, in behalf of themselves and their constituents, *do claim, demand, and insist on, as their indubitable rights and liberties;* which cannot be legally taken from them, altered or abridged, by any power whatever, without *their own consent,* by *their representatives* in *their several* provincial legislatures." 1 Journ. Cong. 28, 9.

*An association* was formed and signed by the members from the different colonies, beginning, "We, his majesty's most loyal subjects, the delegates of the *several colonies* of New Hampshire," &c. &c. "And therefore we do, for ourselves and the inhabitants of the several colonies whom we represent, firmly agree and associate under the sacred ties of virtue, honour, and love of country, as follows." 1 Journ. 32.

The letter to the people of Great Britain was headed in the same manner, and signed by *the delegates* of the *several colonies.* 1 Journ. 36. So were their other letters and addresses at that time, 62.

These proceedings cannot be mistaken in the distinct assertion, that all the powers of government were vested in the *several* provincial legislatures, subject only to the restraints mentioned in the fourth resolution. There was no *state* or *nation*, to which the several colonies stood in the same relation, as the counties and towns of England did; they had no separate powers of government within a county, &c.; the aggregate population composed the state or nation, so did the population of a colony, so now does that of a state. The counties, cities, and townships thereof, exist only for local purposes, have nothing to do in matters of government, except to elect representatives to the legislature of the state or colony, to whose laws they are subject. Hence there can be no analogy between the people of the different districts of a colony, who are the people of the colony, and the colonies themselves in their political capacity, and the people thereof separated from all others by territorial boundaries. To unite them as one, is to erase the line of separation, and make one *colony* and one *legislative body* out of thirteen, acting by the power of one people, inhabiting the former divisions, and the *separate colonies*, as merely the *counties of the one.* Let us suppose, that in the congress of 1774, an additional resolution had been offered to this effect. *" Resolved, N. C. D.* That these thirteen colonies are *one nation,* the people thereof *one people,* and that *this congress* is a *national government,* as the representatives of *the one people,* having the power of *enacting laws* to *bind* the said thirteen colonies and the people thereof, without their separate consent:" it need not be asked what would have been the result.

THE ACTS OF THE CONGRESS, THE STATES AND PEOPLE, IN 1775, AND 1776.

The spirit and principles of this declaration were adopted by the colonies and congress. In October, 1775, congress, on the application of the provincial convention of New Hampshire, recommended them to call a full and free representation of the people, to establish such government as they thought proper, to continue during the dispute with Great Britain. 1 Journ. 206, 15. This was done in a convention of the people in January, 1776, by a constitution which remained in force till 1784; declaring the dissolution of all connection with the British government, and "assuming that *equal rank* among *the powers of the earth,* for which nature had destined us, and to which the voice of reason and providence loudly called us." Vide 2 Belk. Hist. N. H. 303, 5, 9, 335.

The royal government had ceased in South Carolina in September, 1775, under the recommendation of congress in November: 1 Journ. 219: the people of that state formed a constitution in March, 1776, which all officers were sworn to support, "till an accommodation with Great Britain, or they should be released from its obligation by *the legislative authority of the colony."* 2 Drayton's Mem. 171, 186, 196.

In April, 1776, congress resolved, "that trade was subject to such duties and impositions as by *any* of the colonies, and such regulations as may be imposed by the *respective* legislatures," &c., which resolution congress directed to be communicated to foreign nations. 2 Journ. 117, 25.

In May they resolved, "that every kind of authority under the crown should be totally suppressed, and all the powers of government under the authority of the people of these colonies should be exerted. That it be recommended to the *respective assemblies* and *conventions* of the united colonies, where no government sufficient to the exigency of their affairs hath been hitherto established, to adopt such a government, as shall, in the opinion of the representatives of *the people,* best conduce to the happiness and safety of *their constituents in particular,* and America in general." 2 Journ. 158, 66.

On the 24th of June they declared, by their resolutions, "that allegiance was due to *the several colonies,* that adherence to the king was treason against *the colony* within which the act was committed;" and recommended that laws should be passed for punishing treason, and counterfeiting the continental bills of credit. 2 Journ. 217, 18.

In June, the people of Virginia, in full convention, adopted a constitution; declaring that all power is vested in and derived from *the people,* who have an indefeasible right *to institute, reform, alter,* or *abolish* government; that none *separate from,* or *independent of* that of Virginia, ought to be erected or established *within the limits thereof;* and that the government, under the British crown, is totally dissolved. 1 Rev. Code Va. 1, 7. This constitution remained unaltered till 1830. Vide 1 Journ. Cong. 260.

On the 2d of July, 1776, the people of New Jersey, in convention, declared the authority of the crown to be at an end; the *royal government dissolved in all the colonies;* and adopted a constitution, to become void on a reconciliation with Great Britain, Patt. Laws. App. 5; Book of Con. 154, 5, which is yet unchanged. In June 19th, deputies from the cities and counties of Pennsylvania, approved the resolutions of congress passed in May; resolved that a convention be called to form a government on the authority of *the people only;* and declared, on the 24th, their willingness to concur in a vote of the congress, declaring *the united colonies* free and independent *states:* provided, the forming the government, and regulating the internal police of *the colony,* be always reserved to the *people of the colony.* Con. of Penn. 35, 39, 43. The convention assembled on the 15th of July the constitution was adopted in September, 1776, and continued in force till 1790.

As there never was any other political connection between the colonies, than such as resulted from their common origin, by separate charters from the crown, in virtue of the royal prerogative, and the general supremacy of parliament, which extended to all the dominions of Great Britain; it was a necessary consequence of the extinction of both the prerogative and legislative powers of the mother country, that there could remain no restraint on the legislation of the colonies, save what the people thereof should impose. No extraneous power could act, within their respective limits, without their consent: from the moment that the authority of Great Britain ceased to operate, that of each colony became absolute and sovereign; and no government could exist thereout, which could prescribe laws within it. Such was the unanimous expression of the universal sense of the people, in primary assemblies, in conventions of counties and states, legislatures and congress, from 1774: four colonies had become states by the adoption of constitutions of government by the inherent power of the people; the formation of a fifth was in progress on the same principles, which were solemnly promulgated by the original declaration of the rights of the several colonies, and the people thereof. In June, 1776, there was not a colony in which any authority under Great Britain was exercised, except in warfare: and when congress resolved that allegiance was due to the several colonies; that treason was punishable in the colony wherein the act was committed; and that the regulation of trade was subject to the laws of the respective legislatures; it was tantamount to a declaration, that they were then independent, and had, in fact, " assumed their equal station among the powers of the earth." Congress had recommended that all the colonies should do so, by the establishment of a government on the authority of the people only; four states had exercised, a fifth had entered upon the exercise of this authority; and a convention of the people thereof was assembled, before the declaration of independence, by congress, was engrossed or signed by any member. Vide 1 Dall. Laws, App. 54.

THE POLITICAL SITUATION OF THE COLONIES AND STATES BEFORE
THE FOURTH OF JULY, 1776.

From these proceedings, the political results were plain and self-evident; each colony, by the uncontrollable exercise of all the powers of self-government, had in fact become an independent state; five were so, by their declarations of independence in the most solemn manner. No sovereignty did, or could exist over them, unless that of Great Britain should be restored by a reconciliation; which not happening, their declaration of independence, in their separate conventions, became absolute; and these states were independent according to the universal opinion of the country, which is most clearly expressed in the language of this Court. 4 Cr. 212, M'Ilvaine v. Cox. " This opinion is predicated upon a principle, which is believed to be undeniable, that *the several states* which composed this Union, so far at least as regarded their municipal regulations, became entitled, from the time when they declared themselves independent, to all the *rights and powers of sovereign states,* and that they did not derive them from concessions by the British king. The treaty of peace contains a recognition of their independence, not a grant of it. From hence it results, that the laws of *the several state* governments were *the laws of s*overeign states; and as such were obligatory upon the people of such states, from the time they were enacted. We do not mean to intimate an opinion, that even a law of a state, whose form of government had been organized prior to the 4th of July, 1776, and which passed prior to that period, would not have been obligatory. The present case renders it unnecessary to be more precise in stating the principle, for although the constitution of New Jersey was formed previous to the general declaration of independence, the laws passed, on the subject now under consideration, were posterior to it." (They were for the punishment of treason against the state.)

### THE DECLARATION OF INDEPENDENCE.

Such being the political condition of the colonies and states, it becomes a question of easy solution whether congress intended to make a solemn promulgation of these principles to the world, by declaring the great result of the revolution to have been, or to be, the establishment and continued existence of thirteen independent nations and states, with the powers of government separate and sovereign in each; or of one nation, one state, with one national government. Whether this great and crowning act of the revolution was intended to perpetuate, or prostrate, the rights and powers of the colonies, the states, and the people thereof, and to substitute one government, in place of thirteen then in existence. To absolve the people of those states not only from their allegiance to the British crown, but from that allegiance which congress, ten days before, had resolved the people owed to the several colonies; to abolish as well the royal, as the colonial and state governments, within the boundaries of the United States; to suppress alike the British constitution, and those state constitutions, which, two months before, they had recommended to be formed, by the authority of the people of the several colonies alone; to proclaim to foreign nations in April, that the power to impose duties, impositions, and regulations on trade, was in the respective legislatures of the colonies; yet, in July, to declare to the world that the power " to establish commerce," &c. existed in one state, in one government, acting over all the states in their unity of political power, as the representatives of one people, of the one state. Taken in this sense, there must have been *two* American revolutions; one to suppress the government of Great Britain, the other to suppress the governments of the states, each of which was by the right of revolution; for there is no more pretence of any authority by the people of the states, or in the credentials of the members of congress, who were appointed by colonial or state legislatures, to abolish state governments, and constitute a national one, invested with supreme legislative powers over all the states, than there was by the king and parliament to abolish their supreme legislative, or prerogative powers, by any act of the several colonies or states, or when they were assembled in congress by their deputies. The states, by their several representatives, effected the first revolution in an assembly of the states; the congress effected the second, by imposing on the states— people, a new sovereign—*themselves*. Taken in the other sense, the declaration of congress, on the 4th July, 1776, announced one great revolution; on the great principles solemnly declared in 1774, and reiterated in every political movement by the people, whenever they expressed their opinion, in large or small popular assemblages, or through their representatives at home, or those deputed by their local legislatures, to consult, deliberate, and resolve in a congress. Congress could declare the existing political condition of the colonies and states, as their delegates or deputies: but as congress was not a convention of the people, nor had that body any pretence of power to alter the existing state of things; to assume to themselves any legislative power; or take away any from the states; we must therefore read their great and solemn act, as one done by a delegated, rather than by an usurped authority. Its very front is stamped with an impression of intention, which cannot be mistaken.

"In Congress, July 4, 1776." (Vide ante, 44.)
" The unanimous declaration of the thirteen United States of America." It declares self-evident truths; the right and power of the people, to alter and abolish existing government, and to institute new government, on such principles, and organizing its powers in such form, as to them shall seem most likely to effect their safety and happiness: it sets forth the grievances of the colonies, and concludes thus: "We must, therefore, acquiesce in the necessity which denounces our separation, and hold them as we hold the rest of mankind, enemies in war and in peace friends."

" We, therefore, the representatives of the United States of America, in general congress assembled, appealing to the Supreme Judge of the world for the rectitude of our intentions, do, in the name, and by the authority of the good people of these colonies, solemnly publish and declare, that *these united colonies* are, and of right ought to be, *free and independent states;* that *they* are absolved from all allegiance to the British crown, and that all political connection between *them* and *the state* of Great Britain, is and ought to be totally dissolved; and that as *free* and *independent states, they* have full power to levy war, conclude peace, contract alliances, *establish commerce,* and to do all other acts and things which independent states may of right do. And for the support of this declaration," &c. &c.

An unanimous declaration of the thirteen states must necessarily mean an union of action between separate states, in declaring their separate rights. It was a self-evident truth, that the "*one people*" of *each state,* could alter, abolish old, and institute new government at their pleasure: but on every principle of the revolution, it was as self-evident a falsehood, to declare, that "one people" could do so for another; or that the people of any number of states, could, in any way, control the power of any single state. It would be equally untrue, that congress held or could exercise the power of the people in relation to government, either separately or collectively; all their votes, acts, and resolutions, were *by states;* not *per capite,* as a body representing or legislating for one people. They professed to declare only what did exist; not to alter or abolish any present, or to institute any new government. They declared these united colonies to be independent *states,* not *one state,* as the "*state of Great*

*Britain;"* that *they* are absolved from all allegiance to the British crown; but did not declare, that *the people of the several states* were absolved from their allegiance to their state, or held them bound to allegiance to the United States, as a state.

## THIRTEEN COLONIES BECAME THIRTEEN STATES, EACH SOVEREIGN WITHIN ITS TERRITORIAL BOUNDARY.

It remained still a self-evident truth, that by the absolution of all allegiance to the crown, and the dissolution of all political connection between them and the state of Great Britain; the thirteen United colonies, became thirteen United States, in consequence thereof; and that as free and independent states they had the powers declared, as the necessary result of each colony having then, or previously, become freed of all restraint, by the removal of all incumbrance on their independence. This was the meaning of their separate declaration of independence, as declared by this Court, in Coxe v. M'Ilvaine, "that the several states from the time when they declared themselves independent," were entitled to all the rights and powers of sovereign states. It would be strange, indeed, if, by their afterwards uniting with the other states, in their unanimous declaration in congress assembled, they had lost their separate independence, were again dependent, and ceased to hold those rights and powers. This Court has expressed their opinion to the contrary, in Harcourt v. Gaillard, 12 Wh. 526, 7. "There was no territory within the United States that was claimed in any other right, than that of some one of the confederated states." "Each declared itself sovereign and independent, according to the limits of their territory." Georgia insisted on that line (the 31st degree of north latitude,) as the limit which she was entitled to, and which she had laid claim to, when she declared herself independent; or which the United States had asserted *in her behalf*, in the declaration of independence. "The treaty of peace" has been viewed only as a recognition of pre-existing rights, and on that principle, the soil and sovereignty within their (the states of South Carolina and Georgia,) acknowledged limits, were as much theirs at the declaration of independence, as at this hour. So, in the Dartmouth College v. Woodward, 4 Wh. 651; this Court say: "by the revolution, the duties, as well as the powers of government, devolved on the people of New Hampshire. It is admitted, that among the latter, was comprehended the transcendent power of parliament, as well as that of the executive department."

If the authority of this Court is respected, the declaration of independence is to the judicial mind what it is to the common eye; a proclamation to the world, by the separate states assembled in congress by their respective deputies, voting for, and signing the instrument by states; a publication of their existing political condition, each as an independent state, the people of each, "one people;" the state on an equal footing with the other powers of the earth, united in a common struggle against oppression. The voice of the people, whenever, and however expressed, and their action by their appropriate agents, in their domestic, federal, or foreign relations, shows that this declaration was so received and understood by the whole country; from the time it was made, till the adoption of the constitution. Each of those states which had not before done it, proceeded to institute government for itself, by written constitutions; declaring all power to be inherent in the people of the state, and denying the existence of any other, with the exception of Connecticut and Rhode Island. Those states, which had previously adopted constitutions, continued to act under them, without a doubt felt or expressed, that the governments so organized, were as competent, and in all respects on the same footing, as those which were constituted after the 4th of July, 1776. Vide 4 Cr. 212, 13.

The two states, which were exceptions, furnish a still more conclusive illustration of this universal opinion. Connecticut had no constitution till 1818; Rhode Island has none to this day: both states continued to exercise their legislative power, under their respective charters from the king, in virtue of his prerogative. The people of those states had never assembled in convention to abolish the British government, or to institute one of their own; they made no separate declaration of independence, or conferred any new authority on their state legislature; but they silently acquiesced in the course of legislation, founded on the unquestioned existence of a supreme sovereign legislative power, by which legislative usage was, by the tacit assent of the people, a constitution in effect. Herein they departed from the great principle of the American system of government, which was to define, limit, and distribute the powers by written constitutions, instead of doing it according to usage and precedent; but this very departure shows the force of a principle fundamental in all free states and governments; that all power emanates from the people of the state. That legislative usage, by the implied consent of the people, makes such usage as much a supreme law; and to all intents and purposes, the constitution of a state; as if one had been ordained and established by an instrument in writing, adopted in a convention of the people, by their expressly delegated authority. So this Court have held the usage of Connecticut, 3 Dall. 398, 400, &c., and of Rhode Island, 2 Pet. 656, 7, under their respective charters; and their political condition, by the results of the revolution, as defined in 4 Wh. 661, is precisely the same as that of the state of Great Britain. The usage of the legislative body, is the only supreme law of the land, and the only evidence of the constitution of the state. That the force of such usage in these two states, was in no wise impaired by the declaration of independence in congress, is therefore a self-evident truth; and as they had made no separate declaration, either in form, or in any writing constituting government, it is as a political or judicial truth equally clear, that the declaration by congress, was made by the delegates of these states, in the name and behalf of each, of the rights and powers of each, as well as the others of the thirteen, by the unanimous act of all. So it was considered by congress, from the 4th of July onwards; all their proceedings show that their declaration of rights in 1776, differed from their declaration of rights in 1774, only in this. The latter referred to the rights of the colonies, when first united, to obtain a redress of their grievances, by petition and remonstrance; an appeal as British subjects for justice, by the principles of the English constitution, magna charta, and the common law: in the hope of reconciliation, by the repeal of the obnoxious laws, and a disavowal of what the colonists held to be unconstitutional power. The former referred to the then existing rights and powers of the states and people, resulting from the principle declared in 1774: which, after all hope of redress or conciliation had became extinct, and the appeal to arms taken by both parties, were in 1776 applied to the states; who being ipso facto independent, by the suppression of the authority of Great Britain, the fact was declared and proclaimed, together with its effect on the condition of the several states. The people of the states were no longer the subjects of the king, but were thenceforth the citizens of a free state, owing allegiance to it, but to no other state or power; and were thereby on an equal station with the other powers of the earth, as states.

In October, 1776, congress directed that every officer should swear, that "I do acknowledge the thirteen United States of America, namely, New Hampshire, &c. to be free, independent, and sovereign states, and declare that the people thereof owe no allegiance to George the Third, king of Great Britain," 2 Journ. 400. That allegiance is the unerring test of sovereignty, existing in the state to whom it is due, is a truth too evident to be discussed or denied.

In November, congress agreed on the frame of the articles of confederation; and in their circular letter addressed to the respective legislatures of the states, refer it to them, as "so many sovereign, independent communities;" and "to each respective legislature, it is recommended" to invest its delegates with competent powers, in the name and behalf of the state, to subscribe articles of confederation and perpetual union; 1 Laws U. S. 12, 13. These proceedings suffice to show the sense of congress as to the domestic relations of the states before they had adopted the articles of confederation: their federal relation or connection had assumed no definite form; each state made out its own credentials to its deputies in such form as they chose; and congress had hitherto acted by an authority, assumed as exigencies required, calculating on the acquiescence of the separate states.

If congress was, in 1776, a national legislature, with power to pass laws independently of the several states, and to control state legislatures, all subsequent acts were worse than useless; for the government was more absolute than the present. The declaration of independence admits of no qualification of the unlimited powers of a state. Taking it as the creation or the recognition of a government, instituted by one people of one state, as guarantied by the treaty of alliance with France, and acknowledged by the treaty of peace with Great Britain; it was " absolute and unlimited in matters of government, commerce, and possessions;" and all the rights of the crown, and powers of parliament, devolved upon, and passed definitively to the one state and nation, as well to the soil as the jurisdiction of the whole territory within the boundaries of the United States. That this view of the declaration of independence is contradicted by historical facts, by all the political events of the revolution, the proceedings of congress, the general and state conventions, and the adjudications of this Court is, I think, fully apparent in the preceding view. It also appears to me, that this declaration has been as much perverted, as the passage from Blackstone, in its application to the then political situation of the colonies, or states; its intention and effect, connected with the history of the times, is so plainly expressed, that it seems incapable of being misunderstood.

That there were thirteen colonies, with separate governments in each, without any control by one over another, is admitted; that they assembled by different representations; that they voted, acted, and signed the declaration by their separate delegates, is apparent on the journals of congress, and the face of the paper. The members who assembled as the delegates of colonies, were the same, who, as the representatives of the states, made the declaration in the name, and by the authority of the good people of these colonies; which was:—"That these united colonies are, and of right ought to be, free and independent states."

If this declaration had no bearing on the constitution, or if that instrument was not the most ill-fated one that was ever devised and written by man, not only by being itself perverted, but made the cause of perverting every other instrument in writing which forms a part of its history, or can be referred to for illustration; there would be the same union of opinion as to its meaning, as there has been for one hundred and fifty years in England, as to the declaration of rights, wrongs, and the effects thereof, in 1688. That it consummated a revolution in government, whereby all colonial dependence having ceased, each political community assumed, as a state, that separate and equal station among the powers of the earth, which other independent states held, and which each state then and thenceforth had and enjoyed; would have been the universal opinion, if no question of political power was involved in mystifying it. If this paper is taken as it reads, and means what it says, it contains neither a grant or recognition of the existence of any legislative powers within the limits of the once colonies and then states; other than what was and had been in the several legislatures thereof, from their first settlement; and if it cannot be made so by bold assertion, or misinterpretation, there is no foundation for the theory of the *unity of power* in the " one people," in constituting a government for the United States. To my mind, it seems a contradiction in terms and sense, that the declaration could be true in fact, in principle, or historically; if the several states could be made subject to a constitution, ordained by " an absolute sovereignty" in the people of all the states, in the aggregate. It is to me, wholly repugnant to the declaration itself, as to two great grievances set forth: "For taking away our *charters,* abolishing our most valuable laws, and *altering,* fundamentally, the *forms of our government:*" "For *suspending our own legislatures,* and declaring themselves invested with power to legislate for us in all cases whatsoever."

This is the precise effect of the modern interpretation of this great act of the revolution; by which commentators make congress declare, that the very acts of oppression, committed by the king and parliament, against which the states and people contended as violations of their rights, were no longer so when exercised by congress. If the result of the revolution was a change of masters; a mere substitution of a supreme national government over states, with powers more absolute than were ever asserted by king or parliament; then the charters of the states were virtually annulled; their forms of government altered fundamentally, and their own legislatures not only suspended but superseded. It will be left to theorists to reconcile the commentary with the text.

### THE ALLIANCE BETWEEN THE STATES BY THE CONFEDERATION.

By these articles, the nature of the confederation, and its objects, were clearly defined: the relations of the states to each other, their separate powers, and those of congress, explicitly declared. They were adopted, not by *the people of the states,* but by delegates, who were the representatives of the *respective state legislatures;* who were expressly named as the *constituents,* who had authorized them to be ratified and confirmed, and in the name and in behalf of each; and which was so done by the delegates who signed the same accordingly; 4 Laws U. S. 19, 20. For present purposes it is necessary to refer only to three articles.

"Art. 3. The said states, hereby *severally* enter into a firm league of friendship with each other, for their common defence, the security of their liberties, and their mutual and general welfare; binding themselves to assist each other against all force offered to, or attacks made upon them, or any of them, on account of religion, *sovereignty, trade,* or any other pretext whatever."

"Art. 9. The United States, in congress assembled, shall have the sole and exclusive right and power of sending and receiving ambassadors, and entering into treaties and alliances; provided, that no treaty of commerce shall restrain the legislative power of *the respective states,* from imposing such imposts and duties on foreigners, as their own people are subjected to; or from prohibiting the exportation or importation of any species of goods or commodities whatsoever." 1 Laws U. S. 16.

This alliance, league, or confederacy of the states with each other, can leave no doubt, that up to the time of the final ratification in March, 1781, each state was separately sovereign in its own inherent right; and so remained as to all power not expressly delegated, as was declared in the second article. The third article is also conclusive, that the object of the alliance was to maintain and perpetuate their separate sovereignty. This is the more manifest, when these articles are taken in connection with the alliance of the states with France.

ALLIANCE BETWEEN THE STATES AND FRANCE; AND THE GUARANTY TO THEM, BY FRANCE, BY THE TREATY OF 1778.

On the same day, when a committee was appointed by congress to prepare and digest the form of a confederation, to be entered into between these colonies, a committee was also appointed to prepare a plan of treaties to be proposed to foreign powers, June 12, 1776; 2 Journ. 198; the instructions to the commissioners were agreed to in September following; 2 Journ. 361. In the same month, plans of these treaties were submitted to and approved by congress, who made out letters of credence and commissions to the commissioners; 2 Secret Journ. Cong. p. 7.

As the 9th article of confederation, as drawn up, would give to congress the sole and exclusive power of entering into alliances, on their adoption, it was a sufficient guaranty for its observance by the states; but as congress could not restrain the legislative power of the states over commerce, as resolved in April, 1776, and declared in this article, provision was made on the subject in the 6th article: " No state shall lay any imposts or duties, which may interfere with any stipulations in treaties, entered into by the United States in congress assembled, with any king, prince, or state, in pursuance of any treaties already proposed by congress to the courts of France and Spain;" 1 Laws U. S. 15. Those of commerce and alliance with France were made in 1778. The commissions, credentials, and treaties, were in the name of "the thirteen United States of North America, to wit: New Hampshire," &c. 2 Secret Journ. 7; 1 Laws, 74, 95; and the 2d article of the treaty of alliance declares its object most explicitly.

" The essential and direct end of the present defensive alliance, is to maintain, effectually, the liberty, sovereignty, and independence, *absolute* and *unlimited,* of the said United States, as well *in matters of government,* as *of commerce.*" In the 11th article, the parties make a mutual guaranty; in that of France, " His most Christian majesty guaranties, on his part, to the United States, their liberty, sovereignty, and independence, *absolute* and *unlimited,* as well *in matters of government as commerce; also their possessions,* and the additions or conquests that *their confederation* may make during the war," &c. 1 Laws, 95, 98.

This guaranty was fulfilled by the treaty of peace, in which " His Britannic majesty acknowledges the said United States, to wit: New Hampshire, &c., to be free, sovereign and independent states." 1 Laws, 196. This recognition, relating back to the separate or unanimous declarations by the states, as this Court have held it; has the same effect, as if the states had then assumed the same position, by the previous authority of the king; the treaty not being a grant, but a recognition, and subsequent ratification of their pre-existing condition; and all acts which had declared and defined it previous to the treaty, related back to 1776.

Such being the relations of the several states, in their federal and foreign concerns, it follows, that as to their internal concerns, they were in the same attitude of absolute and unlimited sovereignty, before the articles of confederation, as they were afterwards, except so far as they abridged it. Each was a party to the treaty of alliance and peace, and each was bound by the guarantee to France, after the confederation was abolished, and the constitution was established, as firmly as before: the states who delayed their ratification remained so bound, for they could by no act of their own, impair the rights of France: and they were equally entitled to the effects of the treaty of peace, whether they became constituent parts of the Union, by ratifying the constitution, or remained foreign states, by not adopting it. Their state constitutions and governments, remained unimpaired by any surrender of their rights; so that of consequence, their sovereignty was perfect, so long as they continued free from any federal shackles; so the states acted, and so the people of each declared, in all their conventions, from 1776 to 1780.

## EACH STATE INSTITUTED A GOVERNMENT BY THE AUTHORITY OF THE PEOPLE.

Congress has recommended to the colonies to form governments, "on the authority of the people alone:" this was done by the states who adopted constitutions before, and after the declaration of independence; by the assertion of the people in the separate conventions of each state, that they had by nature and inherent right, all the powers of government, and that none could be exercised by any body unless by their authority. They applied to themselves all the principles announced in their unanimous declaration in congress, in terms incapable of being misunderstood.

The people of Pennsylvania declared, "that all power being originally in and consequently derived from the people;" the community hath an indubitable, unalienable, and indefeasible right to reform, alter, or abolish government, in such manner, as shall be by that community judged most conducive to the public weal."

The *supreme legislative power* shall be vested in a house of representatives, &c. Con. of Pennsylvania 55, 6, 7. September, 1776.

The people of North Carolina declared, that all the territory within the bounds of the state, was the right and property of the people, to be held by them *in full sovereignty*. Laws of N. C. 275, 6. Book Const. 234, 5. December, 1776.

Those of New York. "That no authority shall, on any pretence whatever, be exercised over the people or members of this state, but such as shall be derived from, or granted by them." 1 Rev. Laws, 249. M'Cauley's Hist. N. Y. 231, 2. April, 1777.

In Massachusetts. "The people of this commonwealth, have the sole and exclusive right of governing themselves, as a free, sovereign, and independent state, and for ever hereafter shall exercise

11

and enjoy every power, jurisdiction and right, which is not or may not hereafter be by them expressly delegated to the United States of America in congress assembled." Book Const. 53; Laws Mass. 6. March, 1780.

Delaware, Maryland, and Georgia, adopted constitutions in 1776, and 1777, and the people of Vermont, though not a state, made a declaration of their political rights in July, 1777, and adopted a constitution. Vermont St. Pap. 241. The governments which were instituted, were all on the same principles as those which have been specified, and the states were each in the same political situation; "sovereign, independent communities," as they were styled by congress, in their letter recommending the adoption of the confederation. 1 Laws U. S. 12.

In this, their sovereign character, the people of each state could create what corporations they pleased for their own government, either by written or tacit delegation of power, as best pleased them; their action in either mode had the same effect, whether the body politic to be created was for one, or all the states, it was the exertion of the same sovereign authority, as the people; within the limits of their own state, empire, or kingdom. Both corporations, state and federal, were formed on the same authority and in the same right; and as in England, the three states of the kingdom, comprising all the people thereof, acting, whether by organic, or administrative power, in their several and distinct estates, by their representatives respectively; had formed, "the *great* corporation or body politic of the kingdom." The parliament. The legislative power. *The government established by the people.* 1 Bl. Com. 153, 162.

So has *our* new constitution in writing, signed by the separate estates or *states* of the *Union,* created *its* great corporation; not as our *old* one did, a supreme *consolidated* government of *the states,* but "*the federal* government of these states," as the framers thereof called it in their letter to congress; and as the several *states* declared in the heading, by ordaining and establishing this constitution *for* the *United* States of America, as the *several* states, each for itself, had done before, with the two exceptions. When the people of all the states, suffering under oppression, acted by their rights of inheritance from their ancestors, followed their example by drawing their swords upon their sovereign in defending them; declared, as had been done in time immemorial: "*Nollumus leges angliæ mutare.*"

The people of those two states, in their own characteristic way, by deeds rather than words, content with what their representatives in congress had declared for them, and in their name, independence in fact; adhered not only to the laws, but the usages of old, and established their great corporation, by their silent consent, in submitting to the supreme legislative power of the states; as exercised by their representatives chosen in *towns:* a governor and the members of the upper house, by the people of the state at large. Thus, their charter and legislative usage, became their constitution, and so continued; the tacit practical consent of the people, being taken as equivalent to a formal delegation of power in convention; and so considered by this Court. 3 Dall. 398, 400; 2 Pet. 656, 7.

A reference to the other eleven state governments, will show by what people, and of what state, they were constituted by organic power, original, inherent, and sovereign, whether single or connected, in one or thirteen *potentates*. It will also show, that if there is, or is to be, any harmony between the state and federal systems, it arises by the power which created both, being the same; and that the constitutions of government, over and within both, must be so construed, as to avoid any discrepancy between them, in their origin, organization, or action.

EACH STATE WAS " A SINGLE SOVEREIGN POWER," IN ADOPTING THE CONSTITUTION.

When we thus find that each state had thus separately, either in their conventions or practically, declared, asserted, and exercised their power of instituting a government for each, before 1787; and a federal government for, and over all, for federal purposes, as then proposed and adopted, in 1788; we can look back, and in reviewing their progress from their dependent condition as colonies, to their independence as states, see and understand the power which effected the conversion by the people of each state, who transferred from their local, to their federal legislature, federal powers, by their cession, in the grant. And in its provisions we can also see, that the congress has accepted it; is organized under it; acts and must continue to act pursuant to its ordinances, through all time, as the constituent of the whole agency delegated to the government. Then, taking the relation of the states to each other, as it exists under the constitution, and as declared by this Court, in one uniform and consistent series of adjudication, from 6 Cr. 136, to 2 Pet..590, 1; that " The several states are still *foreign* to each other, for all but *federal* purposes;" their position, as " a single unconnected sovereign power," before and without any *federation* between them, is an inevitable consequence.

THE CONSTITUTION IS A CESSION OF POWER BY THE PARTICULAR STATES; OPERATING AS A TREATY OF CESSION, BY A FOREIGN STATE TO THE UNITED STATES.

The operation of the constitution then, must, of necessity, be like that of a treaty of cession, by a foreign state to the United States. As the states are still foreign to each other for all but federal purposes, (they were entirely so before the confederation of 1781, and remained so after its dissolution, till they severally entered into the new one;) the United States could have neither a right of soil or jurisdiction, propriety or dominion, within any particular state, but by a cession from the state by its legislature, or a convention of the people. The act or deed of cession is the title to power or property, according to its terms, operating by way of grant; a treaty, compact, or contract, transferring the subject matter thereof from one party to another; whether they are states foreign to each other, or states connected by federal relation, the effect is the same.

The constitution is a cession of jurisdiction only, made by the people of a state; the cession of territory included, in terms, soil and jurisdiction; so did the treaties of Louisiana with France, and Florida with Spain, by the grant of those provinces, in full sovereignty; each grant performed its proper office, either to transfer legislative power from the sovereign in whom it was vested, or territory from its former proprietor. When power or property thus passed to the United States, it is held subject to the terms and stipulations of the grant; and federal power is exercised over all the territory within the United States, pursuant to the constitution and the conditions of the cession. Whether it was a part of the original territory of a state of the Union, or of a foreign state ceded by deed or treaty; the right of the United States in or over it, depends on the contract of cession, which operates to incorporate as well the territory as its inhabitants, into the Union; placing both under the jurisdiction of its constitution and government. So the constitution operated to incorporate such of the old states as ratified it: so it did as new states have been admitted: so it must operate in future. It was a cession, by nine states, of so much of their separate power as was necessary for federal purposes, to the body politic, called the United States, the "American Confederacy," "Republic," or "Empire;" as a term of designation, including states and territories. The constitution was the charter of this federal corporation, as those of the different states were the charters of their state corporations of government; each with power to legislate according to the terms of their respective charters, subject only to that charter which had been made supreme for its designated purposes.

All charters and grants of power or property, are governed by the same rules of construction; all questions touching the boundaries of territory, or lines of jurisdiction, must be referred back to the original sovereign in whom both were vested; and thence deduced by a regular chain of title, to the contending parties. So this Court has done, as to controversies between the United States and foreign states; 2 Pet. 299, 314, passim; and in controversies arising from the collision of state laws with those of the Union. Adopting the principle, that all governments are corporations, they apply it to those of the territories of the United States, in such a manner as to give a key to unlock any part of the constitution, which can admit of a doubt as to the granting power; they point to and identify that sovereign power, in which was united property and dominion, within its own original territorial limits, as the supreme lord and proprietor thereof. The Court remark: "Yet all admit the constitutionality of a territorial government, which is a corporate body;" 4 Wh. 422. This short sentence, connected with that part of the constitution to which the Court refer, will tend more to solve doubts than any reasoning can do.

### THE POWER OF CONGRESS OVER TERRITORIES, THE DISTRICT OF COLUMBIA, FORTS, ARSENALS, DOCKYARDS, &c.

" The congress shall have power to dispose of, and make all needful rules and regulations respecting the territory or other property belonging to the United States; and nothing in this constitution shall be so construed as to prejudice any claims of the United States, or of any particular state." Art. 4, sect. 3, cl. 2.

Here the power to *dispose* of *property*, or *regulate territory*, by the establishment of a corporation to *govern it*, is identical; in what right, and by what means, either is considered as " belonging to the United States," depends on the right by which *they* were made a corporation, capable of holding, disposing of, or regulating, what belonged to them as a government. This was the cession of soil, and the grant of legislative powers to *a congress* of the United States, who could dispose of, or regulate by law, their territory, or other property, however acquired; how then was it acquired, is the only question; as their right over it is unquestionable, when acquired. The opinions of this Court, concurring with the 16th clause of the 8th section of the 1st article of the charter, point to the grantors, who had the dominion, and the propriety, in and over whatever was granted, whether " to exercise exclusive legislation in all cases whatever, over such district, and such places, for forts, arsenals," &c. " as may *by cession of particular states*, and the *acceptance of congress*, become the seat of government of the United States," or " purchased by *the consent* of the legislature of *the state* in which the same *may be;*" or " to *dispose of*, and make all needful *rules* and *regulations* respecting the territory or other property belonging to the United States;" the right is acquired in the same manner, " cession," or grant, " by particular *states*," or purchase with the assent of the local legislature of *one*.

In relation to this district, this Court say: " On the extent of those terms, according to the common understanding of mankind, there can be no difference of opinion;" and they held, that congress had the same power of taxation in the *district*, as they have in the *territories;* by the same rules of apportionment and uniformity, as in the *states.* 5 Wh. 324. That the power did not depend solely on the grant of exclusive legislation, but was given in the grant of the 1st clause, 8th sect. 1st art. " to lay and collect taxes," &c. as a general one, " without limitation of place," extending " to all places over which the government extends;" in the words of the grant, " throughout the United States." This term designates the whole " American empire." It is *the name* given to our great republic, which is composed of states and territories; all of which are alike within " the United States:" and it is not less necessary, on the principle of our constitution, that uniformity in the imposition of imposts, duties, and excises, should be observed in the one than in the other. 5 Wh. 318, 19. Its language comprehends the territories, and District of Columbia, as well as the states, 523. So, under the confederation, (vide post.) It is therefore clear, that as the taxing power of congress operates in all respects uniformly, "throughout the United States," it must be derived from the same grant; the territories never made any grant; they were then the "property" of the United States, by the devolution of the right of the crown by the treaty of peace, or by cession from particular states, or the one in which it was situated and owned, as an *original* state. The powers of legislation over *the states*, is by the constitution; over the district it is exclusive, by uniting the legislative power of "the particular states," (Maryland and Virginia,) by their "cessions;" which authorize the exercise of *federal* and *state* powers, by one consolidated government. Over forts, dockyards, and arsenals, it is by *purchase* from the owners of *the soil*, with the consent of the local legislature, who may make the power exclusive by ceding their own, or consent to the purchase, and ceding *a* concurrent, or retaining *the* jurisdiction of the states over the territories; it is by making rules and regulations respecting their property, but the power is legislation; regulations by laws, which are "rules of action prescribed by the legislative power," whether for the disposition or government of property within the *territories* of the United States, which belonged, or should belong to them thereafter.

## ALL THE TERRITORY WITHIN THE UNITED STATES, AT THE TREATY OF PEACE, BELONGED TO THE PARTICULAR STATES.

This Court has decided, " That there was no territory within the United States, that was claimed in any other right than that of some one of the confederated states; therefore, there could be no acquisition of territory made by the United States, distinct from, or independent of, some one of the states; the soil and sovereignty were as much theirs at the declaration of independence, as at this hour." (1827.) "Thus stood the rights of the parties at the commencement of the revolution; and when, by the treaty of peace, the southern boundary of the United States was fixed at the ancient boundary of South Carolina or Georgia, (it matters not which,) Georgia insisted on that line, as the limit which she was entitled to, and which she had laid claim to, when she declared herself independent; or which the United States had asserted *in her behalf*, in the declaration of independence," and "the right to it was established by the most solemn of all international acts, the treaty of peace. It has never been admitted by the United States, that they acquired any thing, by way of cession from Great Britain, by that treaty. It has been viewed only as a recognition of pre-existing rights." 12 Wh. 526, 7: Harcourt v. Gaillard, S. P. 534, 5: Henderson v. Poindexter, 4 Cr. 212. It could be viewed in no other way, when we look to the assertion of her claims by Georgia, in 1783, as "a sovereign independent state;" whose "true and just limits," "as secured" "by their charter, and guarantied as well by the articles of confederation, as by the treaty of alliance" with France. Laws of Georgia, 264. That treaty has been referred to, to show what was guarantied to the several states; it also shows what was guarantied to the United States, as a confederation of the several states.

Art. 5. " If the United States should think fit to attempt the reduction of the British power, remaining in the northern parts of America, or the islands of Bermudas; those countries or islands, in case of success, shall be confederated with, or dependent upon, the said United States." By art. 6, France renounces any claims to those islands or those countries, or to *the United States*, heretofore called *British colonies*, or which are at this time, or have lately been, under the power of the king and crown of Great Britain.

Art. 11. France guaranties to the United States, their liberty and "also their possessions;" "and the *additions* and *conquests* that *their confederation* may make during the war, from any of the dominions, now or heretofore possessed by Great Britain in North America, conformable to the 5th and 6th articles above written; the whole as their possession shall be fixed and assured to the *said states*, at the moment of the cessation of their present war with England," 1 Laws, 97, 8. On this ground the states stood in their separate existence, and the United States, as a confederation; and as a consequence of this position, this Court held, that neither the United States or Spain could, in the revolution, acquire by conquest, a territory within the limits claimed by an ally during the war, 12 Wh. 524, 6. These great principles have been as authoritatively settled by this Court as they can be; and have been the basis of their adjudications in all cases save those of the Cherokees. " On the 7th of October, 1763, the king, exercising a right which was never questioned, over what were then called the·*royal* provinces, issued his proclamation by which he established the northern boundaries of Florida, at the 31st degree of north latitude," 12 Wh. 524: his right to legislate over a conquered country, was never denied in Westminster Hall, or questioned in parliament; 9 Pet. 748. By the revolution, the duties as well as the powers of government, *devolved* on the people of New Hampshire, 4 Wh. 651; and, of course, to the people of each separate state. By the treaty of peace, " the powers of government, and the right of soil, which had previously been in Great Britain, *passed definitively* to these states." 8 Wh. 584.

There then could be no mode, by which the United States could acquire, either " the powers of government," or the " right of soil, in any territory, but by a cession from the states, on whom both rights *devolved* by the revolution, and passed to them *definitively*, by the acknowledgment and renunciations of the treaty. And it was held by this Court, that the only territory which in fact belonged to the United States in 1787, (that which lay west of Pennsylvania, and north of the Ohio,) was acquired by the cession from Virginia, &c. 5 Wh. 375, &c.

As to places purchased by the United States, for forts, dock-yards, &c. the same principles apply; and have been applied by this Court, in terms and language appropriate alike to all cessions, by putting and answering the all-important question,

"What then is the extent of jurisdiction which a state possesses? We answer, without hesitation, the jurisdiction of a state is co-extensive with its territory, co-extensive with its legislative power."

"The place described is unquestionably within the original territory of Massachusetts; it is then within the jurisdiction of Massachusetts, unless that jurisdiction has been *ceded* to the United States."

That *original* territory means the charter boundaries of the state, cannot be questioned; from which it must follow, that jurisdiction and legislative power being concomitant with territorial rights, the United States cannot exercise any federal, or exclusive legislation within these boundaries; unless it has been ceded by the particular state, in its original sovereign capacity, as a constituent of the Union.

THE ORDINANCE OF 1787, AND THE ADMISSION OF NEW STATES.

Though these opinions of the Court have been delivered in cases arising in the old states, they are equally applicable to the new states which have been admitted into the Union, pursuant to the ordinance of 1787; which declares, that they shall be admitted on an equal footing with the *original* states, in all respects whatever; 1 Laws, 480. *Such* states are thus referred to in the 4th art. 3d sec. cl. 1. "*New* states may be admitted by the congress into this union." They have been admitted, and now are constituent parts thereof, in virtue of, and according to the terms of this ordinance, which declares what such equal footing is, and shall remain.

The North Western Territory was part of the original territory of Massachusetts, Connecticut, New York, and Virginia; in 1787, it belonged to the United States, by separate deeds of cession made by those states: it was thus the property of the confederation, subject to the exceptions, conditions, and reservations in the respective deeds. The "particular states," had ceded their jurisdiction, and thereby annulled their legislative power over it. The articles of confederation were drawn up in November, 1777, before any cession was made; consequently, there was no provision made for the exercise of any legislation by congress over any territory within the boundaries of those states, while they retained both soil and jurisdiction. But after the cession, from the necessity of the case, congress assumed and exercised the power to pass "an ordinance for the government of the territory of the United States, north-west of the Ohio;" the first clause of which shows in what capacity they did so, on the 13*th July*. "Be it ordained by the United States, in congress assembled," &c. As an act of the states, by their several ambassadors, it was binding on them in their legislative capacity, if done by their authority, or subsequently ratified; the act of cession was in effect to authorize it; the acquiescence of the states was in law a ratification by the states, which the people thereof confirmed by the constitution, as proposed on the 17*th September*, 1787. In the interval, a committee of congress had made a report on the respective powers of congress, and the states, to regulate Indian affairs; in which the general legislative power of any state, "*in all parts of it,*" is most distinctly admitted on all subjects, except Indian affairs, which were asserted to have been delegated to congress, by the 9th article of the confederation; 12 Journ. Cong. 82, 84, &c. The whole subject was thus before congress, and the convention, at the same time; nine of the members of the convention were members of congress, when the report of the convention containing the proposed constitution, resolutions, and letters, was submitted to, and unanimously accepted by congress. Vide 12 Journ. 99, 100. Rhode Island was not present in either body; but the members of both bodies, on the behalf of the twelve states who were present, acted in perfect concert and unity of opinion, on the appropriate subjects confided to them. Congress exercised the organic power of the states, without any express delegation; the convention proposed an organic act, to be done by the people of each state, as the constituent power thereof; and both were "done," accordingly, by *ordinance;* the states in congress using the term, "*be it ordained;*" the people using this: "*we do ordain.*" The effect is, a government is established by the states collectively; in congress, in one case, and separately, in the other, in conventions. By one ordinance, it was established for the government of a territory, and new states to be formed out of it; by the other, for the government of all the territories, and all the states, old and new, which may be included in the Union at that time, or afterwards: one ordained by states, in a *convention, or congress;* the other, by each state, in a *convention of the people.* After providing for the temporary government of the territory, as one district, the ordinance of July, 1787, contains a preamble worthy of note. " And for extending the fundamental principles of civil and religious liberty, which form the basis whereon these republics, their laws, and constitutions, are erected; to fix and establish those principles as the basis of all laws, constitutions, and governments, which for ever hereafter shall be formed in said territory; to provide for the establishment of states, and permanent governments therein, and for their admission to a share in the federal councils, on an equal footing with the original states, at as early periods as may be consistent with the general interest:"

" It is hereby ordained and declared, by the authority aforesaid, (congress,) that the following articles shall be considered as articles of compact between the original states, and the people and states in the said territory; and for ever remain unalterable; unless by common consent;" to wit: (art. 1 and 2, was for the security of persons, property, and contracts; art. 3, relates to the Indians within the territory.)

Art. 4. " The said territory, and the states which may be formed therein, shall for ever remain a part of this confederacy of the United States of America; subject to the articles of confederation, and to such alterations therein, as shall be constitutionally made, and to all the acts and ordinances of the United States in congress assembled, conformable thereto," &c. &c.

12

Art. 5. "There shall be formed in the said territory, not less than three, nor more than five states," &c. "And whenever any of the said states shall have sixty thousand free inhabitants therein, such state shall be admitted by its delegates into the congress of the United States, on an equal footing with the original states, in all respects whatever; and shall be at liberty to form a permanent constitution and state government, provided the same shall be republican, and in conformity to the principle contained in these articles," &c. 1 Laws U. S. 479, 480.

This was the constitution for the territory; and with the articles of confederation, formed one constitution for the territory, and for the old and new United States of America: being the ordinances, one, of the states assembled in congress; the other, of each state in their respective general assemblies, or state legislatures, authorizing their delegates to assent to, and sign it.

THE ORDINANCE OF 1787 IS INCORPORATED INTO THE CONSTITUTION, AND YET REMAINS A PART OF IT, BY DECLARING ITS VALIDITY.

In September following, a convention of all the states but one, after they had been in session from May preceding, proposed an ordinance to be adopted, by the people of each state, in their separate conventions.

### " CONSTITUTION OF THE UNITED STATES."

" We, the people of the United States, in order to form a more perfect Union, establish justice, ensure domestic tranquillity, provide for the common defence, promote the general welfare, and secure the blessings of liberty to ourselves and posterity, do ordain and establish this constitution for the United States of America."

Its provisions have been noticed, so far as is necessary for present purposes, except the 6th article, which incorporates the ordinance of July, 1787, into the constitution, as a compact or engagement, subject as the other parts of it are, to amendments, pursuant to the 5th article.

Art. 6. 1. " All debts contracted, and engagements entered into, before the adoption of this constitution, shall be as valid against the United States, under this constitution, as under the confederation."

This was a confirmation of the ordinance, giving it the same binding effect, ab initio, as if it had been a constitutional provision in all its terms. It was perfectly consistent with the ordinance, which made the territory and new states " subject to the articles of confederation," and alterations "therein constitutionally made," and the acts of congress, &c. conformable thereto; that when these articles were abolished, and the confederation was converted into a federal government, the constitution which established it should declare;

2d. " This constitution, and the laws of the United States which shall be made, in pursuance thereof, and all treaties made, or which shall be made, under the authority of the United States, shall be the supreme law of the land."

Thus there are now, as there were under the confederation, two constitutions : one for all the territory belonging to the United States, by cessions from particular states, or foreign states, in which a territorial government exists, under the authority of congress; all of which have been established, organized, and administered, pursuant to the ordinance from 1787 to this day : and until a territory becomes a state, by the formation of a constitution therefor, by the people thereof in convention, and its admission into the Union by congress. "The territory and states which may be formed therein, forever remain a part of the confederacy, subject to the ordinance and to the constitution, &c., as, under the confederation, they were a part of the former confederacy of the United States of America," subject to the articles thereof. When new states are so admitted into the Union, in fulfilment of the stipulations in the deeds of cession by the original states, or of the treaties with foreign powers; they are admitted according to the " articles of compact," the " engagements entered into before the adoption of this constitution," " between the original states and the people and states of the said territory," " on an equal footing with the original states, in all respects whatever." Then the constitution of the state, having superseded the articles of the ordinance, as that of the United States did the articles of confederation, 1 Wh. 332; each state still has two constitutions of government, one for state, the other for federal purposes; both ordained by the same people, and in the same manner, in a convention of their representatives, elected by the electors of the states, for the special object, whereby in the simple, impressive, instructive, and strictly constitutional language of this Court, " The national and state systems are to be regarded as one whole." 6 Wh. 419. " The powers of government are divided between the government of the Union, and those of the states." " They are each sovereign, with respect to the objects committed to it; and neither sovereign, with respect to the objects committed to the other." 4 Wh. 410.

In this union of political and judicial authority, we must know what was "a state," an "original state," a "new state," "the United States," "the congress of the United States," and "states so admitted into this Union." We also know, what was the territory belonging to the United States in 1787, by cession from the states, by deeds of cession executed by their agents or delegates in congress, specially authorized; of New York, in 1781, 1 Laws, 469, 72; of Virginia, in 1784, Ib. 472, 5; of Massachusetts, in 1785, Ib. 482, 4; of Connecticut, in 1786, Ib. 485, 6; of South Carolina, in 1787, Ib. 486. We further know, from the cession of Louisiana and Florida, by treaties with foreign states, how the soil and jurisdiction of the new territories passed definitively to these states; and that pursuant to the stipulations thereof, and the ordinance of 1787, new states have been admitted into this Union, on an equal footing with the original states down to the present time. Nay, at this session, (1837) "the congress" has admitted the state of Michigan, formed out of the territory north-west of the Ohio, ceded by the states of the Union; and another, the state of Arkansas, formed out of that ceded by a foreign state, of territory not in the United States, into this Union, on the principles of the ordinance.

The territorial government of those states, had been founded on the ordinance, and it is now the basis of the governments existing in the territories of Ouisconsin and the Floridas, under the authority of Congress; according to the terms and conditions thereof. Congress is therefore bound, and the faith of the present states pledged, by the 6th article of the constitution, to fulfil all its stipulations; whenever these territories shall be entitled to be admitted into the Union as states. Now then, it may be most confidently assumed as a self-evident truth, manifest in the history, the solemn acts of the colonies, the states in congress, the people thereof in conventions, directly asserted in the ordinance, and confirmed by the constitution in language, plain, clear, and visible to every eye, and impressing on every mind this fact—

THE OLD AND NEW STATES ARE ON AN EQUAL FOOTING; AND ADOPT-ED THE CONSTITUTION IN CONVENTIONS OF THE PEOPLE OF EACH STATE.

That all the new states which have been admitted, pursuant to the 1st clause of the 3d section, 1st article of the constitution, "formed of parts of a state with the consent of the legislature of the state concerned, as well as of the congress," or pursuant to the ordinance and 6th article; have adopted it by the act and power of the convention of such new state, wholly independent of the action of any of the old states or people thereof.

There are now thirteen new states which have been admitted into the Union, confessedly on an equal footing with the thirteen old states, in all respects; it is therefore a political impossibility, that the people of the United States in the aggregate, could ordain a constitution for them, while the ordinance, and the 6th article validating it, remain in force. The people of a territory may, at their pleasure, continue under a territorial government, after they are entitled to become a state; it is a privilege which they may exercise or waive; and there is no power in the existing states, the people, or the constitution, to compel them to adopt any other government, than that prescribed by the ordinance. It is idle then to contend, that a new state comes into the Union by any other act or power, than of the people within its limits by their own volition; so that the only question which remains is, whether the original states became constituent parts of the United States, by ratifying the constitution in the same manner as the new. If they did, it was by the act of the people of each state; if they did not, then the constitution was made a supreme law within their territory, by an "external power;" of consequence, the old states had not and have not an equal station or footing with the new, but were subordinate to a paramount power; while the new states have voluntarily adopted it, in the plenitude of absolute sovereignty.

This conclusion is inevitable from the premises assumed, and the interpretation given to the declaration of independence, in late commentaries and expositions of the events of the revolution, in their bearing on the condition of the states in 1776, and thence till 1787.

It is not pretended, that any legislative power was ever granted to congress, unless by the articles of 1781, the ordinance of 1787, and the constitution; the separate states, therefore, never had any such powers, or if they were vested in them by original right, congress could not exercise any legitimate authority within the states, unless by their cession.

## EACH STATE WAS THE ABSOLUTE PROPRIETOR OF THE VACANT LANDS WITHIN ITS BOUNDARIES.

By connecting the foregoing view, which principally relates to the right of dominion, jurisdiction, or legislative power of the several states, within their territorial boundaries, with their rights of soil to the lands, which remained unappropriated at the revolution; the same results will become manifest.

The original right of the crown to grant the right of soil, and the powers of government, in and over the proprietary provinces, and the right of soil in the vacant lands, in the royal and chartered colonies, was never drawn in question after the revolution, by any of the states on behalf of the confederacy; for whenever the crown had made a grant, it was universally admitted that it was valid. When the proprietary governments were superseded by those of the states, the proprietaries were left in the quiet enjoyment of their rights of property, as in New Jersey to this day; or the states were suffered to resume their vacant lands, and to hold them without any claim by the other states, for any share, as in Pennsylvania. Vide 1 Dall. L. Pa. 822; and in Delaware, 2 Laws, D. 1074, 5. But the states which had no vacant lands, denied the exclusive right of those states whose right of boundaries extended originally to the South sea, and after the treaty of peace of 1763, to the Mississippi; and set up a claim to a proportion of the unappropriated lands within the limits of those states, as a common acquisition by the confederation, for the common benefit, in right of conquest, and from Great Britain. But admitted the legislative power of the states over them, making no claim to jurisdiction. Those states, however, claimed the lands, on the grounds before stated, as their own, by the devolution of the crown to them, the guarantee by the proposed articles of confederacy, and of the treaty with France.

To put an end to all future controversy, it was, by the 9th article of the former, *provided,* " that no state should be deprived of territory for the benefit of the United States." Connecting this proviso with the 3d article, and the 2d and 11th articles of the treaty of alliance with France; it is clear, that when the confederation became the act of all the states, congress could neither by treaty, or otherwise, do any valid act to affect the territorial rights of the states, without a direct violation of the express stipulations of both guarantees, and this proviso. This was the principal reason why the final adoption of these articles was delayed from November, 1777, till March, 1781. Various attempts were made in congress, to strike out, or so modify this proviso, that the vacant lands should be deemed to be the property of all the states, as a common fund for defraying the expenses of the war; which having all failed, some of the states refused to adopt them. In March, 1780, congress, finding that the controversy could be no otherwise terminated, recommended to the states to make liberal cessions of their western lands to the United States; to which Virginia and New York agreeing, the articles were signed, and cessions accordingly made, by those and other states, which were deemed satisfactory. Vide 1 Laws U. S. 11, 12, 20, 22, 24, 467 to 482; 5 Wh. 376, 7.

From this time, that dangerous controversy which had threatened to dissolve the confederacy of the revolution, ceased by this compromise; vide 6 Cr. 142: it was no longer a political question after the cessions of the states had been accepted, and congress made no claims to soil or jurisdiction that were not in conformity to the deeds from the respective states. But the United States had not relinquished their claims, within the boundaries of those states which had made no cessions; though they made no grants of land within the boundaries of such states, yet, from the necessity of the case, they established a territorial government within the state of Georgia, over the territory between the Chatahoochie and Mississippi. It was done, however, with the assent of Georgia, who was willing to surrender the jurisdiction, retaining the right of soil. By the first section of the act, there was a provision for the appointment of commissioners to adjust the claims to territory with Georgia, and to receive proposals for the cession of the whole or part thereof, "out of the ordinary jurisdiction thereof:" by the second section, the lands "thus ascertained as the *property* of the United States, shall *be disposed of*," &c. To avoid all controversy by so doing, it was declared by the fifth section, that the establishment of this government shall, in no respect, impair the right of Georgia to the jurisdiction or soil of the territory: but the same were declared to be "as firm and available as if this act had never been made;" 1 Story, L. U. S. 494, 5; act of 1798. This, it will be seen, was in precise conformity to the 2d clause, 3d sect. 4th art. of the constitution.

In 1802, an adjustment was made between Georgia and the United States, of all matters between them; by cession, and an acceptance on the terms and conditions therein specified; 1 Laws U. S. 488, &c. which seems to preclude any future controversy about the right of soil or jurisdiction: but unhappily they have arisen on the Indian question, in the cases of the Cherokees living east of the Chatahoochie.

Georgia having made no cession, and claiming, as has been seen, to the Mississippi, had, by the act of 1795, made sale of a large tract on the Yazoo river; on the validity of which sale the old question arose, whether those lands belonged to the United States, or to Georgia, at the time of the grant in 1795?

This was one main point directly made in Fletcher v. Peck, on which this Court decided that the title to the land was in Georgia; that she had a right to grant it; and that the grant was valid, to pass a title in fee simple to the purchasers; 6 Cr. 142. The United States acquiesced in that decision, by making a compromise with the purchasers, and paying them a certain sum.

In Harcourt v. Gaillard, the same question came up, and was decided in favour of Georgia, as has been shown before; vide 12 Wh. 524, &c. Herein will be found another strong illustration of the accordance of the opinions of this Court, with the great acts of the revolution. Their judgment is founded on the declaration of independence, the treaties of the states with foreign powers, and the treaty of peace. The guarantee of the states with each other, by the third article of confederation, and by France to each, was of their *possessions*, as well as in matters of government; the guarantee to the confederacy was only of such conquests or acquisitions, as should be made from Great Britain, without the boundaries of the particular states; "the whole, as their *possession*, shall be *fixed* and assured to the said states, at the moment of the cessation of their present war with England;" 1 Laws, 98, 9. Now, as no conquests were made by the confederacy, and the possessions of the several states were fixed by the treaty of peace, according to their original boundaries, the confederacy could acquire no territory as possessions, or jurisdiction in matters of government; and this Court have declared, in four solemn decisions, that they did not; 4 Cr. 212; 6 Cr. 142; 12 Wh. 524; Ib. 534.

Taking, it therefore, as a political, or judicial question, it has long since been put at rest; not only by the authority of the constitution, and all the departments of the government; but in public opinion. It may then be assumed as an unquestioned proposition, that the United States can have no right of soil within any of the states of this Union, unless by a cession from the particular states, or a foreign state, who was the original, absolute, proprietary thereof; from this proposition another equally unquestionable one necessarily results.

THE RIGHTS OF SOIL AND JURISDICTION, ARE CONCOMITANT AND INSEPARABLE, UNLESS BY THE STATE IN WHOM BOTH WERE VESTED.

It is not deemed necessary to enter into any course of reasoning, or any reference to authority, to prove that *the state* which is the absolute owner of the territory within its boundaries, has the absolute power of government over it; or that if the legislative jurisdiction was by original right in a paramount power, that the right of soil was in the same power. If these propositions are true, a third is self-evident; that if the right of soil or jurisdiction, is legitimately exercised by any other than such paramount power, it must be by its grant or authority, otherwise it must be void as an usurpation. Grants of land or power, must then derive their validity from the same sovereign, who alone can separate the one right from the other;

and his grant must testify what he has granted, and to whom: the separation is not to be made by theory, assertion, or construction. If the existing condition of the country is such, that the right of soil is in a single state in full propriety, and the dominion over it is absolute or qualifiedly in the United States; the original sovereign was the people of the state, or the people of all the states, as one " single sovereign power." I have traced the right to property and power to the people of each state, and deduced the title to both from them to the United States, by their deeds of cession, and constitution of government; let those who assert that the right was not in each state, show how the rights of the crown devolved on the one people, and how they have made their grant of territory, or the powers of government over the several states. On the first organization of the federal government in 1789, there were only eleven states within the Union; yet the constitution was then ordained and established by "We, the people of the United States." If they were the whole people in the aggregate, in their unity of power, the congress of that day evinced their most profound ignorance of the origin and nature of the government they were administering. As North Carolina and Rhode Island had not ratified the constitution, the revenue laws put those states on the same footing as foreign states, kingdoms, or countries; 1 Story, L. U. S. 30, 50. No provision was made for the operation of the judiciary act of 1789: vide 1 Story, 53, &c.: and if the three branches of the legislative power were not demented, these two states were no more constituent parts of the American empire at that time, than Canada and Nova Scotia.

The whole Congress were demented, if the same paramount power, which made the constitution the supreme law of the land in the eleven states, had not the same power over those two states, to force them into the Union, and make them subject to its laws; without any act of a convention of the people thereof.

Should this be deemed by theorists a proposition too bold to advance, they must give some good reasons to show why the constitution and laws have now any more force in those states, than in 1789; unless it has been by the ratification of the people, in a capacity wholly separate and distinct from the people of the other states, who having previously done the same act, were *functi officio;* and could not act jointly with them. For myself, I am utterly unable to imagine any middle position to be assumed, by which to account how North Carolina and Rhode Island, are now constituent parts of the United States: that they became so by the consent of each, as the other states did, is to me an intelligible proposition; but how it has been, or could otherwise be done, is incomprehensible to a mind not accustomed to search for mysteries in plain words.

## THE PREAMBLE OF THE CONSTITUTION IS PROSPECTIVE, REFERRING TO THE PEOPLE OF THOSE STATES WHICH SHOULD RATIFY IT FROM TIME TO TIME.

I have only to add one other consideration, to illustrate the meaning of the preamble. All agree that the constitution was to be established by *the people* of the United States, whenever the conventions of nine states should ratify it; all must agree, that when it was proposed for adoption in 1787, it could not be foreseen which of the states would so ratify it; the states therefore could not be named till their separate ratifications were given. It provided for the admission of new states, but no one could divine their names or locality; states could be " formed by the junction of two or more states," but none could say of which. The constitution was intended for posterity, through all time; and for " the land," the whole territory, and all the states, old and new; as one law, speaking in the same words, and with the same intention, at the time it was proposed, and at each period when any state ratified it, and thus became one of " the United States of America," by the act of the people of the states respectively.

When the terms " we, the people," " of the United States," are thus applied, they seem to me not only appropriate to the instrument, but the only terms that would be so; it uses terms in all its parts, yet we find no definitions or explanations; it was not intended for a code; and the term " people," was a mere designation of the power by which the constitution was made, as " the states" were designated by their separate ratifications. Hence it referred, in 1789, to eleven only, then to the old thirteen states, and now refers to the thirteen new states: and when others shall be admitted into the Union, it will refer to them as it did to the old, and now does to the new. " The people" " of the several states, which may be included within this Union," as the constituent power of the federal government.

## CONGRESS HAS NO RIGHT OF SOIL, OR JURISDICTION IN ANY STATE; UNLESS IT IS BY THE GRANT OF THE STATE.

I can adopt no course of reasoning, or use any language that so well supports these positions, as that of the late Chief Justice of this Court. " It is in the 8th section of the 1st article we are to look for cessions of territory, and of exclusive jurisdiction. Congress has power to exercise exclusive jurisdiction over this district, and over all places purchased by the consent of the legislature of the state in which the same shall be, for the erection of, &c. It is observable, that the power of exclusive legislation, (which is jurisdiction,) is united with cession of territory; which is to be the free act of the states."

" It is difficult to compare the two sections together, without feeling a conviction, not to be strengthened by any commentary on them, that in describing the judicial power, the framers of our con-

13

stitution had not in view any *cession of territory, or, which is essentially the same,* of general jurisdiction."

" It is not questioned, that whatever may be necessary to the full and unlimited exercise of admiralty, and maritime jurisdiction, is in the government of the Union. Congress may pass all laws which are necessary and proper, for giving the most complete effect to this power. Still, the general jurisdiction over the place, subject to this grant of power, *adheres to the territory,* as a portion of sovereignty *not yet given away.* The *residuary powers of legislation* are still in Massachusetts. Suppose, for example, the power of regulating trade, had not been given to the general government; would this extension of the judicial power to all cases of admiralty and maritime jurisdiction, have divested Massachusetts of the power to regulate the trade of her bay?" 3 Wh. 388, 89.

Alluding to the powers of congress, wherever, and however exercised, the Court use this language: " This power, like all others which are specified, is conferred on congress as the legislature of the Union; for, strip them of that character, and they would not possess it; in no other character can it be exercised;" 6 Wh. 424.

"Since congress legislates in the same forms, and in the same character, in virtue of powers of equal obligation, conferred in the same instrument, when exercising its *exclusive* powers of legislation, as well as when exercising those which are *limited,*" &c. Ib. 426. The Court put their finger on that power which enabled congress to legislate in the states, or elsewhere.

" The American states, and the American people, had been taught by the same experience, that this government would be a mere shadow, that must disappoint all their hopes, unless invested with large portions of that sovereignty which belongs to independent states. Under the influence of this opinion, and thus instructed by experience, the American people in the conventions of their *respective* states, adopted the present constitution;" 6 Wh. 380, 1. " A judicial system was to be prepared, not for *a consolidated people,* but for distinct societies, already possessing distinct systems, and accustomed to laws, which, though originating in the same great principle, had been variously modified;" 10 Wh. 46. " The power having existed prior to the formation of the constitution, and not having been prohibited by that instrument; remains with the states, subordinate to the power granted to congress on the same subject;" 5 Wh. 16, 17, S. P.; 9 Wh. 198, 9; 4 Wh. 425; 12 Wh. 448; 2 Pet. 466.

" It is not the want of an *original power* in an *independent sovereign state,* to prohibit loans to a foreign government, which restrains the (state) legislature from direct opposition to those made by the United States. The restraint is imposed by our constitution;" 2 Pet. 468.

Had the constitution not been adopted, the Court points to that power which alone can restrain " a single sovereign unconnected power;" 6 Cr. 136; a state, a nation, over whom no external power can operate; 7 Cr. 136; an independent sovereign state; 2 Pet. 468; which can restrict itself, and open its territorial boundaries to another jurisdiction. In these, and the opinions of the Court already referred to, I find in my judgment the most ample support of the preceding views.

That the rights of soil, and general jurisdiction over the whole territory, within the boundaries of the several states, was invested in the people of each, as absolute sovereigns of both; that neither right can be exercised, but by a grant from them, and that what is not given away by cession, still remains with them. *Residuary sovereignty* is also defined to be what each state has reserved to itself, or excepted from the grant; and not as commentators define it, what " the people of the nation," have been pleased to leave, to " the people of the states respectively."

If, in the course pursued, I have used plain terms in relation to those theories which appear to be in direct contradiction to the whole political history of the country, to all the declarations of the rights of the states and people, by themselves, by conventions, legislatures, congress, as well as all the great principles of government, thus announced and sanctioned by this Court; if in testing the constitution by these fundamental principles, and the old established maxims of the common law, I have arrived at conclusions which do not suit the spirit of the times, and the habits of the day, in constitutional discussions; it has been in submission to the constituted authorities of the country, political and judicial, whose union of opinion, and their striking coincidence with the words, provisions, and history of the constitution, leave no doubt on my mind as to its meaning and intention. In expressing my views, in terms of perfect conviction, of their correctness, it is not from any reliance on my own opinion, or train of reasoning; but having found fundamental principles, too clearly established to be shaken by any authority, subordinate to that of this Court, I feel with them; that " this concurrence of statesmen, legislators, and of judges, in the same construction of the constitution, may justly inspire some confidence in that construction;" 6 Wh. 421. In one respect, my conclusions differ from those of the late Chief Justice. To my mind he has given no *construction* to the constitution; he has only declared what it says, by carrying out the definition of the general terms it uses, and making a practical application thereof, to the various cases, in which he has delivered the opinion of the Court.

On inspecting the constitution judicially, no one can fail to be impressed with the truth and force of his remarks.

" A constitution, to contain an accurate detail of all the subdivisions of which its great powers will admit, and of all the means, by which they may be carried into execution, would partake of the prolixity of a legal code, and could scarcely be embraced by the human mind. It would probably never be understood by the public. Its nature, therefore, requires that only its great outlines should be marked, its important objects designated, and the minor ingredients which compose those objects, be deduced from the nature of the objects themselves. That this idea was entertained by the framers of the American constitution, is not only to be inferred from the nature of the instrument, but the language. Why else were some of the limitations found in the 9th section of the 1st article, introduced? It is also, in some degree warranted by their having omitted to use any restrictive term, which might prevent its receiving a fair and just interpretation. In considering this question then, we must never forget that it is *a constitution* we are expounding;" 4 Wh. 407. S. P. 1 Wh. 326.

This great and good judge, never forgot, or disobeyed this injunction: no commentator ever followed the text more faithfully, or ever made a commentary more accordant with its strict intention and language; he never brought into action the powers of his mighty mind, to find some meaning in plain words, of known import, and in common use, that would be above the comprehension of ordinary minds. He knew the framers of the constitution, who were his compatriots; he was the historian of his country; so that, as the expositor of its supreme law, he knew its objects, its intentions; could and did apply to it the rules of interpretation, as the principles of law, then understood, according to the political condition of the people, the states, and the state of the times. Though it is now the fashion of the day, to practically consider his opinions, as less worthy of attention in and out of Court, than is paid to others; the time is not distant, in my opinion, when public opinion will unite, in considering the constitution, and the *judicial* commentaries upon it, made by this Chief Magistrate, the best evidence of the law of the land. What lord Coke said of the civil law, in his time, may, with great truth, be applied to the constitution, in the present, and the glosses upon it.

" Upon the text of the civil law, there be so many glosses and interpretations, and again, upon these, so many commentaries, and all these written by *doctors* of equal degree and authority, and therein so many diversities of opinion, as they do rather increase, than resolve doubts and uncertainties; and the professors of that noble science say, That it is like a sea full of waves. The difference, then, between those glosses, and commentaries, and this which we publish, is, that their glosses and commentaries, are written by *doctors* which he *advocates*, and so, in a manner, private interpretations. And our expositions, or commentaries upon *magna charta, and other statutes*, are the resolutions of judges, in Courts of justice, in judicial causes of proceeding; either related and reported in our books, or extant in judicial records, or in both; and therefore, being collected together, shall, (as we conceive,) produce certainty, the mother and nurse of repose and quietness, and are not like to the waves of the sea, but *satio benefida peritis*, for *judicia sunt tanquam jurisdicta*." 2 Co. Inst. *proeme finis*.

What this judge would have said, had he lived in our time and country, and seen the glosses and commentaries which have been written within the present century here, and in England, upon the constitution and the common law, is not difficult to imagine. His motto was *qui patiens qui prudens;* his patience and prudence would have been put to a severe trial, if he was compelled to undergo the infliction of listening to these glosses, which, *like the waves of the sea,* beat upon us in a constant flood, increasing in size with every foreign importation, or home production of books.

That they will not produce that certainty in the law, which is the *mother* and *nurse* of *quietness* and *repose,* must be well ascertained: that it will be produced by looking into, and adhering to the decision of this Court on constitutional questions, I am well assured; and have therefore referred to them as safe commentaries upon its text.

There is another consideration of conclusive weight on my mind.

By taking the constitution as the grant of the people of each state; as the depositories of the absolute and unlimited powers of government, in their original sovereignty; their grant conveys the same power which was in the grantor before its execution: of consequence, the powers of the federal government will have a supremacy proportioned to the supremacy of the grantor.

It will bind the states by the sovereign power which they all acknowledge; it will be their own voluntary act, their full and free cession of jurisdiction; so that the more absolute the sovereignty is, which grants the power, the greater will be the strength of the grant, and the security from violation. By adopting the opposite principle, which ascribes the creation of the government to the people in the aggregate, the doctrine of consolidation is necessarily introduced as its foundation; this is so repugnant to the constitution itself, and the universal opinion of the conventions which framed and the people who adopted it, that it will never be acquiesced in. The principle itself is so utterly repugnant to all American ideas of government, that it will be resisted and opposed even in theory; when it is once made the foundation for the action of the government, and referred to as the source of its powers, and we must expect to witness the reality, of what has once threatened its existence. If the states of the Union were sovereign and independent states, before the adoption of the constitution, and the grant of legislative powers by it was not made by the several states who ratified it; then they retain all their pre-existing powers, and congress act by an usurped authority. On the theory then of the unity of political power in one people, there will be fastened the antagonist principles of consolidation, and nullification; under the pressure of which the government must fall. On the other hand, if the government is admitted to be the work of the separate people of each state, there can be no pretext for nullification: the sovereign power of the state has made the grant; has declared it the law of the land, supreme in obligation over its own laws and constitution; has commended its judges to obey it; has appointed a tribunal to expound it; and bound itself to abide by changes to be made by alterations or amendments. The people and the states will, like individuals, submit to the privation of those rights which they have granted to another; but when any claim of property or power, is made under an adversary or paramount right, they will call for the exhibition of the muniments of original title, and its regular deduction to whoever claims its exercise; if not produced, they may and will resist.

No danger can assail the constitution, which will be so difficult to avert, as by the professed friends of its supremacy, renouncing and disclaiming a title perfect in itself, and endeavouring to place it upon a grant by a power which exists only in theory; and from whom no title can be deduced by any visible or tangible act.

THE CONSTITUTION PRESCRIBES THE RULE OF ITS INTERPRETATION.

I cannot close this view of the constitution, without again referring to that clause of the instrument, which, connected with its exposition by this Court, I have said is the key to its meaning; it is also the rule prescribed by its framers, whereby to ascertain the extent of the grant of territory or jurisdiction, the rights of soil, the powers of government, as well as the restrictions on the states. "The congress shall have power to dispose of, and make all needful rules and regulations respecting the territory or other property belonging to the United States;" *and nothing in this constitution shall be so construed, as to prejudice any claims of the United States, or of any particular state.*

It has always seemed to me, that the latter part of this clause is one of the most, if not the most important sentence in the whole instrument; though it has received but little, if any attention. Its words are most comprehensive, extending to the whole constitution, as well as to every subject to which the United States, or any particular state, had any claim; they must not be deemed senseless, but have some meaning and application, which will correspond with the preceding part of the clause; the intention with which they were introduced, and the subject matter of reference. By this clause, a power was given to dispose of, and regulate the territory or other property belonging to the United States, acquired, as has been seen, by cession from the particular states of the Union, or foreign states; and that regulation was but another word for legislation, and the power of creating territorial governments, or corporations. It has been also shown, that this Court have uniformly held, that the right to property and jurisdiction, or legislative power, are concomitant, and vested in the same original proprietor of the soil of a state or territory; and that all the powers of congress, whether exclusive over their own property or territory, or limited over the several states; is of the same nature and character, conferred by the same instrument, as one uniform law throughout the United States. To regulate, implies power over the thing to be regulated, 9 Wh. 209; to prescribe rules, to make laws; it is exclusive over the ceded territories, because the cession of soil carries with it jurisdiction; unless otherwise expressed. It is exclusive within this district, because the states in their cession made it so; it is exclusive, concurrent, or federal only, over forts, arsenals, &c., according to the terms of the cession by a state, or its consent to the purchase; it is federal over the states, its territory, or the property of its citizens, limited by the constitution to enumerated objects: but in whatever mode, or to whatever extent it is, or can be exercised, the power arises from the cession, by a legislative act, and the constitution. This clause, therefore, of necessity refers to whatever power or property has been in any way granted to the United States by the constitution, or which had been previously, or should thereafter be ceded to them, so that it *belonged* to them; and the proviso, limitation and prohibition, must have a reference as broad as its subject matter and express terms. It is a declaration, that the claims of the grantee to what is granted, shall not be prejudiced by any construction of any thing contained in the constitution; so that in the language of this Court, the powers of the government shall not be construed and refined down to insignificance. It is also a declaration, that the claims of a grantor to what was ungranted and not prohibited, should remain unprejudiced by any broad construction of the grant, which would take away the reserved powers of the states or the people: the intention of which is apparent, by recurring to the second article of the confederation, in which each state retained "all power, right, and jurisdiction, not expressly delegated to the United States;" and to the ninth, which protected their territory.

Such a clause would have defeated the great objects of the constitution, unless all powers intended to be granted had been enumerated in detail; "the minor ingredients," as well as "the great outlines;" which would have made it a prolix code, unintelligible to those for whose regulation it was intended; Vide 4 Wh. 407. On the other hand, it would have been almost a hopeless effort, to have effected its adoption without some clause of limitation, by which a rule of interpretation should be laid down as fundamental. We know, as an historical fact, that it was not adopted by all the states, till after the amendments were made, among which the tenth was deemed the most important. No men could better know, or more deeply feel the dangerous effects to the Union, of contests between particular states and the confederacy; the danger of conflicting claims to territory, had been imminent; it was averted by cessions, by the states, made in the spirit of compromise. Six years of experience under the confederation, had taught them the necessity of cessions of legislative power, in the same spirit.

During the revolution, the contest was for property, which was settled by the adoption of the articles of confederation, which prohibited the United States from depriving a state of territory for their benefit. It did not require the spirit of prophecy to foresee, that under the constitution, there would be a similar contest for power; and it would have been strange if some endeavour had not been made to avoid it. It was a most delicate effort to so frame a constitution, as to define the precise line by which the granted and reserved powers of government should be so separated, as to avoid any collision; the necessity of the case requires it to be on some point, between a delegation to congress by express words, and such general terms, as by construction might be held to comprehend such as were not granted to them. Perhaps a better term could not have been used, than the one adopted, to avoid both difficulties. "Shall be adjudged," is a parliamentary term of great significancy: a word of command that such a construction shall be given, as in the 12 Cor. 2, prohibiting the king from granting land by any other than the tenure of soccage. His grants must be so taken as to convey such tenure, whatever may be their words; Vide ante, and 3 Ruff, 192: "*Shall not be construed,*" is a term in the 11th amendment, the meaning and effect whereof has been settled by this Court, as before stated; and must receive the same interpretation when it is found in the body of the instrument.

When, therefore, we find a declaration, "*nothing* contained in this constitution *shall be so construed,*" &c., it can have no meaning, unless it be to prohibit any interpretation of the grant, by which it shall operate to the prejudice of the grantor, or grantee, *by construction merely*. Taken in connection with the 10th amendment, such intention is apparent; by reserving what is not granted or prohibited, that which is granted or prohibited, is not reserved; whereby the grant must be interpreted according to the import of its language, without straining it beyond, or within its obvious meaning.

This Court has carried out the rule prescribed by the constitution, according to its spirit and intention. "The powers actually granted must be such as are expressly given, or given by necessary implication." "The instrument is to have a reasonable construction, according to the import of its terms." "Where a power is given in general terms, it is not to be restrained to particular cases, unless that construction grow out of the context expressly, or by necessary implication;" 1 Wh. 326. Words which import a power should not be restricted by a forced construction; 6 Wh. 423. A similar rule is applied to cessions of property. A term used in connection with, and explained by the other parts of the instrument, so as to show a clear intention, will be considered as a part of, and explanatory of it, to carry the intention into effect. "But if no such conclusion can be drawn, the term must receive its legal and appropriate interpretation;" 10 Pet. 53. "There must be something to take the term out of the strict, legal, and technical interpretation; it must appear, in the instrument, to warrant any other construction;" Ib. 54.

These rules are those of the common law. An implication which necessarily results from the words used, is of the same effect as express words; because they equally serve to show the intention of the grantor. Words are but the evidence of intention; their import is their meaning, to be gathered from the context, and their connection with the subject matter. "It is proper to take a view of the liberal meaning of the words to be expounded, of their connection with other words, and the general object to be accomplished by the prohibitory clause, or the grant of power;" 12 Wh. 437.

In thus ascertaining the meaning of an instrument of writing, by the express words thereof, or their necessary implication, it is not mere construction; it is following the intention apparent on its face, if not in words; it is their plain meaning, taking the whole together. It wholly differs from that mode of construction which is resorted to in order to infer or imply the grant of one thing by the grant of another; to raise an implication on the words of a grant, by matter extraneous, to which no reference is made in any part of it; to seek, *aliunde*, for an intention, which the words do not import. That implication or construction which the law permits, is what the judicial eye can perceive, by inspection, to be the intention of the writing and the parties; not that which can be gathered only from matter not contained in it, by assumption, supposition, ingenious reasoning, or conjecture, of motives, objects, or intentions. The first is applied to all instruments; the latter is rejected, as mere parol evidence; which the law repudiates whenever it is offered to contradict, explain, or control a writing.

By keeping in view this distinction between the necessary implication apparent in the writing, or, as Blackstone expresses it, " the evident consequence," 1 Bl. Com. 250, or conclusion which results from its inspection, and that which is made by construction alone, founded on extraneous matters, the meaning of the constitution and this Court is the same.

One power, restriction, prohibition, or reservation, is not to be implied from another; it is incompatible with a grant by enumeration of the things granted, and which " deals in general language." If it is once a settled rule of construction, that any power can be infused into it, which on its face does not appear to be granted; or any power restricted by mere construction, which is granted, the system becomes utterly deranged. Nothing can more clearly indicate the intention of its framers, to exclude the doctrine of constructive powers, or constructive restraints, than the 17th clause of the 8th section of the 1st article.

Not willing to leave to the congress, the exercise of any powers not enumerated, however indispensable to their efficient action, or to paralyse the legislative power, by withholding the power of executing its laws, a distinct and express grant was made, " to make all laws which shall be necessary and proper for carrying into effect the foregoing powers," &c. Not to extend the jurisdiction of congress, to any subject matter of legislation not enumerated in the grant, but to enable it to execute the laws it was authorized to pass. The great and incurable defect of the confederation was, the dependence of congress on state laws to execute and to carry into effect their resolutions and requisitions: generally speaking, the jurisdiction of the old and new congress was the same, except as to the regulation of commerce and a judicial system. The states would not delegate the power of execution to operate directly on the subjects of its jurisdiction; the people of the states granted this power, by the constitution, by which alone the federal government became efficient and com-

14

petent to the objects of its creation. It has been said, that congress would have had this power without an express grant, according to the rule of law, that the grant of a thing is a grant of the means necessary for its enjoyment. But however true this may be, as a mere legal proposition, it never was a principle of American government, but a contrary rule applied to the powers delegated by the confederation; it required the invocation of the sovereign power of the people of each state to change it, by making an express grant of a power, which no state would have permitted to be exercised within its limits but by its own consent. I am well aware that this clause has been viewed otherwise by this Court; they have held it to be a grant, by its terms, of the means or the powers necessary and proper to carry the powers of congress into effect, as a collateral rather than a direct power, authorizing the use of instruments or subordinate agents, to effect the objects and purposes of the constitution. Herein they have, in my opinion, departed from their accustomed course: they have applied to this clause a construction which it does not admit, consistently with its terms, and their own settled rules of interpretation.

That the power is express, and its objects definitely declared, is plain, " to carry into effect," to pass " such laws as may be necessary and proper," for the executing and enforcing the powers granted by the constitution to the federal government, its departments and officers; and not by that of the states, as under the confederation. That it is the all-important and vital power of the federal government, which must exist in full vigour, and be exercised with firmness, in order to perpetuate its existence, is admitted by all. In my opinion, this power is weakened, by making it by construction, an implied, and not an express power, and extending it to other objects than those of execution; and if it is so extended, there can be no limits assigned to its exercise, than the discretion and judgment of congress, as to the degree of necessity, or propriety, in the given case. No power is so dangerous as that which makes necessity its source; for necessity will always be assumed, when a pretext is wanted. When the constitution gives a discretionary power, depending on the necessity of the case or its urgency, it does so in terms; as suspending the writ of habeas corpus; and a state laying duties on imports or exports, or engaging in war: but, this discretion differs, essentially, from that which is confided by the clause under consideration. It is confined to the necessity of making a law, *appropriate* for the execution of specific powers, over the enumerated subject matters of legislation: whenever a new subject of jurisdiction is introduced, congress act by no legitimate authority. This Court has declared, that *confidence* in the *discretion* of *the States,* was not a principle of the constitution, 6 Wh. 388, &c.; *confidence* in congress is equally unknown to its provisions, unless in those parts which expressly declare it, in certain cases which are exceptions, applied alike to the federal and state legislatures.

There is another powerful objection to considering this clause in any other aspect than an express grant of legislative powers of execution. In referring it to the means of execution, by the assumption of jurisdiction over nonenumerated subjects, there necessarily arises a collision of opinions about the degree of necessity for using such means, which no reasoning can settle; it is but opinion, the correctness of which can be tested by no fixed or determinate standard of authority. Those who think a power necessary, will exercise it; those who think otherwise, will oppose it: hence we find that from the time of the adoption of the constitution, this clause has been, and yet continues to be, the debateable ground of contending parties, and remains as unsettled in public opinion, as the preamble to the constitution. One gives it such a construction as will enlarge, the other construes it so as to contract, the powers of the government to the utmost possible extent to which plain language can be perverted, by refined, ingenious, and powerful minds, reasoning under the influence of political opinion, each overlooking the declared import, and necessary implication of the words.

It cannot be doubted that these contests for power were foreseen by the framers of the constitution, and I have always been satisfied, that they intended to guard against both constructions; so as alike to prevent the powers of congress from being frittered down to inefficiency for the objects of the grant, or the reserved powers of the several states from being usurped—*by construction.* No clause could be more appropriate to the purpose, and none could more clearly express the intention, than that "nothing in this constitution shall be so construed." I do not feel at liberty to expunge one word from it, or to give it a more narrow application than it imports; it embraces every thing in the constitution, whether by way of grant or restriction, and prescribes for the interpretation of all its provisions, the only rule by which its true meaning can be ascertained, and the movements of the state and federal systems be preserved in harmony as one great whole. It ought, in my judgment, to receive the most liberal and benign interpretation which the words admit of; and if so taken, will effectuate the most salutary result—" certainty, the mother and nurse of the repose and quietness" of the Union.

These are my general views of the constitution, extracted from those sources of political and judicial authority which have been followed as safe guides; for their prolixity or tediousness, I have no apology to offer to the profession, other than my sense of the necessity of resorting at large to some better mode of expounding the constitution than has been hitherto pursued. It was necessary to explain my own peculiar opinion, on the cases depending and decided at the last term, as well as in some previous ones, wherein I have hitherto differed from the other judges; for which position, it was proper that my reasons should be understood by those who should desire to know them. Having now done this, I have only to show, that in combatting propositions and theories which I considered as unsound as dangerous, as repugnant to the provisions of the constitution, as the judicial exposition of its great principles, and the definition of its terms, I have not made them from fancy; and in such form as to enable me to put them down.

In the following extracts will be found the antagonist propositions to those which I have endeavoured to establish. The exalted character and stations of the eminent persons who have given their expositions of the constitution, entitle them to the most grave consideration and profound respect; and forbid the imputation of an intention to refer to *names*, and not to *things*. The following extracts from an able and learned commentary on the constitution, published in 1833, thus defines a state constitution:

" It is a fundamental law, prescribed by the will of a majority of the people of the states, (who are entitled to prescribe it,) for the government and regulation of the whole people. It binds them as a supreme compact, ordained by the sovereign power; and not merely as a voluntary contract," &c.; 1 Story Com. 317, 18; sec. 349.

He thus defines the constitution of the United States. " It is not a compact; on the contrary, the preamble emphatically speaks of it as a solemn ordinance and establishment of government. The language is, ' We, the people of the United States, do *ordain* and *establish* this *constitution* for the United States of America.' *The people* do *ordain* and *establish*, (not contract,) and stipulate with each other. The people of the *United States*, not the distinct people of *a particular state*, with the people of the other states. The people ordain and establish a *constitution*, not a *confederation;*" Ib. 319; sec. 352. " It was, nevertheless, in the solemn instruments of ratification by the people of the several states, assented to as a constitution;" Ib. 323; sec. 356. " But that it is, as the people have named and called it truly, a constitution; and they properly said, We, the people, &c. do ordain, &c. and not we the people of each state;" Ib. 327; sec. 360.

" The doctrine then that the states are parties, is a gratuitous assumption. In the language of a most distinguished statesman, the constitution itself, in its very front, refutes that. It declares that it is ordained and established by the people of the United States. So far from saying that it is established by the governments of the several states, it does not even say that it is established by *the people of the several states;* but it pronounces, that it is established by the people of the United States, in the aggregate. Doubtless the people of the several states, taken collectively, constitute the people of the United States. But it is in this, their collective capacity; it is as all the people of the United States, that they establish the constitution;" Ib. 332, 333; sec. 363. These propositions are laid down in terms so explicit, as to be susceptible of no misunderstanding as to their meaning; it is, therefore, unnecessary to pursue the remarks of the author any further, in order to develope his ideas as to the origin of the present governments.

The learned commentator thus notices and defines the origin and nature of the two governments which preceded the present, as the correct conclusions drawn from the political history of the country, from the assembling of the first congress of the revolution, till the adoption of the articles of confederation, and thence till the adoption of the constitution.

"The congress of delegates (calling themselves in their more formal acts, the delegates appointed by the good people of these colonies), assembled on the 4th of September, 1774, and having chosen officers, they adopted certain fundamental rules for their proceedings. Thus was organized, under the auspices, and with consent of the people, acting directly in their primary sovereign capacity, and without the intervention of the functionaries to whom the ordinary powers of government were delegated in the colonies, the first general or national government; which has been very aptly called the revolutionary government, since, in its origin and progress it was conducted upon revolutionary principles. The congress thus assembled, exercised *de facto*, and *de jure*, a sovereign authority; not as the delegated agents of the governments, *de facto*, of the colonies, but in virtue of original powers derived from the people. The revolutionary government thus formed, terminated only when it was regularly superseded by the confederated government, under the articles finally ratified, as we shall hereafter see in 1781;" 1 Story's Com. 185, 6, sec. 200, 201.

"In the first place, antecedent to the declaration of independence, none of the colonies were, or pretended to be, sovereign states, in the sense in which the term sovereign is sometimes applied to states;" Ib. 191, sec. 207. "Strictly speaking, in our republican forms of government, the absolute sovereignty of the nation is in the people of the nation, and the residuary sovereignty of each state, not granted to any of the public functionaries, is in the people of the state;" Ib. 195, sec. 208. "Now, it is apparent, that none of the colonies before the revolution, were in the most enlarged and general sense, independent or sovereign communities;" Ib. 196, sec. 210.

"In the next place, the colonies did not severally act for themselves, and proclaim their independence;" Ib. 197.

"But the declaration of independence of all the colonies, was the united act of all; it was a declaration by the representatives of the United States of America, in congress assembled, by the delegates appointed by the good people of the colonies, as in a prior declaration of rights they were called. It was not an act done by the state governments then organized, nor by persons chosen by them. It was emphatically, the act of the whole people of the United States, by the instrumentality of their representatives, chosen for that among other purposes. It was an act not competent to the state governments, or any of them, as organized under their charters, to adopt. Those charters neither contemplated the case, or provided for it. It was an act of original inherent sovereignty by the people themselves; resulting from their right to change the form of government, and to institute a new government whenever necessary for their safety and happiness. So the declaration of independence treats it. No state had presumed, of itself, to form a new government, or to provide for the exigency of the times, without consulting congress on the subject; and when they acted, it was in pursuance of the recommendation of congress. It was therefore the achievement of the whole, for the benefit of the whole. The people of the united colonies made the united colonies free and independent states; and absolved them from all allegiance to the British crown. The declaration of independence has, accordingly, always been treated as an act of paramount and sovereign authority, complete and perfect, *per se;* and *ipso facto,* making an entire dissolution of all political connection with, and allegiance to Great Britain. And this not merely as a practical fact, but in a legal and constitutional view of the matter by courts of justice;" Ib. 199, sec. 211.

"The same body, in 1776, took bolder steps, and executed powers which can, in no other manner, be justified or accounted for, than upon the supposition, that a national union, for national purposes, already existed, and that the congress was invested with sovereign power over all the colonies, for the purpose of preserving the common rights and liberties of all."

"Whatever, then, may be the theories of ingenious men on the subject, it is historically true, that before the declaration of independence, these colonies were not in any absolute sense sovereign states; that that event did not find or make them such: but that at the moment of their separation, they were under the dominion of a superior controlling national government, whose powers were vested in and exercised by the general congress, with the consent of the people of all the states; Ib. 202, sec. 214.

"From the moment of the declaration of independence, if not for most purposes at an antecedent period, the united colonies must be considered as being a nation de facto, having a general government over it, created and acting by the general consent of the people of all the colonies. The powers of that government were not, and could not be well defined; but still its exclusive sovereignty in many cases was firmly established; and its controlling power over the states, was in most, if not in all, national measures, universally admitted;" Ib. 203, sec. 215.

It is unnecessary to follow the learned author through his history of the confederation, or his views of the nature of the government which existed under it; as he has copied into his work, from a most interesting state paper; "some of its important passages, as among the ablest commentaries ever offered upon the constitution;" Vide 2 Story's Com. 543.

"In our colonial state, although dependent on another power, we very early considered ourselves connected by common interest with each other. Leagues were formed for common defence; and before the declaration of independence, we were known in our aggregate character as the United Colonies of America. That decisive and important step was taken jointly. We declared ourselves a nation, by a joint, not by several acts; and when the terms of our confederation were reduced to form, it was in that of a solemn league of several states, by which they agreed that they would, collectively, form one nation, for the purpose of conducting some domestic concerns, and all foreign relations. In the instrument forming that Union, is found an article which declares that every state shall abide by the determination of congress, on all questions which by that confederation shall be submitted to them;" 2 Story's Com. 546.

"The people of the United States formed the constitution, acting through the state legislatures, in making the compact, to meet and discuss its provisions; but the terms used in its construction, show it to be a government, in which the people of all the states, collectively, are represented. We are one people in the choice of president and vice president. Here the states have no other agency than to direct the mode in which the votes shall be given. The candidates having the majority of all the votes, are chosen. The electors of a majority of states may have given their votes for one candidate, and yet another may be chosen. The people, then, and not the states, are represented in the executive branch;" 2 Story's Com. 551.

"The unity of our political character commenced in its very existence. Under the royal government, we had no separate character; our opposition to its oppressions began as united colonies. We were the United States under the confederation, and the name was perpetuated, and the Union rendered more perfect, by the federal constitution. In none of these stages did we consider ourselves in any other light than as forming one nation. Treaties and alliances were made in the name of all. Troops were raised for the joint defence. How, then, with all these proofs, that under all our changes of position, we had, for designated purposes, with defined powers, created national governments? how is it, that the most perfect of those several modes of union, should now be considered as a mere league, which may be dissolved at pleasure?" 2 Story's Com. 554.

It is proper here to add an extract from the opinion of Chief Justice Jay, in the case referred to, at the end of sec. 211, 1 vol. Com. 199, part of which is given in sect. 216, p. 204, 5; as it will show the coincidence of views entertained and declared by him in 1793, and those of the learned commentator forty years afterwards.

"Afterwards, in the hurry of the war, and in the warmth of mutual confidence, they (the people,) made a confederation of the states the basis of a general government. Experience disappointed the expectations they had formed from it; and the people, in their collective and national capacity, established the present constitution. It is remarkable, that in establishing it, the people exercised their own rights, and their own proper sovereignty; and, conscious of the plenitude of it, they declared, with becoming dignity, we, the *people* of the *United States*, do ordain and establish this 'constitution.' Here we see the people acting as sovereigns of the whole country: and, in the language of sovereignty, establishing a constitution, by which it was their will that the state governments should be bound, and to which the state constitutions should be made to conform. Every state constitution is a compact, made by and between the citizens of a state, to govern themselves in a certain manner; and the constitution of the *United States* is likewise a compact, made by the people of the *United States*, to govern themselves as to general objects, in a certain manner.  By this great compact, however, many prerogatives were transferred to the national government; such as those of making war and peace, contracting alliances, coining money," &c. &c.

"If, then, it be true, that the sovereignty of the nation is in the people of the nation, and the residuary sovereignty of each state in the people of each state, it may be useful," &c.; 2 Dall. 270, 271.

The only difference of opinion between these two most learned jurists, is in the constitution being a compact; it is, however, only a difference about a name; they agree in the thing; the power which created, the nature and origin of the federal government, those of the states, and the thing created; a constitution, not a league.

These extracts are made more at large than would be required on an ordinary occasion; in order to present a full view of the ground on which the doctrine of the unity of power, in the one people, of one nation, existing from the beginning of the revolution, is asserted; and that no supreme sovereign power was in the people of the several states, competent to ordain and establish the constitution, is maintained; so that there can be no misapprehension as to meaning or intention.

It was intended to publish the preceding view, with the four opinions which follow, in an appendix to the eleventh volume of Mr. Peters' Reports, which contains the opinions of the Court, and the judges who dissented. But it was found that, by so doing, the publication of the Reports would be delayed beyond the time at which they would otherwise have been before the public. Unwilling to be the cause of such delay, I have adopted this mode of submitting my views and opinions to the profession.

H. B.

---

### BRISCOE ET AL. V. THE COMMONWEALTH BANK OF KENTUCKY.

IT has so happened, that I am the only member of the Court, who composed one of the majority in the case of Craig v. Missouri, and now concurs with the majority in this case, in affirming the judgment of the court of appeals; in this respect my situation is peculiar, as well as in another particular. After an argument in the former case, two of the judges had died; of the remaining five, three were of opinion that the paper issued by the state of Missouri were bills of credit, and two of a contrary opinion; on the argument in 1830, there were two judges present who had not before sat in the cause, and on whose opinion the result depended. If they agreed with the minority, the judgment was of course confirmed; if they divided, it was reversed; so that the one who joined the three made the judgment of the Court: this was my case; agreeing in opinion with the three who were for reversing, I concurred in the judgment and general course of the opinion and reasoning of the Court, though my opinion was formed on grounds somewhat different. It was my intention to have assigned my reasons in a separate opinion, but as it was the first term of my sitting in the Court, the business was new and pressing, and want of time prevented it; but at my suggestion a clause was added to the opinion prepared by the chief justice, which would enable me afterwards to show the reasons of my judgment should a similar question occur. In this case, too, I fully concur in the judgment rendered, yet not in the course of reasoning or the authority on which the opinion of the Court is based; so that my position is as peculiar in this as it was in Craig v. Missouri; and in one respect is in marked contrast with that of the other three judges who sat in that case. The judge who was in the majority then, and now dissents, was and is of opinion, that the paper emitted in both cases came within the restriction of the constitution as bills of credit; two who then dissented and now are in the majority, were, and are of opinion that the papers in neither case are bills of credit, so that no imputation of inconsistency can rest upon them. With me it is

15

[Briscoe et al. v. The Commonwealth Bank of Kentucky.]

different; my judgment has led me to different results in the two cases, and therefore it cannot be deemed improper for me to explain the reasons why, though forming one of the majority in both cases, I stand in some measure alone.

A judge who now dissents, may find reasons therefor in the opinion delivered in Craig v. Missouri; those who now concur, may rest on their dissenting opinions in that case; but the same course of reasoning and deduction which shows the consistency of others, may lead to a very contrary conclusion as to mine.

These considerations must be my apology for the course now taken.

In Craig v. Missouri, the subject of controversy, were certificates signed and issued by the auditor and treasurer pursuant to a law of that state, which were on their face receivable at the treasury for taxes and debts due the state, bearing interest at the rate of two per cent. per annum. One-tenth the amount of said certificates were directed to be withdrawn annually from circulation; they were made a legal tender for all salaries and fees of office, in payment for salt to the lessee of the public salt works at a price to be stipulated by law, and for all taxes due the state, or to any county, or town therein. They were to be loaned on personal security by joint and several bonds bearing interest; the proceeds of the salt springs, the interest accruing on the bonds, all estates purchased under the law, all debts due or to become due to the state, were pledged and constituted a fund for their redemption, and the faith of the state was also pledged for the same purpose.

It seemed to a majority of the Court, to be impossible to disguise the character of this paper, or to change its nature or effect by substituting the word *certificate* on its face for the word *bill;* the change was only in name, the thing was the same. Connected with the law under which the paper was issued, it was a bill, note, or obligation, emitted by the state, with the avowed purpose of circulating as money for all the purposes referred to in the law; the funds and faith of the state were pledged for its payment with interest from its date, and it was made a legal tender in payment of certain debts to individuals, and of taxes to towns and counties. No member of the Court was more clearly of opinion, that these self-called certificates were bills of credit to all intents and purposes, and that that part of the constitution which declared, that no state should emit them, would be a dead letter if they were not held to be within it, than I was. On this subject, my opinion went to the full extent of that which was delivered by the chief justice, and has been fully confirmed by subsequent reflection.

There was between the concurring judges and myself, no other difference of opinion, or in the reasons of our respective judgments, than in the definition of a bill of credit, which is thus given in the opinion, 4 Pet. 432: "To emit bills of credit conveys to the mind the idea of issuing paper, intended to circulate through the community, for its ordinary purposes, as money, which paper is redeemable at a future day. This is the sense in which the terms have been always understood. If the prohibition means any thing; if the words are not empty sounds, it must comprehend the emission of any paper medium by a state government for the purpose of common circulation."

To this broad definition I could not assent; in my opinion, no paper medium could be deemed a bill of credit emitted by a state, unless it contained on its face, or the law under which it was emitted gave a pledge of its faith or credit for its redemption; nor then, unless it was made a legal tender in the payment of some debts to individuals. Though the opinion is silent as to the pledge of the faith of the state, being a requisite to constitute a bill of credit, and negatives the necessity of the paper being made a legal tender; yet these matters entered into the character of the paper, and were a part of the case before the Court, as appears in the opinion, 4 Pet. 432, 3. The first sentence in the latter page, shows the ground on which my opinion turned; the paper was a tender, and the faith of the state was pledged. This last clause was added to the opinion at my request. " It also pledges the faith and funds of the state for their redemption."

Thus there was a perfect union of opinion between the judges who composed the majority, on the whole case presented for judgment, as well in the result as the course of reasoning which led to it; the only variance was as to the requisites of a bill of credit. Three judges holding that " any paper medium emitted by a state government for the purpose of common circulation," filled the constitutional definition of a bill of credit, while one judge held that there were two additional requisites; that the emission should be on the credit of the state, and the paper declared a legal tender. But as the certificates or bills, taken in connection with the law directing their emission, contained all the requisites to constitute bills of credit, on the most limited construction which could be given to the constitution, there could be no other difference of opinion than in the reasons for judgment.

Had the opinion and reasoning been applied to the whole case, to paper not only emitted by a state for common circulation, but emitted on its faith and credit expressly pledged, and made a tender, the reasons would have been in perfect accordance with the views of the majority and their judgment. But though this was requested by me, the opinion was confined to only a part of the case on the record, taking no notice, in the reasoning, of the pledge of the faith of the state in direct terms, or giving to it any declared effect in fixing the character of the paper. If this pledge had not appeared on the certificate or in the law, my opinion would have been for affirming the judgment of the state court; and as three judges held that even with this pledge, the certificates were not bills of credit, it is evident that the judgment of this Court depended on this part of the law.

[Briscoe et al. v. The Commonwealth Bank of Kentucky.]

With this explanation, the case of Craig v. Missouri, so far from being an authority in favour of the proposition, that it is not necessary to constitute a bill of credit, that the faith of the state should be pledged for its payment, it must be taken as negativing it by the opinion of four judges. On the other hand, four judges were of opinion, that it was not necessary that the certificates should have been made a legal tender for any purpose, in order to make them bills of credit. Thus understood, I adhere to the decision of the Court in that case, as it was judicially before it on the record; and yet retaining the same opinion now, which I then expressed to the judges, I cannot feel myself precluded from acting on it in this case, because the opinion of the Court, as delivered, did not take the same course as mine, in leading the majority to the conclusion they formed. To now abandon the deliberate result of my best judgment, formed and expressed in that case, which has been confirmed on the successive arguments in this, would look more like yielding to a train of reasoning on a part of a case, than respecting the judgment of the Court on the whole record. It would also place me in a position of inextricable difficulty, to now surrender my judgment to the same reasoning and illustrations, which failed to convince me seven years since, the more especially when the intervening investigations which it has been my duty to make on this subject, has led my mind to the conclusion it first formed.

With these remarks, the profession will understand the reason why I concurred in the judgment of the Court in this, and the former case, in that the faith of the state of Missouri was pledged for the payment of the paper which she emitted, and made a legal tender; in this, Kentucky has not pledged her faith to redeem the notes of the bank, nor made them a legal tender in payment of a debt. I also concur with the opinion of the Court in this case, that these notes cannot be deemed to have been emitted by the state, and have no desire to add any views of my own on this part of the case, my object being to defend my own peculiar position as to the definition of a bill of credit, according to the true interpretation of the first sentence of the tenth section of the first article of the constitution.

It is in these words—" No state shall enter into any treaty of alliance or confederation; grant letters of marque and reprisal; coin money; emit bills of credit; make any thing but gold and silver coin a tender in payment of debts; pass any bill of attainder, or ex post facto law, or law impairing the obligation of contracts, or grant any title of nobility."

In analyzing this sentence, it is apparent that these restrictions on the states relate to three distinct subjects. 1. To those on which the constitution had granted express powers to the federal government; to make treaties, grant letters of marque and reprisal, coin money. 2. To those on which the constitution made no grant of any power, by either express words, any necessary implication, or any reasonable interpretation; to emit bills of credit, make any thing but gold and silver coin a legal tender in payment of debts, or pass any law impairing the obligation of contracts. 3. To those subjects on which the 9th section of the first article had imposed the same restriction on the United States and congress, as the tenth section did on the separate states; to pass any bill of attainder, ex post facto law, or grant any title of nobility.

On the last class of cases any comment is useless; there has never been any difference of opinion' as to the meaning of a bill of attainder, or a title of nobility; and though there have been doubts as to the meaning of an ex post facto law, they have long since been settled, so that we can safely assume, that as to those parts of the ninth and tenth sections of the first article, the meaning of the constitution is as plain and definite as its language.

By referring the terms to a standard of admitted authority, from which they have been adopted in the constitution, they become as intelligible as if their settled definition had been added by the convention which framed the instrument. What the standard of definition shall be, depends on the term used; if it is one of common use in the ordinary transactions of society and so applied, it shall be taken in its common ordinary acceptation by those who use the term; if it relates to any particular art, science, or occupation, its meaning is its common understood sense, according to the usage and its acceptation among men so employed. If it is a term appropriate to the common, or statute law, or the law of nations, it must be taken as intended to be applied according to its established definition as a known legal term.

Hence the term *bill of attainder*, means the conviction of a person of a crime by legislative power; an *ex post facto* law, is one which makes an act criminal which when committed was no offence; *a title of nobility* is a term which defines itself. Thus the terms used as to the third class of cases, have been considered as defined by a reference to their understanding in a legal sense.

In passing to the first class of cases, it will be found that the terms *treaty, alliance, confederation,* and *letters of marque and reprisal,* when referred to the law of nations, are perfectly defined; so is the term *coin money,* when referred to the words in their common acceptation, or their legal sense. There is no ambiguity in the words; taken separately or in connection, as a term or phrase, they require no other interpretation than is to be found in the known and universally received standard by which they are defined, nor can they be taken in any other sense, or by any other reference, unless there appears from the context or other parts of the same instrument, an obvious intention to use and apply them differently from their ordinary or legal acceptation. These are the established unvarying rules of interpretation which assign a meaning to language, that requires explanation not contained in the words themselves; the want of certainty is cured by a reference to that which is certain, and when any word, term, or phrase, has acquired a definite meaning, its use without explanatory words, is always deemed to be so intended. With the universal consent of every statesman and jurist, the terms used in these two classes of cases in the tenth section, with the exception of an ex post facto law, have been received and taken according to their known definition, by municipal or national law, and common understanding; and there is now the same common assent to the meaning of an ex post facto law, as settled by the repeated adjudications of this Court. The same rules have also been applied to all other parts of the constitution, in which terms of known import are used, as the *writ of habeas corpus, trial by jury*, &c. No man ever doubted that they were used according to their definition by the common law, or that the words *taxes, commerce, money, coin*, were used and must be taken in their ordinary meaning and acceptation. It is indeed an universal rule, applied to all laws supreme or subordinate, to all instruments of writing, all grants or reservations of power, property, franchise or immunity, and all contracts; that the words and language used, shall be interpreted by such reference, accordingly as the subject matter is made certain by their legal or commonly received definition or acceptation. There is another rule of interpretation equally universal, that the whole instrument shall be examined, to ascertain the meaning of any particular part or sentence, so as to avoid any discrepancy, and the same standard be applied to all its terms, and every word which can bear upon its intention, referring each to the appropriate subject to which it relates, the standard is furnished for the interpretation. Thus the word *bill* has a meaning depending on the subject matter to which it is applied; a *bill of credit* refers to the payment of money; a *bill of attainder* refers to the conviction of an offence by a legislature; so of the word *law*, an *ex post facto law* refers to one which inflicts a punishment; a law impairing the obligation of a contract, refers to *money* or *property* due or owned in virtue of a *contract*.

Taking it then as an undoubted proposition, that the same rules of interpretation must be applied to all parts of the tenth section, taken in connection with the whole constitution, as one instrument of writing, I shall endeavour to ascertain what is the meaning of the terms used in reference to the second class of cases.

The first term is " No state shall emit bills of credit."

That by state is meant a state of this Union there can be no doubt. Next comes the word *emit*, which, referring to bills of credit, means an emission of paper; a putting off, putting out, putting forth, or issuing bills by a state, for the payment of money, at some time, by some person, and on credit.

The time of payment, the fund out of which it is payable, the faith or credit reposed in, or pledged by those who emit it, depends on the law under which the state made, or authorized the emission.

[Briscoe et al. v. The Commonwealth Bank of Kentucky.]

Then comes the term *bills of credit*, without any reference or explanatory words; but as it necessarily relates to the payment of money, the word *bill* must be taken as a paper, containing some evidence that a certain sum is due, to the person to whom it was emitted or issued, or by whom it is held. It is a word of legal import, as well defined as any in the English language, according to the subject matter to which it is applied. " A *bill* is a common engagement for money given by one man to another; when with a penalty it is a penal bill, when without one it is a single bill;" Toml. L. D. 230; " and it is all one with an obligation, saving that it is commonly called a bill when in English, and an obligation when in Latin. But now by a bill, we ordinarily understand a single bond without a condition; by an obligation, a bond with a penalty and condition;" Cow. L. I. Tit. Bill; 5 D. C. D. 191. Obl. A.; or according to the definition of C. B. Comyns, " a single bill is when a man is bound to another by bill or note, without a penalty;" ib. 194. C.

A *bill of credit* is also a well known term of the law; in its mercantile sense, it means a letter addressed by one merchant to another, to give credit to the bearer for money or goods, such letter being in the nature of a bill of exchange, is called a bill and so treated; Beawes, L. M. 483; S. P. 5, D. C. D. 131; Merchant, F. 3. When the word *bill* refers to paper emitted by a bank, there will be found a most marked adherence to the distinction between an obligation and a bill, as appears in the clause of the original charter of the Bank of England, read by plaintiffs' counsel, " That all and every *bill* or *bills obligatory* and of *credit* under the seal of the said corporation, made or given to any person or persons, shall and may by endorsement thereon, &c. be assigned," &c., 5 W. & M. ch. 20, sect. 29; 3 Ruff. 563. So in the twenty-sixth section of the same act, " The corporation shall not borrow or give security by *bill, bond, covenant* or *agreement,* under their common seal," &c. ib.; the word bill denotes a sealed paper, either a bill obligatory which is an obligation, or a bill of credit which is a single bill; or if they are taken as synonymous, the words of the act are expressly confined to sealed bills, which require endorsement to make them assignable. Taking the term *bills obligatory* and of *credit,* under the common seal of the corporation, to be what they are declared in the charter, they are in their legal sense, and in common acceptation, the *bills of the bank* or *bank bills,* issued under their seal. This leads to another distinction between the different kinds of paper issued by the bank, worthy of all observation in the present case; the notes issued by the bank were not under its common seal; they were payable to bearer on demand, and passed from hand to hand by delivery merely, without endorsement. They can, therefore, in no just sense be deemed *bills of credit under seal,* requiring a special act of parliament to make them assignable; and so well was this known and fully understood, that we find throughout the extended charter to the bank in 8 and 9 W. 3, *bank bills* and *bank notes* are referred to in the same marked contradistinction which exists between a sealed bill assignable only by endorsement, and an unsealed note payable to bearer and transferable by delivery only.

In providing for enlarging the capital of the bank, the subscribers were authorized to pay one-fifth of their subscription " *in bank bills* or *bank notes,* which have so much money bona fide resting due thereupon," &c., 3 Ruff. 657, sect. 23. The same words, " in *bank bills* or *bank notes,*" are three times repeated in the twenty-fifth section, and are carried through the whole act. In the thirty-sixth section, the discrimination is too strongly marked to admit of any possible doubt; in this section it is declared, " That the forging or counterfeiting of any *sealed bank bill,* made or given out *in the name* of the said governor and company for the payment of any sum of money; or of any *bank note,* of any sort whatever, *signed for* the said governor and company of the Bank of England, &c., shall be felony;" ib. 659. The act of 3 & 4 Ann, ch. 9, is also most explicit in its provisions, which embrace all notes in writing, signed by any person, "or the servant or agent of any corporation," payable to order or bearer, and puts them on the footing of inland bills of exchange, according to the custom of merchants, but neither in terms or by construction, can be applied to bills under seal; 4 Ruff. 180; or has ever been attempted to be so applied or construed. We must, therefore, take the term *bills of credit,* when applied to the paper issued by a bank, to mean an instrument under its corporate seal, payable to some person, and assignable by endorsement, and not a note payable to order or bearer, and transferable as an inland bill of exchange, according to the universal acceptation of the term in England.

There is another class of bills of credit in England, known by the name of exchequer bills, which are issued by the officers of the exchequer when a temporary loan is necessary to meet the exigencies of government. They were first termed *tallies of loan and orders of repayment,* charged on the *credit of the exchequer in general,* and made assignable from one person to another. 5 W. & M. ch. 20, sect. 39; 3 Ruff. 566. By a subsequent act, the officers of the treasury were authorized to *cause bills to be made forth* at the receipt of the exchequer, in such manner and form as they shall appoint, &c., and to issue the same to the uses of the war, they were made receivable for all taxes and money due at the exchequer, bore an interest, a premium was given for giving them circulation, the nation was security for their payment. Vide 8 and 9 W. 3, ch. 20, sect. 63, 4, 5, 6; 3 Ruff. 667, 8; 7 Ann, ch. 7, sect. 22; 4 Ruff. 345; 9 Ann, ch. 7, passim; 4 Ruff. 431; and they were called *bills of credit,* 3 Ruff. 679. Such is the nature of the three classes of bills of credit in England, whether they are *letters* or *bills of credit* of merchants in the nature of a bill of exchange, the *bills obligatory* or of *credit* of a bank, or *exchequer bills;* they all partake of the same character, and are the *bills of credit* of the person, corporation, or government, which emits, makes forth, issues, or puts them into circulation. The name given to the paper, its form or the mode of giving it currency or circulation is immaterial; its substance consists in its being an engagement to pay money at a future day, and that its payment rests on the security, faith, credit or responsibility, of those who put it into circulation, pledged on the face of the bills of individuals and corporations, and the law of the nation which emits or issues them. Bills of credit were viewed in the United States in the same way, before the adoption of the constitution and immediately afterwards. That the definition of a *bill* by the common law and common acceptation, is the same here as in England, and has ever been so accepted, is a proposition which needs only to be asserted; the same reasoning also attaches to a letter of credit in a mercantile sense, and the same distinction which has been shown to exist there, between *bank bills* and *bank notes*, was in the most explicit manner recognised during the revolution.

On the 31st December, 1781, congress passed an ordinance to incorporate the subscribers to the Bank of North America, and recommended to the legislatures of the several states, to pass such laws as were necessary to give the ordinance full operation, agreeably to the resolutions of congress on the 26th May preceding; 7 Journals Cong. 197, 199.

In the proceedings of that day, we have the plan of the bank which was then approved; in the twelfth article it is provided, " That the *bank notes payable on demand*," shall by law be made receivable in every state for duties and taxes, and by the treasury of the United States as specie; congress also resolved, that they should be received in payment of all debts due the United States, and recommended to the states to make the counterfeiting bank notes a capital felony; 7 Journals Cong. 87, 90; 26 May, 1781.

Pursuant to this recommendation, Pennsylvania passed an act to prevent and punish the counterfeiting the *bank bills*, and *bank notes* of the bank, made or to be made or given out. Hall and Sellers L. vol. 2. p. 11; 18 March 1782. In 1783 Delaware passed an act to punish the counterfeiting the *bank bills*, and *bank notes* of the bank; 2 Laws D. 773. But the law of Massachusetts passed the 8th March, 1782, contains the most unequivocal evidence, that the distinction between *bank bills* and *bank notes* was well known and understood, for it copies the thirty-sixth section of the acts of 8 and 9 W. 3, before referred to, " That if any person shall counterfeit any *sealed bank bill or obligation* made or given out for or in the name of the said P. D. & Co. for the payment of any sum of money; *or any bank note of any sort whatsoever*, signed for or in the name of the said P. D. & Co." Thomas' L. Mass. 187. In all these acts the words *note, bill* or *obligation*, are put in the same contradistinction from each other, which the common law assigns to them, and so are the acts of congress for chartering the Bank of the United

16

States, which were patterned from the acts of parliament chartering the Bank of England.

By the ninth fundamental article of the charter of 1791, it is provided, that " The total amount of the debts which the said corporation shall at any time owe, whether by *bond, bill, note,* or other contract, shall not exceed, &c." 1 Story L. 172. S. P. 8th article of charter of 1816. 3 Story, 1554. In the 13th article, the 29th section of the 5 W. & M. ch. 20, chartering the Bank of England is copied, declaring that " *The bills obligatory* and *of credit under the seal* of the said corporation," &c. shall be assignable by endorsement, &c. And *bills* or *notes* issued by the corporation, signed by the president and countersigned by the cashier, promising the payment of money, to any person or his order, or to bearer, though *not under the seal of the corporation*, shall be as binding on them as on a private person, and be negotiable by endorsement if payable to order, or by delivery only if payable to bearer; 1 Story, 173, 4. S. P. 12th article of charter of 1816; 3 Story, 1554, 5; thereby adopting the provisions of the 3d & 4th Ann, ch. 9, before referred to as to notes.

In the twelfth article of the charter of 1816, there is this proviso, " That said corporation shall not make any *bill obligatory,* or *of credit,* or *other obligation* under its seal, for the payment of a less sum than five thousand dollars." In the seventeenth section we find the paper issued by the bank placed in contradistinction no less than five times, by the denomination of *bills, notes,* or *obligations,* and the same distinction is made throughout the acts of 1791, and 1816. It is also carried into the acts of 1798, (omitting the word obligation,) by which the counterfeiting of *any bill,* or *note,* issued by order of the president, directors, and company, of the bank, is made a felony; 1 Story, 518; the act of 1807; 2 Story, 1048; and the eighteenth and nineteenth sections of the act of 1816; 3 Story, 1557, 8, in each of which the words *bill* and *note* are used to refer to the two kinds of paper, the word bill being used in its comprehensive sense as a known legal term, embracing *bills, bonds, obligations of all kinds,* when under the corporate seal, according to their settled and unvaried acceptation.

In considering the third species of bills of credit which are issued by the government, I will first refer to their definition by parliament, as the best evidence of the meaning and acceptation of the term in England, and as it was adopted in the United States.

The authority for issuing *tallies, orders,* or *bills,* from the exchequer, and the manner of doing it, are pointed out in the acts of 5 W. & M. ch. 20; 8 & 9 W. 3, ch. 20, before referred to, and 8 & 9 W. 3, ch. 28; 3 Ruff. 677, 9; also in Gilbert Hist. Exch. 137. When money is paid into the exchequer for debts due, or on a loan to the government, the teller who receives it gives a *bill* for the amount, which is an *exchequer bill,* or *a bill of credit;* a substantial definition of which will be found in the eleventh section of the 8 & 9 W.

3, ch. 28; 3 Ruff. 679.  " Provided also that this act, or any thing herein contained, shall not extend to alter or change any method of *receipts* or *payments* by *bills of credit* in the exchequer, allowed, or to be allowed by parliament," referring evidently to two species of such bills which are issued from the exchequer, according to the prescribed mode of accounting for all moneys paid.  *A bill of credit* given to a debtor who pays his debt, is merely the evidence of its payment; but *a bill of credit* given to one who lends money on the credit of the exchequer, allowed to be pledged by act of parliament, is a bill *made forth* on the credit of the government, who is a debtor to the holder for the amount with interest thereon as directed by the law.

It is evident that the constitution did not intend to prevent the emission by a state of a bill of credit of the first description, which in effect would be no more than a receipt for a debt due the state; it clearly refers only to that class of *bills of credit* which were emitted by a state, for the purposes declared in the law authorizing them to be emitted and put into circulation.   Taken in this sense, the term *bill of credit,* will be found to have been as well defined in the United States before the adoption of the constitution, as it was in England, or as the term *bill of credit,* in reference to bank bills, had been there and here from the time when the first charter of a bank was granted.

By the ninth article of the confederation, congress were authorized " to borrow money or *emit bills* on *the credit* of *the United States;*" but unless nine states consented, could not "*coin money,*" nor *emit bills,* nor *borrow money on the credit of the United States."*  By article twelve, *all bills of credit emitted, moneys borrowed,* and *debts contracted,* by or under the authority of congress, &c. shall be deemed a charge against the United States; for payment and satisfaction whereof, the said United States, and *the public faith,* are hereby solemnly pledged; 1 Laws U. S. 18, 19.

If there is certainty in language it would seem to be in this, as a definition of a "*bill of credit,*" and was evidently copied in the tenth section of the first article of the constitution; the prohibition against any less than nine in number of states acting on certain subjects is in the precise words, "*nor coin money,*" "*nor emit bills;*" if it is asked what bills, the answer is, "*bills on the credit of the United States, bills of credit emitted by the authority of congress on a pledge of the public faith."*  By substituting *state,* for "*United States* in congress assembled," the meaning of the words is identical, and cannot be mistaken when they are transferred into the constitutional prohibition, "*No state shall coin money, emit bills of credit,*" means *bills on the credit of the state.*  Plain words must be perverted by something inconsistent with reason, if they mean any thing else; if they do not refer to bills emitted on the credit of the state, we must be informed on whose credit.   It must be that of an individual, a corporation, or of the United States;

those who assert such a proposition, can have no respect for the constitution or its framers. Yet they can in no other way evade the obvious meaning of plain words; the prohibition was intended, and does prohibit *a state* from *emitting bills* on *its own credit*, and not on any other credit.

The prohibition is confined to a state, to an emission by a state, of bills of credit, emitted on the faith of a state, which can be pledged only by the law of a state, and no more exquisite torture can be inflicted on plain words, than in the endeavour to make them mean more, mean less, or mean any thing else than the credit of a state. When we look to the names affixed to the articles of confederation, and the constitution; when we consider that the former, after being long discussed in congress, and approved by that body, was submitted to the state legislatures, who deliberated nearly four years before its adoption, and that every word, phrase, and sentence, was fully discussed and most anxiously considered, it cannot be considered as a bold or rash assertion, that the framers of both instruments, comprehended the language they used, said what they meant, meant what they said, and stamped upon their work an impress of intention, which they at least designed should be intelligible to all capacities.

If the definition of a bill of credit, as given in both instruments, is not authoritative, I know of none higher to which to appeal as a more certain standard of political or judicial truth. In following such leaders in a path which they have plainly marked, I feel perfectly conscious of avoiding that disrespect for the solemn muniments of title on which the Union rests, which would be a cause of severe self-reproach, if in this tribunal I should rest my judgment on any contradictory authority. As however it cannot derogate from the respect due to the framers of those instruments, or the instruments themselves, to refer to authority subordinate only to that of state legislatures who made the confederation, and the people of the several states who ordained the constitution, in affirmance of the definition of bills of credit, as given by all, I shall refer to the resolutions of the old congress, and the acts of the new immediately after the adoption of the constitution.

By the third section of the act of July, 1790, making provision for the debt of the United States, among other evidences of debt which were to be received as subscription to the proposed loan were the following: " Those issued by the commissioners of loans in the several states, including certificates given pursuant to the act of congress of the 2d January, 1779, for *bills of credit* of the several emissions of 20th May, 1777, and 11th April, 1778. And in the bills of credit issued by the authority of the United States, at the rate of one hundred dollars in the said bills for one in specie." 1 Story, 110, 111.

The general term *bills of credit*, as used in the act of 1790, are defined in the resolutions of congress on the days respectively referred to.

20th May, 1770. " Resolved, that the sum of 5,000,000 of dollars, *in bills on the credit* of the United States, be forthwith *emitted,* under the direction of the board of treasury." 3 Journ. 194.

11th April, 1778. " Resolved, that 5,000,000 of dollars be *emitted* in *bills of credit,* on the *faith* of the United States."

" That the thirteen United States be pledged for the redemption of *the bills of credit* now ordered to be *emitted.*" 4 Journ. 149.

2d January, 1779. In the preamble and resolutions of this day, bills of credit are thus referred to. The United States have " been under the necessity of *emitting bills of credit,* for the redemption of which the *faith* of the United States has been pledged." " That any of the *bills emitted by order of congress,* &c." " That *the bills* received on the said quotas," &c. " That the following *bills* be taken out of circulation; namely, the whole *emissions* of 20th May, 1777, and 11th April, 1778." 5 Journ. 5, 6.

When, therefore, we find, that in the confederation, the acts and resolutions of congress, these various terms are used as synonymous, all referring to the same species of paper, as well known and defined as the term coin, money, or any other term, could be, and the same term, *bills* of credit, used in the constitution, it is not a little strange that those who framed the instrument, should be supposed to have used it in a different sense, without adding some words denoting such intention. That the term being adopted without explanation, was intended to be taken with the same meaning which had been so long and universally accepted, would, on any other than a constitutional question, be deemed conclusive evidence of their intention, cannot be doubted. If the term could admit of two interpretations, the members of the convention would adopt that which comported with the meaning given to the term by themselves, while members of congress, before, as well as after the adoption of the constitution, rather than any other standard of interpretation to be found elsewhere. These reasons are strengthened by a reference to other parts of the constitution, the terms of which are copied from the articles of confederation, as to *coin money, regulate the value thereof, borrow money on the credit of the United States, fix the standard of weights and measures,* and numerous others, apparent on inspection.

As the constitution was intended to be a supreme fundamental law, and bond of union, for ages to come, it was of the last importance to use those terms in the grant, or prohibition of power, which had acquired a precisely defined meaning, either in common acceptation, or as terms known to the common, the statute, or the law of nations, and infused, by universal consent, into the most solemn acts of congress, and the alliance of the confederation, which expressed the sense in which the whole country understood words, terms, and language. The framers of the constitution did not speak in terms

[Briscoe et al. v. The Commonwealth Bank of Kentucky.]

known only in local history, laws or usages, or infuse into the instrument local definitions, the expressions of historians, or the phraseology peculiar to the habits, institutions, or legislation of the several states. Speaking in language intended to be "uniform throughout the United States," the terms used were such as had been long defined, well understood in polity, legislation, and jurisprudence, and capable of being referred to some authoritative standard meaning; otherwise, the constitution would be open to such a construction of its terms as might be found in any history of a colony, a state, or their laws, however contradictory the mass might be in the aggregate. If we overlook the language of acts and instruments which express the sense in which it is understood by all the states, and seek for the true exposition of the constitution in those which speak only for one state, we have the highest assurance in the course and range of the argument in this case, that certainty cannot be found in the almost infinite variety of laws which had been passed by the states in relation to the emission of paper money. Nor is there more certainty in referring to the opinions of statesmen and jurists, in debates in conventions, or legislative bodies, to political writers, or commentators on the constitution, among all of whom there is a most irreconcilable contradiction and discrepancy of views, on every debateable word and clause in the constitution, the result of which has been strongly exemplified in the argument of the cases at this term, depending on its true interpretation. Whether the remark made in the senate of the United States, by a profound and eminent jurist, in a debate on a most solemn constitutional question, is particularly applicable to the mass of what has been offered to the Court as authority in this case, or not, yet its general practical truth must be admitted.

"If we were to receive the constitution as a text, and then to lay down in its margin the contradictory commentaries which have been made, and which may be made, the whole page would be a polyglot, indeed. It would speak in as many tongues as the builders of Babel, and in dialects as much confused, and mutually as unintelligible."

Fully convinced that the constitution is best expounded by itself, with a reference only to those sources from which its words and terms have been adopted, I have always found certainty, and felt safety in adhering to it as the text of standard authority to guide my reasoning to a correct judgment. In expounding it by opinion, or on the authority of names, there is, in my opinion, great danger of error; for, when it is found that from the time of its proposition to the people, to the present, the wisest, and best men in the nation, have been, and yet are, placed foot to foot on all doubtful, and many plain propositions in relation to its construction, it is as difficult as it would be invidious, to select as a consulting oracle, any man, or class of statesmen or jurists, in preference to another.

On the question involved in this case, of what are bills of credit, my judgment is conclusively formed on the authority herein referred to; if it is not conclusive, I have neither found, or have been directed to that which is paramount, or, in my judgment, at all coordinate, or to be compared with it. Resting on this authority, it was my deliberate opinion, that the certificates issued by a law of Missouri, pledging the faith of the state for their redemption, were bills of credit, prohibited by the constitution. On the same authority, and as the result of subsequent researches, it is now my most settled conviction, that the notes of the Commonwealth Bank of Kentucky, are not bills of credit emitted by the state of Kentucky, inasmuch as the state has pledged neither its faith, or credit, for their payment. And the notes not being payable at a future day, or issued on any credit as to time, either on their face, or by the law under which they were issued, but directed to be paid on demand, in gold or silver, they were not emitted to obtain a loan to the state, or to meet its expenditures, and cannot be deemed its bills of credit. On a careful consideration of the mischiefs against the recurrence of which the constitution interposed this prohibition, of its language, the bearing of the three phrases on each other, their evident spirit, and the meaning deducible therefrom, I cannot abandon my first impression, that one requisite of a bill of credit is, that it be made a tender in *payment* of debts.

The crying evils which arose from the issue of paper money by the states, cannot be so well described as they are in the language of the constitution. The emission of bills of credit by the states, making them a tender in payment of debts, impaired and violated the obligation of contracts. The remedy is an appropriate one, reaching both the cause and effect, by three distinct prohibitions; no state shall emit bills of credit, make any thing a tender but gold and silver, or pass any law impairing the obligation of contracts. Thus the remedy covers the whole mischief, and goes beyond it if applied literally to its full extent; the mere emission of bills of credit was no evil; if no law coerced their circulation or reception by individuals, they are as harmless as certificates of stock, emitted on a voluntary loan to the state, which are admitted not to be the prohibited bills of credit. So long as they were not made a tender, they could produce no evils not common to all paper, whether of a state, a corporation, or individual, which by common consent, passes from hand to hand in the ordinary transactions of life. To prevent the circulation of such a medium, it was not necessary to call into action the high power of the constitution; the evil would cure itself; when the paper ceased to pass by consent, it would pay no debt, nor lead to the violation of any contract. The prohibition could not have been intended to prevent the people from taking as money, what would answer all the purposes of money in the interchanges of society, or to deprive them of the exercise of their free will; on the contrary, it was made to prevent the coercion of their free will by a tender law, and leave them free to enforce the obligation of their contracts for the payment of money, and the enjoyment of their property.

In the construction of all laws, we look to the old law, the mischief and the remedy, and so expound it as to suppress the mischief, and advance the remedy; no just rule of interpretation requires a court to go further, by applying the remedy to a case not within the mischief, unless the words of the law are too imperative to admit of construction. I know no class of cases to which the rule is more appropriate, than those embraced within those prohibitions of the constitution on the exercise of powers reserved by the states, over subjects on which congress have no delegated power; there can be no collision between the laws of a state and the laws of the Union, as there would be where a state would legislate on those subjects that had been confided to congress or any department of the federal government. Taking the first class of cases in the tenth section, relating to treaties, letters of marque and reprisal, and coining money, which are subjects over which the constitution grants express powers as an example, it is evident, that to make the prohibition effectual to the object in granting the powers, it must be total, so as to exclude the exercise of any power by a state over the subject matter. From the nature of these subjects, there can be no concurrent power in the two governments; hence we find that the two first were, even by the article 6, of confederation, expressly prohibited to the states, without the consent of the United States. The same reasons apply to the third, because the express power in congress to *coin money, regulate the value thereof,* and of *foreign coin,* coupled with the prohibition to a state to coin money, is a decisive expression of the intention, that it shall not exercise the power, as in the case of a treaty, or a letter of marque and reprisal. The evils to be guarded against had not existed under the confederation; the states separately had not made treaties, granted letters of marque or reprisal, or coined money, in violation of those articles; the evils were wholly prospective, but were to be apprehended if any doubt whatever could be raised on the terms of grant of those powers. Hence the prohibition.

Touching the third class of cases, bills of attainder, ex post facto laws, and titles of nobility, they were not subjects of any delegated powers to congress; but as they were opposed to the whole spirit of the people, and the constitution, it annulled all power, state and federal, to do these things; and the prohibition is, in its nature and object, absolute and illimitable.

But the second class of prohibited cases, emitting bills of credit, tender laws, and those impairing the obligation of contracts, are widely different; the evils had existed, did exist, and must recur, if not prevented.

Congress could not legislate on these subjects, much less control the states, on whom the powers of parliament, in all their transcendency, as well as the prerogative of the crown, devolved by the revolution; 6 Wh. 651; 8 Wh. 584. Each state had the power of emitting bills of credit, of passing tender laws, 4 Pet. 435, and exercised both, by annulling contracts and grants, the right to do which could not be contested by any authority; 4 Wh. 643, 651. These were the acts which called aloud for the remedy given by the prohibitions, to prevent their recurrence, which would have been certain if it had not been made.

This Court has declared the intention of the constitution on the subject of contracts. " It was intended to correct the mischiefs of state laws, which had weakened the confidence between man and man, and embarrassed all transactions between individuals, by dispensing with a faithful performance of engagements; to guard against a power which had been extensively abused, and to restrain the legislature in future from violating the rights of property. It protected contracts respecting property, under which some person could claim a right to something beneficial to himself; and since the clause must, in construction, receive some limitation, it ought to be confined to the mischiefs it was intended to remedy. Not to authorize a vexatious interference with the internal concerns or civil institutions of a state; to embarrass its legislation in the regulation of internal government, or to render immutable those institutions for these purposes, which ought to vary with varying circumstances. The term contract must be understood in a more limited sense, so as not to embrace other contracts than those which respect property, or some object of value, and confer rights which may be asserted in a court of justice;" 4 Wh. 428, 429; Dart. College case. " The principle was the inviolability of contracts. The plain declaration that no state shall pass any law impairing the obligation of contracts, includes all laws which infringe the principle the convention intended to hold sacred, and no further. It does not extend to the remedy to enforce the obligation of a contract; the distinction between them exists in the nature of things, so that without impairing the obligation, the remedy may be modified as the state may direct;" 4 Wh. 200; Sturgess v. Crowninshield. It is also a principle declared by this Court, that the prohibition does not extend to the passage of a state law, which does not affect contracts existing when the law was enacted, and which operates only on the obligation of posterior contracts; 12 Wh. 369; Ogden v. Saunders; and no exposition of the constitution is better settled, or commands more universal assent, than that the prohibition does not extend to the passage of retrospective, unjust, oppressive laws, or those which divest rights, antecedently vested, if they do not directly impair the obligation of a contract; 2 Pet. 411, 13; 3 Pet. 289; 8 Pet. 110; and that " The interest, wisdom, and justice of the representative body, and its relations with its constituents, furnish the only security where there is no express contract, against unjust and exclusive taxation, as well as against unwise legislation generally;" 4 Pet. 563.

Let these principles of constitutional law be applied to the con-

17

[Briscoe et al. v. The Commonwealth Bank of Kentucky.]

struction of the clause against emitting bills of credit, as they have been applied to the clause concerning the obligation of contracts, the conclusion seems to me inevitable. That the same construction, which imposes a limitation to the corrective remedy against the future violation of the sanctity of contracts, which it was the great object of the prohibition to protect, should be extended with at least as much liberality, to limit the operation of that clause of the same article, which prohibits an evil which by no possibility could impair the obligation of a contract, without a tender law. The mischiefs of a mere emission of bills of credit, are trivial in their consequences, compared with the effect of tender laws; their combined effect is to violate a contract: surely then the restriction on a state, ought not to be construed more rigidly against an act, which cannot of itself produce the mischief intended to be remedied, than a law which wholly annuls a contract. If each clause is taken according to an universal rule, that laws should be construed *subjectam materiam,* the lesser evil requires the more gentle corrective; but in assigning to the emission of bills of credit, without their being made a tender, a more restrictive meaning than to the direct violation of a contract, we act on the inverse rule. The protection is lessened in the same proportion as the danger is increased; the greater the mischief the milder and less inefficient is the remedy: reason and established principles alike require, that a prohibition should be limited, as far as can be done, without producing the mischief intended to be remedied, and expanded so far as is necessary to correct it. The construction must be according to the subject matter of the law, strict or liberal as the nature of the case requires, and the object to be effected will be defeated or accomplished, *ut res magis valeat quam pereat;* that which will effectuate all the objects of the prohibition cannot be too narrow, that which goes beyond the express word, or necessary implication, to effect an object not within the mischief, must be too broad.

On the same rule which confines the prohibition as to contracts, to state laws passed affecting existing contracts, and excluding from the protection of the constitution, all posterior contracts; a law making bank notes a legal tender in payment of debts contracted after the passage of the law, would not be within the prohibition. On the same principle by which an unjust, oppressive, retrospective law, or one which divests vested rights, is held not to impair the obligation of a contract per se, it must be held that a mere emission of bills of credit is not within the mischiefs intended to be corrected. There is no more danger in the exercise of this power, at the discretion of the legislature, than in these unrestrained powers, to modify the *remedy* to enforce the *obligation* of a contract, which this Court hold not to be affected by the prohibition. There is in the nature of things, the same distinction between bills emitted which are not made a tender, and those which are a tender, as between the remedy and the obligation of a contract; nay the distinction is more marked.

[Briscoe et al. v. The Commonwealth Bank of Kentucky.]

The obligation of a contract, without an effective remedy to enforce it, would be " a name," and not "a thing;" the word obligation would be an " empty sound," and the protection of the constitution a solemn mockery. Yet if it is held to prohibit the emission only, of bills of credit which were not a tender, it would prevent none but imaginary evils, and leave real practical ones unredressed. To emit the notes of an individual or a private corporation, for the purposes of circulation, would be productive of the same evils as the bills of credit of a state; the mischief does not depend on who is the owner of the stock pledged for its payment, or on whose credit they are received in circulation. Yet it is conceded by counsel and agreed by all the judges, that bank notes are not within the prohibition, though they are as much " paper money," " paper medium," as the bills of credit of a state. Why then should the prohibition extend to the mere emission of the latter, and not to the former species of paper money, when neither are a tender in payment of debts? What good reason can be assigned, why the constitution did not prohibit the emission of both, if it prohibits one, and on what ground does the discrimination rest? It cannot be that there is less danger, in having the paper medium of the country based on the funds, faith, and credit of the state, which can by taxation, levy a contribution *ad libitum*, on all the property of all its citizens, for its redemption, 4 Wh. 428; 4 Pet. 563, than when a bank emits it on the mere credit of their corporate stock. Nor that a state will more readily sport with and abuse its plighted faith, than a corporation, an individual, or a banking association.

These questions are not unworthy the consideration of those who hold that it is not necessary to bring bills of credit within the prohibition, that they be made a tender in payment of debts. That all " paper intended to circulate through the community for its ordinary purposes as money, which paper is redeemable at a future day, the emission of any paper medium by a state government, for the purpose of common circulation," though not made a tender, and though the faith, funds, or credit of the state are not pledged for its redemption, are bills of credit. They are also worthy of notice by those who hold that paper emitted by the officers of a state, under the authority of a law, which paper is of the precise character above defined, which is made a tender, and for the redemption of which the funds and faith of the state are both most solemnly pledged in the law directing its emission, are not bills of credit within the prohibition. It will not suffice, that a disclaimer is made of its extension to bank notes, or a declaration that they are not included within the mischiefs, without assigning the reasons, or referring to the authority on which the discrimination is made on just principles of construction. For myself, I rest on the most solemn adjudications of this Court, as well prior as subsequent to the case of Craig v. Missouri, settling the rules and principles on which the most important prohibition in the tenth article has been construed; and in applying them to the

clause now in question, find abundant authority for holding it necessary, that bills of credit be made a tender in payment of debts, to
come within the prohibition. Taking my definition of bills of credit of a government, from acts of parliament, of the old and new
congress, the articles of confederation, and the constitution, I held
in Craig v. Missouri, that certificates emitted by a state, for circulation, payable in future on the faith and funds of the state, which certificates were made a tender, were prohibited as bills of credit. On
the same authority I now hold, that the notes in question are not
such bills of credit, because not emitted by the state, not made a tender in *payment* of any debts to individuals, nor the faith or general
funds of the state pledged for their redemption. And further; On
the authority of acts of parliament, of the old congress, of state legislatures before the adoption of the constitution, and acts of congress since, and of the common law, I make the distinction between
the *bills of credit*, issued under the seal of a bank, and *bank notes*
payable to bearer on demand, and hold that the latter can by no just
definition, or legal construction, come within the prohibition. I have
resorted to these sources of information, as the fountain of constitutional law and have found in them abundant cause of justification of
the opinions which I formed in the former case, and adhere to in this.

The plaintiffs have relied much upon the pleadings in this record,
as presenting the question in controversy in an aspect different
from what it would have been, if the averments of the plea had been
denied by a replication, instead of being admitted by a demurrer.

These averments are in the first plea. 1. That the state, by the
law establishing the bank, declared that the capital stock thereof
should be 2,000,000 dollars. 2. "But which capital stock the said
bank never received, or any part thereof, as these defendants aver."
From the admission of these averments, it is contended, that inasmuch as the capital stock was not made up and paid into the bank
by the state, pursuant to the declaration contained in the law, the
faith and credit of the state was legally, virtually, and morally
pledged to provide this amount of capital, as a fund for the redemption of the notes issued by the bank. And that having violated this
pledge, the state was bound, and, if suable, was compellable to pay
them; whereby the notes of the bank became bills of credit of the
state, as effectually as if they had been emitted on an express pledge
of its faith or credit for their redemption.

The first averment is founded on the law of incorporation, and is
an averment of mere matter of law as to which it is among the oldest and best settled rules of pleading, that the law will not suffer an
averment of that to be law, which is not law; such averment or
pleading is to no effect or purpose, though admitted by demurrer;
Pl. 168, a, 170, b. On an inspection of the law, it appears that this
averment refers only to the section which declares what the amount
of the capital shall be; but the plea wholly omits any reference to
the section which specifies the items which shall compose that capi-

[Briscoe et al. v. The Commonwealth Bank of Kentucky.]

tal as a fund for the redemption of the notes. It is the proceeds of the lands belonging to the state, its surplus revenue, the stock of the state in the bank of Kentucky, and the securities taken by the bank, on a loan of its notes to individuals. The mode of redemption was in making these notes receivable in payment for lands, taxes, debts due the state, the Bank of Kentucky, and the Bank of the Commonwealth. This was the only pledge given by the state, and it is not averred in the pleas that this pledge was in any way violated, by any refusal to receive the notes for any such purposes; on the contrary, it is admitted that they were always so received; consequently, the state has faithfully kept its faith, as entire as it was pledged by the law. This part of the plea, therefore, is *to no purpose or effect*, so far as it avers that to be law which is not law.

The notes of the bank constituted no part of its capital; while they remained on hand, they were worthless to the bank; when loaned out, they became the evidence of a specie debt, due by the bank on demand, to the holder; the securities taken for repayment, were part of the capital for their redemption. But as they were taken only for the precise amount of the notes loaned, the amount of debt due by and to the bank was equal, with only this difference, that the bank paid no interest on their notes, while they received interest on their loans; the accretion of interest, therefore, was the only means of increasing the capital, by the issue of their notes. If they were burnt, according to the direction of the law, after they had performed their function, in their reception as payment by the state, or the bank, it was no loss to the bank which issued them; or if the notes were returned to the bank by the state treasurer, or the bank of Kentucky, they were as useless, as capital, as before they were first issued. In reissuing them, their operation was the same, adding nothing to the capital; indeed, the proposition is self-evident, that a bank note is not a fund for its own payment; a debt due by a bank, is not a part of the capital stock, pledged for the payment of the debt.

It thus appears, that by the terms and necessary operation of the law, though the term capital stock is used in the law, the thing which was made the capital was the proceeds of lands, taxes, debt, and bank stock; and as the law and constitution regard *things*, and not *names*, such must be taken to be the spirit, substance, and effect of the law of incorporation. Hence, the second averment is of a fact wholly immaterial, since it was no part of the law that the capital should ever be received by the bank in any other manner than the one pointed out, which was in fact the only manner in which it could be received; that is, as a fund for the redemption of its notes. In virtue of this law, purchasers of land, and debtors of the state, or banks, had the option of making payment in specie, the notes of other banks, or of the Commonwealth Bank; they would, of course, pay in that medium which was the easiest, and cheapest to be obtained, which must have been the notes of the Bank of the Commonwealth, or they would never have been issued. So that the inevitable effect of the law, and the emission of these notes on loan, was to make their receipt in payment, the means of their redemption, in addition to the securities on which the loan was made, and precluded any reasonable probability, or even possibility, that the proceeds of the pledged funds would be paid into the coffers of the bank, in specie, or the notes of other banks, unless the notes of the Commonwealth Bank were more valuable, or more difficult to be obtained than either.

That such a consummation was in the contemplation of the legislature, or can be assumed by the Court, in order to give effect to the plea, is a proposition too extravagant to have been made by counsel; if this assumption is not made, that the state was bound by the law to make up the capital stock of the bank by the actual receipt of the pledged funds, then there can be no pretence of its reception being a material averment. Had this second averment been put in issue, and found for the defendant, the Court must have rendered a judgment for the plaintiff *non obstante veredicto* if he was otherwise entitled to judgment, on the ground that the issue was on an immaterial fact; 1 Pet. 71.

---

### The Proprietors of Charles River Bridge v. The Proprietors of the Warren Bridge.

In this case I entirely concur in the judgment of the Court, as well as the reasons given in the opinion delivered by the Chief Justice; my only reason for giving a separate opinion is, to notice some matters not referred to in that opinion, which I am not willing should pass without expressing mine upon them. The course of the argument, and the nature of several questions involved in the case, gives them an importance deserving attention from these and other considerations, which I cannot overlook.

The first question which arises in this cause, is on an objection to the jurisdiction of the court below, made by the appellees, on the ground of the want of proper parties; and that the state of Massachusetts, being now the owners of the bridge pursuant to the terms of the charter to the defendants, no suit could be sustained which can affect their interest in it. On an inspection of the record, the case is one which does not admit of this objection, if it was well founded otherwise. The bill was filed in June, and the pleadings closed in December, 1828, so that we have no judicial knowledge of any matters which have arisen since; confining itself, as the Court must do, to the pleadings in the cause, and the decree of the court below, we can notice nothing not averred in the bill or answer, nor act on any evidence which does not relate to them.

[Charles River Bridge v. Warren Bridge et al.]

An injunction is prayed for by the plaintiffs, to restrain the defendants from erecting a bridge over Charles river, pursuant to their charter in the act of 1828, which they allege to be a violation of their rights, by impairing the obligation of previous contracts made by the state with the plaintiffs. When the pleadings closed, the defendants had not completed the bridge complained of; they were then the only persons who had any present interest in it; they were constructing it for their own benefit, and were to have the sole and exclusive use of it, till by the terms of the charter it became the property of the state; they were therefore the proper, and the only parties against whom a bill for an injunction could then be sustained. If then the plaintiffs were in June, 1828, entitled to a decree restraining the erection of the bridge, their right cannot be affected by any matter *pendente lite*, or by any reversionary right, which may have accrued to the state. The case must be decided, as it ought to have been decided in December, 1828, and the only question before the court below on the pleadings and exhibits, was on the right of the plaintiffs to the only remedy prayed, which was an injunction; that court had jurisdiction between the parties to the suit, to decide the question of right between them, but could go no further than to grant the injunction against the erection of the bridge, because the bill avers no matter arising subsequent to December, 1828.

Whether on an amended, a supplemental, or an original bill, a decree can be rendered for an account of tolls received, and for the suppression of the bridge, is a question which can arise only after a reversal of the decree now appealed from, and such a state of pleading as will bring subsequent matters before the court below.

It has also been objected that the plaintiffs have a perfect remedy at law, if their case is such as is set forth in the bill, and therefore cannot sustain a suit in equity. If this case came up by appeal from a circuit court, the question might deserve serious consideration; but as the courts in Massachusetts derive their equity jurisdiction from a state law, it becomes a very different question. The supreme court of that state is the rightful expositor of its laws; 2 Pet. 524, 5; and having sustained and exercised their jurisdiction over this case, as one appropriate to their statutory jurisdiction in equity, it will be considered as their construction of a state law, to which this Court always pays great, and generally conclusive respect. Our jurisdiction over causes from state courts, by the twenty-fifth section of the judiciary act, is peculiar; no error can be assigned by a plaintiff in error, except those which that act has specified, and the Court can reverse for no other. It may be a very different question, whether the defendant in error may not claim an affirmance, on any ground which would entitle him to a decree below, which it is unnecessary to consider, as these objections to the jurisdiction cannot be sustained.

The next question is one vital to the plaintiffs' case if decided against them, which is, whether a charter to a corporation, is a contract within the tenth section of the first article of the constitution, which prohibits a state from passing any law impairing the obligation of a contract; or whether this prohibition applies only to contracts between individuals, or a state and individuals. As this question is not only an all-important one, arising directly and necessarily in the case, but in one view of it, is the whole case which gives the plaintiffs a standing in this Court, it will be next considered.

In this country every person has a natural and inherent right of taking and enjoying property, which right is recognised and secured in the constitution of every state; bodies, societies, and communities have the same right, but inasmuch as on the death of any person without a will, his property passes to his personal representative or heir, a mere association of individuals, must hold their real and personal property subject to the rules of the common law. A charter is not necessary to give to a body of men the capacity to take and enjoy, unless there is some statute to prevent it, by imposing a restriction or prescribing a forfeiture, where there is a capacity to take and hold; the only thing wanting is the franchise of succession, so that the property of the society may pass to successors instead of heirs; Terms of the Law, 123; 1 Bl. Com. 368, 72. This and other franchises, are the ligaments which unite a body of men into one, and knits them together as a natural person; 4 Co. 65, a; creating a corporation, an invisible incorporeal being, a metaphysical person; 2 Pet. 323; existing only in contemplation of law, but having the properties of individuality; 4 Wh. 636; by which a perpetual succession of many persons are considered the same, and may act as a single individual. It is the object and effect of the incorporation to give to the artificial person the same capacity and rights as a natural person can have, and when incorporated either by an express charter, or one is presumed from prescription, they can take and enjoy property to the extent of their franchises as fully as an individual; Co. Lit. 132, b; 2 D. C. D. 300; 1 Saund. 345. It bestows the character and properties of individuality on a collective and changing body of men; 4 Pet. 562; by which their rights become as sacred as if they were held in severalty by natural person. Franchises are not peculiar to corporations, they are granted to individuals, and may be held by any persons capable of holding or enjoying property; a franchise is property, a right to the privilege or immunity conferred by the grant; it may be of a corporeal or incorporeal right, but it is the right of property, or propriety, in the thing to which it attaches. Franchises are of various grades, from that of a mere right of succession to an estate in land, to the grant of a county Palatine, which is the highest franchise known to the law, (as has been shown in the preliminary view; vide ante, 49, 50;) the nature and character whereof is the same, whether the grant is to one or many. Corporations are also of all grades, and made for varied objects; all governments are corporations, created by usage and common con-

sent, or grants and charters, which create a body politic for prescribed purposes; but whether they are private, local, or general in
their objects, for the enjoyment of property, or the exercise of power,
they are all governed by the same rules of law, as to the construction, and the obligation of the instrument by which the incorporation is made. One universal rule of law protects persons and property. It is a fundamental principle of the common law of England,
that the term freemen of the kingdom, includes "all persons," ecclesiastical and temporal, incorporate, politique, or natural; it is a part
of their magna charta; 2 Co. Inst. 4; and is incorporated into our institutions. The persons of the members of corporations are on the
same footing of protection as other persons, and their corporate property secured by the same laws which protect that of individuals;
2 Co. Inst. 46, 7. "No man shall be taken," "no man shall be dis-
seised," without due process of law, is a principle taken from
magna charta, infused into all our state constitutions, and is made
inviolable by the federal government, by the amendments to the
constitution.

No new principle was adopted, in prohibiting the passage of a law
by a state, which should impair the obligation of a contract; it was
merely affirming a fundamental principle of law, and by putting contracts under the protection of the constitution, securing the rights
and property of the citizens from invasion by any power whatever.
It was a part of that system of civil liberty which "formed the basis
whereon our republics, their laws and constitutions are erected, and
declared by the ordinance of 1787 to be a fundamental law of all new
states." This was the language of the congress, "And in the just
preservation of rights and property, it is understood and declared,
that no law ought ever to be made, or have force in the said territory,
that shall in any manner interfere with, or affect private contracts, or
any agreements, bona fide and without fraud, previously formed;" 1
Laws U. S. 478, 79. This ordinance was passed during the session
of the convention which framed the constitution, several of the
members of which were also members of congress; it was, therefore,
evidently in their view, and may justly be taken as a declaration of
the reasons for inserting this prohibitory clause. As an important
cotemporaneous historical fact, it also shows that the convention intended to make the prohibition more definite, less extensive in one
respect, and more so in another, than in the ordinance. Omitting
the words "in any manner interfere with or affect," the words "impair the obligation of," were substituted; the word private was
omitted, so as to extend the prohibition to all "contracts," public or
private: as "the constitution unavoidably deals in general terms;"
1 Wh. 326; marks only great outlines, and designates its general objects; 4 Wh. 407; no detail was made, no definition of a contract
given, or exception made.

No one can doubt that the terms of the prohibition are not only
broad enough to comprehend all contracts, but that violence will be

[Charles River Bridge v. Warren Bridge et al.]

done to the plain meaning of the language, by making any exception by construction; it must, therefore, necessarily embrace those contracts, which grant a franchise or property to individuals or corporations, imposing the same restraints on states, as were imposed by the English constitution on the prerogative of the king, which devolved on the states by the revolution; vide 4 Wh. 651; 8 Wh. 584, 8. "The king has the prerogative of appointing ports and havens;" the "franchise of lading and discharging has been frequently granted by the crown," from an early period. "But though the king had a power of granting the franchise of ports and havens, yet he had not the power of resumption, or of narrowing or contracting their limits, when once established;" 1 Bl. Com. 264. It would be strange if the free citizens of a republic did not hold their rights by a tenure as sacred as the subjects of a monarchy; or that it should be deemed compatible with American institutions, to exclude from the protection of the constitution, those privileges and immunities which are held sacred by the laws of our ancestors. We have adopted them as our right of inheritance, with the exception of such as are not suited to our condition, or have been altered by usage, or acts of assembly. No one, I think, will venture the assertion, that it is incompatible with our situation, to protect the corporate rights of our citizens, or that in any state, there is either an usage or law which makes them less sacred than those held by persons who are not members of a corporation. No one can, in looking throughout the land, fail to see that an incalculable amount of money has been expended, and property purchased on the faith of charters and grants, or contemplate their violation by a law, which will not, some day, take his possessions from him, by an exercise of power, founded on a principle which applies to all rights. If a state can revoke its grant of property or power to a subordinate corporation, there can be no limitation; there is no principle of law, or provision of the constitution, that can save the charter of a borough, a city, a church, or a college, that will not equally save any other; of consequence, if all cannot be protected, none can be.

The federal government itself is but a corporation, created by the grant or charter of the separate states; if that is inviolable by the power of a state, each of its provisions is so; each state, in its most sovereign capacity, by the people thereof, in a convention, have made it a supreme law of the state, paramount to any state constitution then in existence, or which may be thereafter adopted. The state has made an irrevocable restriction on its own once plenary sovereignty, which it cannot loosen without the concurrence of such a number of states, as are competent to amend the constitution. So far as such restriction extends, the state has annulled its own power, by a surrender thereof for the public good; if a state can remove that restriction on its own legislative power, and do the thing prohibited, it can also remove the restriction on its sovereignty, by revoking the powers granted to congress. The property and power of the federal government, are held by no other or stronger tenure, than the land or franchises of a citizen or corporation; both rights were inherent in the people of a state, who have made grants by their representatives, in a convention directly by their original power, or in a legislative act, made by the authority delegated in their state constitution. But the grants thus made are as binding on the people and the state, as if made in a convention; they are the contracts of the state, the obligation of which the people have declared, shall not be impaired by the authority of a state; it shall not "pass any law," which shall have such object in view, or produce such effect. An act of a convention is the supreme law of the state; an act of the legislature is a law subordinate; both, however, are laws of the state of binding authority, unless repugnant to that law which the state has, by its own voluntary act, in the plenitude of its sovereignty, made paramount to both, and declared that its judges, " shall be bound thereby," any thing to the contrary notwithstanding. Each state has made the obligation of contracts a part of the constitution, thus saving and confirming them under the sanction of its own authority; no act, therefore, can violate the sanctity of contracts, which cannot annul the whole constitution, for it is a fundamental principle of law, that whatever is saved and preserved by a statute, has the same obligation as the act itself. This principle has been taken from the magna charta of England, and carried into the great charter of our rights of property.

By magna charta, ch. 9, and 7 Rich. II. it is enacted, " that the citizens of London shall enjoy all their liberties, notwithstanding any statute to the contrary. By this act, the city may claim liberties by prescription, charter, or parliament, notwithstanding any statute made before; 4 Co. Inst. 250, 53; 2 Co. Inst. 20, 1; 5 D. C. D. 20, London, M. T. P. Harg. Law, T. 66, 67.

The constitution goes further, by saving, preserving and confirming the obligation of contracts; and notwithstanding any law passed after its adoption; and this confirmation being by the supreme law of the land, makes a contract as inviolable, even by a supreme law of a state, as the constitution itself.

From the beginning of the revolution, the people of the colonies clung to magna charta, and their charters from the crown; their violation was a continued subject of complaint. Vide 1 Jour. Cong. 27, 8; 40, 1; 60, 108, 143, 154, 167, 178; one of the grievances set forth in the declaration of independence is, " For taking away our charters," &c.

One of the causes which led to the English revolution was, " They have also invaded the privileges, and seized on *the charters* of most of *those towns* that have a right to be represented by their burgesses in parliament; and have secured surrenders to be made of them, by which the magistrates in them have delivered up all their rights and privileges, to be disposed of at the pleasure of those evil counsellors," &c. 10 Journ. Commons, 2, b. In the language of congress,

# 140

" The legislative, executive, and judging powers, are all moved by the nod of a minister. *Privileges and immunities* last no longer than his smiles. When he frowns their feeble forms dissolve;" 1 Journ. 59, 60. " Without incurring or being charged with a forfeiture of their rights, without being heard, without being tried, without law, without justice, by an act of parliament, *their charter* is destroyed, their liberties violated, their constitution and form of government changed; and all this upon no better pretence, than because in one of their towns, a trespass was committed on some merchandise said to belong to one of the companies, and because the ministry were of opinion, that such high political regulations, were necessary to compel due subordination, and obedience to their mandates;" 1 Journ. 41.

Such were the principles of our ancestors in both revolutions; they are consecrated in the constitution framed by the fathers of our government, in terms intended to protect the rights and property of the people, by prohibiting to every state the passage of any law which would be obnoxious to such imputations on the character of American legislation. The reason for this provision was, that the transcendent power of parliament devolved on the several states by the revolution; 4 Wh. 651; so that there was no power, by which a state could be prevented from revoking all public grants of property or franchise, as parliament could do; Harg. L. T. 60, 61; 4 Wh. 643, 51. The people of the states renounced this power; and as an assurance that that they would not exercise it; or if they should do so inadvertently, that any law to that effect should be void; the constitution embraces all grants, charters and other contracts affecting property, places them beyond all legislative control, and imposes on this Court the duty of protecting them from legislative violation; 6 Cr. 136; 4 Wh. 625. In the same sovereign capacity, in which the people of each state adopted the constitution, they pledged their faith that the sanctity of the obligation of contracts should be inviolable; and to insure its performance, created a competent judicial power, whom they made the final arbiter between their laws and the constitution, in all cases in which there was an alleged collision between them. These principles have been too often, and too solemnly affirmed by this Court, to make any detail of their reasoning or opinions necessary.

In Fletcher v. Peck, they were applied to a grant of land by a state to individuals, made by the authority of a state law, which was afterwards repealed; 6 Cr. 127; in New Jersey v. Wilson, to an immunity from taxation granted to a tribe of Indians; 7 Cr. 164; in Terrett v. Taylor to a religious society; 9 Cr. 43, &c.; in Dartmouth College v. Woodward to a literary corporation; 4 Wh. 636. In all these cases state laws which violated the grants and charters which conferred private or corporate rights, were held void under the prohibition in the constitution; the Court holding that as it contained no exception in terms, none could be made by construction, the language being clear of all ambiguity, it extended to corporations as well as individuals; 8 Wh. 480 to 490, passim.

But while the Court repudiates all *constructive exceptions* to the prohibition, it equally repudiates its application to *constructive contracts;* it will preserve the immunity from taxation, when it is granted in terms as in 7 Cr. 164; yet they will not raise an immunity by implication, " where there is no express contract;" 4 Pet. 563.

There can be no difficulty in understanding this clause of the constitution, its language is plain and the terms well defined by the rules of law, the difficulty arises by the attempts made to interpolate exceptions on one hand, so as to withdraw contracts from its operation; and on the other hand, to imply one contract from another, to make each implied contract the parent of another, and then endeavour to infuse them all into the constitution, as the contract contained in the grant or charter in question. If human ingenuity can be thus exerted for either purpose with success, no one can understand the constitution as it is; we must wait till it has been made by such construction, what such expounders may think it ought to have been, before we can assign to its provisions any determinate meaning. In the rejection of both constructions, and following the decisions of this Court, my judgment is conclusively formed; that the grants of property of franchise, privilege, or immunity, to a natural or artificial person, are alike confirmed by the constitution; and that the plantiffs are entitled to the relief prayed in their bill, if they have otherwise made out a proper case.

In tracing their right to its origin, they found it on a grant to Harvard college, by the general court, or colonial council, in 1640, of the ferry between Boston and Charlestown, which had belonged to the colony from its first settlement. In 1637, the governor and treasurer were authorized to lease this ferry for three years, at forty pounds a year, under which authority they made such a lease, and gave an exclusive right of ferry between the two towns, though they were not authorized to do more than lease the ferry. The lease expired in 1640, when the ferry reverted to the colony, and was granted to the college by no other description than " the ferry between Boston and Charlestown," which the plaintiffs contend was a grant in perpetuity of the exclusive right of ferriage between the two towns, and from any points on Charles river, at the one or other.

All the judges in the court below, as well as the counsel on both sides agree, that the common law as to ferries was adopted and prevails in Massachusetts; this part of the case then must depend on what were the rules and principles of that law, in their application to such a grant at the time it was made.

It is an admitted principle, that the king by his prerogative was vested with the right of soil and jurisdiction over the territory within which he constituted by his charter the colonial government; their grants had the same validity as his, and must be construed by the same rules which regulate prerogative grants. Vide 1 Pick. 182, &c.

As the king, by his charter put the colonial government in his place, they held the right in and over the arms of the sea, the navigable rivers, and the land in the colony, for the benefit of the people of the colony, as a public trust, not as a private estate; the people of the colony had the right of fishing, navigating and passing freely in and over the public waters, subject to such grants of franchise or property as may have been made, or which should be made in future. But as any grant of a private right in or over public property, is necessarily an abridgment of the public right to the extent of such grants, the law looks on them with great watchfulness, and has prescribed rules for their construction, founded on a proper regard to the general interest.

The prerogative of the king is vested in him as necessary for the purposes of society; it extends to all things not injurious to his subjects, but "stretcheth not to the doing of any wrong;" 1 Bl. Com. 237, 9; the objects for which it is held and exercised, are for the good of the subject, and the benefit of the commonwealth, and not his private emolument. It is a part of the common law; 2 Co. Inst. 63, 496; confined to what the law allows, and is for the public good; Hob. 261; and the increase of the public treasure; Hard. 27; 2 Vent. 268. The king is the universal occupant of the public domain, which he may grant at pleasure; 11 Co. 86, b; 9 Pet. 748; Cowp. 210; but his grants are voidable, if they are against the good of the people, their usual and settled liberties, or tend to their grievance; 2 Bac. Ab. 149; Sho. P. C. 75; holding it for the common benefit as a trust, his prerogative is the guardianship of public property, for the general interest of his subjects.

This is the reason why the king has a prerogative in the construction of his grants, by which they are taken most strongly in his favour and against the grantee, because they take from the public whatever is given to an individual; whereas the grants of private persons are taken by a contrary rule, because the public right is not affected by them. From a very early period, it was the policy of the law of England to protect the public domain from the improvident, or illegal exercise of the royal prerogative in making grants, and to secure to pious and charitable institutions, the benefit of donations made directly to them or for their use, by rules of construction appropriate to each kind of grants, which were a part of the common law. These rules were affirmed by statutes in order to give them a more imposing obligation; these statutes were passed in 1323, 24. By the 17 Ed. II. st. 1, ch. 15, it is enacted that "When our lord the king giveth or granteth land or a manor, with the appurtenances, without he make express mention in his deed or writing, of knights' fees, advowsons of churches and dowers when they fall belonging to such manor or land, them at this day the king reserveth to himself such fees, advowsons and dowers; albeit that among other persons it hath been observed otherwise;" 1 Ruff. 182, 3. By the 17 Ed. II. called the statute of templars, it was declared, that grants and donations for charitable purposes, should be held; " So always that the godly and worthy will of the foresaid givers be observed, performed and always religiously executed as aforesaid;" Keble. St. 86, 7. Subsequent statutes have prescribed the same rule, whereby it has ever since been a fundamental principle of the law of charities, that the will of the donor should be the standard of construction in relation to all such gifts or grants; 8 Co. 131, b; 10 Co. 34, b; 3 Co. 3, b; 7 Co. 13, a; putting them on the footing of a will, in which the intention of the testator prevails over the legal interpretation of the words.

Both classes of cases are exceptions to the general rules of construing private grants. They rest, however, on the strongest grounds of reason, justice, and sound policy, applicable alike to England and this country. In cases of charities the rule has been most liberally applied by this Court, as it has in England in the construction of statutes and grants, in favour of donations to them; 4 Wh. 31, &c. 9 Cr. 43, 331; 3 Pet. 140, 480; 9 Wh. 455, 64; 2 Pet. 580, 85; so of dedications of property to public use, or the use of a town; 12 Wh. 582; 6 Pet. 436, 7; 10 Pet. 712, 13; the rules of which are essentially different from those which relate to grants from one person to another, or laws for private benefit. In cases of grants by the king in virtue of his prerogative, the rule prescribed by the statute of prerogative has ever been a fundamental one in England, " that nothing of prerogative can pass without express and determinate words;" Hob. 243; Hard. 309, 10; Pl. 336, 7. In 1830, it was laid down in the house of lords as clear and settled law, that the king's grants shall be taken most strongly against the grantee, though the rule was otherwise as to private grants; 5 Bligh. P. C. 315, 16; this rule was never questioned in England, and has been adopted in all the states as a part of their common law.

This rule is a part of the prerogative of the crown, which devolved on the several states by the revolution; 4 Wh. 651; and which the states exercise to the same extent as the king did, as the guardians of the public for the benefit of the people at large. It is difficult to assign a good reason why public rights should not receive the same protection in a republic as in a monarchy, or why a grant by a colony or state, should be so construed as to impair the right of the people to their common property, to a greater extent in Massachusetts than a grant by the king would in England. But the grant of this ferry in 1640, was only a prerogative grant by colonial authority, which being derived solely from the charter of the king, and not by act of parliament, could rise no higher than its source in his prerogative, nor could it pass by delegated authority what would not pass in the same words by original grant from the king; consequently the grant must be construed as if he had made it. If, however, there could be a doubt on this subject, by the general principles of the common law as adopted in that colony, there were reasons peculiar to it, which would call for the most rigid rules of construing grants of any franchise, or right of any description, on the waters or shores of the rivers and arms of the sea within its boundaries.

In 1641, the general court adopted an ordinance which was a declaration of common liberties, providing that riparian owners of land on the sea or salt water, should hold the land to low water mark, if the tide did not ebb and flow more than one hundred rods; though this ordinance expired with the charter of the colony, there has been ever since, a corresponding usage, which is the common law of the state to this day; 4 Mass. 144, 5; 6 Mass. 438; 17 Mass. 148, 9; 1 Pick. 182, &c. The riparian owner of land in Charlestown " may, whenever he pleases, enclose, build, and obstruct to low water mark, and exclude all mankind;" 1 Mass. 232; it is therefore a necessary conclusion from the nature and extent of the riparian right, that grants of land on Charles river must be construed by the rules of prerogative grants. Any construction which would extend them beyond the limits described in the grant, must take from the adjoining riparian owner a right which is exclusively in him; it cannot then ever have been the law of Massachusetts, that the grant of the ferry in general terms, between two opposite points on the shore of Charles river, which is an arm of the sea and salt water, would give any right beyond the landings. Had the grant been definite of the landings, describing them by metes and bounds, with the right of ferriage over the river, its construction must be the same as a general grant, for it could in neither case be extended so as to give a right of landing on another man's soil.

Independent, however, of any considerations of this kind, the law of Massachusetts on the subject of the construction of grants, has been settled by the repeated decisions of its supreme court, and is thus laid down by Chief Justice Parsons in language which meets this case on all points. " Private statutes made for the accommodation of particular citizens or corporations, ought not to be construed to affect the rights or privileges of others, unless such construction results from express words, or necessary implication;" 4 Mass. 145. In case of a deed from A to B, the court gave it a strict and technical construction, excluding all the land not embraced by the words of the description; 6 Mass. 439, 40; S. P. 5 Mass. 356; " where a tract of land is bounded on a street or way, it does not extend across the street or way, to include other lands and flats below high water mark;" 17 Mass. 149. In grants by towns no land passes by implication " unless the intention of the parties to that effect, can be collected from the terms of the grant;" 2 Pick. 428; " nothing more would pass than would satisfy the terms;" 3 Pick. 359; " in the absence of all proof of ancient bounds, the grant must operate according to the general description of the estate granted;" 6 Pick. 176.

" By the common law it is clear that all arms of the sea, coves, creeks, &c. where the tide ebbs and flows, are the property of the sovereign, unless appropriated by some subject, in virtue of a grant, or prescriptive right which is founded on the supposition of a grant;" 1 Pick. 182; "the principles of the common law were well understood by the colonial legislature." "Those who acquired the property on the shore were restricted from such a use of it, as would impair the public right of passing over the water." "None but the sovereign power can authorize the interruption of such passages, because this power alone has the right to judge whether the public convenience may be better served by suffering bridges to be thrown over the water, than by suffering the natural passages to remain free;" ib. 184. "By the common law and the immemorial usage of this government, all navigable waters are public property for the use of all the citizens, and there must be some act of the sovereign power direct or derivative, to authorize any interruption of them." "A navigable river is of common right a public highway, and a general authority to lay out a new highway, must not be so extended as to give a power to obstruct an open highway, already in the use of the public;" ib. 185, 87.

From these opinions it would seem, that the interest of the riparian owners and of the public, would require for their protection, the application of such a rule of construing legislative grants of any right in or over the waters of the colony, as would confine them to the description, so that nothing should pass that was not embraced in its terms, and no right be impaired, further than the words of the law had done it. The supreme court of Massachusetts have not shown any sensibility as to the rules of construing grants, because they may be called "*prerogative*" rules, or in permitting the state to avail itself of *prerogative* rights; 6 Pick. 415.

This *prerogative* rule has been adopted in New York, without any fear that it was incompatible with the policy of a republic. "It is an established rule, that when a grant is susceptible of two constructions, that should be adopted which is most favourable to government;" 3 Caines, 295. Per Thompson, Justice: "It is a general rule of law that in the exposition of governmental grants, that construction, when the terms are inexplicit, shall be adopted, which is least favourable to the grantee;" 303. Livingston, Justice: "The idea of *rolling* out the patent, to the extent of four miles from every part of the plains, is literally impracticable, and when so modified as to be practicable, it would give too difficult and inconvenient a shape for location, and in a case of a location vague and doubtful, it would be stretching the grant over all the surrounding patents to an unreasonable degree. A construction more convenient and practicable, better answering the words of the grant, more favourable to the rights of the crown, and to the security of adjoining patents ought to be preferred;" 306. Kent, Chief Justice: "No property can pass at a public sale, but what was ascertained and declared;" 1 J. Cas. 287; a road will not pass by general words thrown in at the end of the

19

[Charles River Bridge v. Warren Bridge et al.]

metes and bounds in a sheriff's deed;" ib. 284, 6; S. P. 13; J. R. 551. "Such construction will be given as will give effect to the intention of the parties, if the words they employ will admit of it, *ut res majis valeat quam pereat;*" 7 J. R. 223. But when the description includes several particulars, necessary to ascertain the estate to be conveyed, none will pass except such as will agree to every description. "Thus, if a man grant all his estate in his own occupation in the town of W, no estate can pass except what is in his own occupation, and is also situate in that town;" ib. 224.

"A right to fish in any water, gives no power over the land," (cites Savill, 11;) "Nor will prescription in any case, give a right to erect a building on another's land. This is a mark of title and of exclusive enjoyment, and it cannot be acquired by prescription;" 2 J. R. 362. "A mere easement may, without express words, pass as an incident to the principal object of the grant, but it would be absurd to allow the fee of one piece of land, not mentioned in the deed, to pass as appurtenant to another distinct parcel, which is expressly granted by precise and definite boundaries." Thus, where land was granted on each side of a public road, by such description as included no part thereof, and the road was afterwards discontinued, the grantee has no right to any part of the site of the road; 15 J. R. 452, 55. This Court has not departed from these rules in expounding grants to corporations. "In describing the powers of such a being, no words of limitation need be used. They are limited by the subject." "But if it be intended to give its acts a binding efficacy beyond the natural limits of its power, and within the jurisdiction of a distinct power, we should expect to find in the language of the incorporating act, some words indicating such intention;" 6 Wh. 442. "It ought not to be so construed as to imply this intention, unless its provisions were such as to render the construction inevitable;" ib. 443. The act must contain words indicating such intention, and "this extensive construction, must be essential to the execution of the corporate power;" ib. 445. "It is an obvious principle that a grant must describe the land to be conveyed, and that the subject granted must be identified by the description given of it in the instrument itself;" 3 Pet. 96. "Whatever the legislative power may be, its acts ought never to be so construed, as to subvert the rights of property, unless its intention to do so shall be expressed in such terms as to admit of no doubt, and to show a clear design to effect the object;" 2 Wh. 203. Where a piece of ground in Charlestown was purchased by the United States for a navy yard, with the assent of Massachusetts, by the following description, "one lot of land with the *appurtenances*," &c., it was held that an adjacent street did not pass, as there was no intention expressed that it should pass; the term *appurtenances*, received a strict, legal, technical interpretation. The Court recognise the English rule as laid down in 15 J. R. 454, and refer with approbation to a case decided in Massachusetts, in which it was held, that by the grant of a grist mill with the appurtenances, the soil of a way, immemorially used for the purpose of access to the mill, did not pass, although it might be considered as a grant of the easement, for the accommodation of the mill; 10 Pet. 53, 4; 7 Mass. 6.

In this opinion, delivered in 1836, we find the rule prescribed by the *statute of prerogative* recognised by this Court, as it had been in the supreme courts of New York and Massachusetts, as to a grant of land *with the appurtenances;* which, with the other opinions herein referred to, would be deemed conclusive evidence of the law, on any other question than one involving the application of the clause of the constitution, against impairing the obligation of contracts. But if this consideration is to have any weight in the construction of a grant by a government, it ought to operate so as to exclude any broader construction than the words thereof import; not only because it may abridge the rights of riparian owners, and the public rights of property, but for a still stronger reason; that every grant is a contract, the obligation whereof is incorporated in the constitution as one of its provisions. Of consequence the legislature is incompetent to resume, revoke, or impair it, let their conviction of its expediency or public convenience be what it may. It is, therefore, the bounden duty of a court, not to make a grant operate by mere construction, so as to annul a state law which would be otherwise valid, and make a permanent irrevocable sacrifice of the public interest for private emolument, further than had been done by the terms of the grant. Such has been the uniform course of this Court.

" The question whether a law be void for its repugnance to the constitution, is at all times a question of much delicacy, which ought seldom or ever to be decided in the affirmative in a doubtful case. The Court, when impelled by duty to render such a judgment, would be unworthy its station, could it be unmindful of the obligations which that station imposes. But it is not on slight implication and vague conjecture, that the legislature is to be pronounced to have transcended its powers, and its acts to be considered as void. The opposition between the constitution and the law, should be such that the judges feel a clear and strong conviction of their incompatibility with each other;" 6 Cr. 128. " On more than one occasion, this Court have expressed the cautious circumspection with which it approaches the consideration of such questions; and has declared, that in no doubtful case would it pronounce a legislative act to be contrary to the constitution;" 4 Wh. 625. " It has been truly said that the presumption is in favour of every legislative act, and that the whole burthen of proof lies on him who denies its constitutionality;" 12 Wh. 436.

From these principles it follows, that no legislative grant can be held void on account of its alleged violation of a former grant, which is not definite in its object, the thing granted, and its extent; if it is so imperfectly described as to leave it doubtful whether the subject matter of both grants is the same, the doubt operates conclusively in favour of the power of the legislature to make the second grant.

This consideration alone necessarily leads to the rule for construing public grants of property or franchise, even  more strictly than in England; the reason exists in the provision of the constitution which prohibits any legislative violation of the obligation of a contract; whereas, in England, parliament can revoke or annul a grant of property or power, as the several states could before they adopted the constitution;" 4 Wh. 628, 651.

It is, however, not necessary for the purposes of this case, to hold the plaintiffs to any other rules of construction, than those laid down by this Court in 6 Pet. 738, to which the Court has referred in their opinion. These rules were extracted from the adjudged cases in England, in this and the highest state courts, as unquestionable principles which were deemed too firmly established to be shaken. Yet the rule thus established, is attempted to be put down, by calling it *"the royal rule of construction;"* vide 6 Pet. 752. The *prerogative rule* and one incompatible with republican institutions. To remarks of this kind I have no reply. It suffices for me that I find the settled doctrine of this Court, to be supported by an uniform current of authority, for five hundred years, without contradiction; it sufficed also for the majority of the Court in this case, to refer to the case in 6 Pet. 638, as to the rules of construing public grants, it not being deemed necessary to lay down the qualifications which applied to particular cases, which are noticed in that opinion.

In the argument of this case the counsel on neither side deemed that case worthy of a reference, nor is it noticed in the dissenting opinion in which the general principle laid down is assailed; yet a most singular course has been pursued in relation to the opinion delivered, in which that principle was sanctioned by six of the judges. *The cases referred to, the principles laid down, the very expressions of the Court,* have been carefully extracted from that case and applied to this, in order to impress upon the profession the belief that the Court had intended to establish a less liberal rule of construing public grants, than the English decisions would warrant. Whether this course has been pursued in ignorance of that opinion, or under an expectation that it was not, or will not be read, is immaterial; it is a duty due to the profession and the Court that their principle should be known. I therefore subjoin an extract, to prevent further misapprehension of their meaning.

" A government is never presumed to grant the same land twice, " 7 J. R. 8. Thus a grant, even by act of parliament, which con-" veys a title good against the king, takes away no right of property " from any other; though it contains no saving clause, it passes no " other right than that of the public, although the grant is general of "the land; 8 Co. 274, b.; 1 Vent. 176; 2 J. R. 263. If land is grant-" ed by a state, its legislative power is incompetent to annul the grant

" and grant the land to another; such law is void; Fletcher v. Peck,
" 6 Cr. 87, &c.  A state cannot impose a tax on land, granted with
" an exemption from taxation; New Jersey v. Wilson, 7 Cr. 164;
" nor take away a corporate franchise; Dartmouth College v. Wood-
" ward, 4 Wheat. 518.  Public grants convey nothing by implica-
" tion; they are construed strictly in favour of the king; Dy. 362,
" a; Cro. Car. 169.  Though such construction must be reasonable,
" such as will make the true intention of the king as expressed in
" his charter take effect, is for the king's honour, and stands with
" the rules of law; 4 Com. Dig. 428, 554; G. 12; 10 Co. 65.  Grants
" of the strongest kind, " *ex speciali gratia, certa scientia, et mero*
" *motu*," do not extend beyond the meaning and intent expressed
" in them, nor, by any strained construction, make any thing pass
" against the apt and proper, the common and usual signification and
" intendment of the words of the grant, and passes nothing but what
" the king owned; 10 Co. 112, b.; 4 Co. 35; Dy. 350, 1, pl. 21.  If
" it grant a thing in the occupation of B. it only passes what B. occu-
" pied; this in the case of a common person, a fortiori in the queen's
" case, 4 Co. 35 b.; Hob. 171; Hard. 225.  Though the grant and
" reference is general, yet it ought to be applied to a certain particu-
" lar, as in that case to the charter to Queen Caroline—*id certum est*
" *quod certum reddi potest*, 9 Co. 30, a. 46, a. 47, b. S. P.  When
" the king's grant refers in general terms to a certainty, it contains
" as express mention of it as if the certainty had been expressed in
" the same charter; 10 Co. 64, a.  A grant by the king does not
" pass any thing not described or referred to, unless the grant is as
" fully and entirely as they came to the king, and that *ex certa*
" *scientia*, &c.; Dy. 350, b.; 10 Co. 65, a.; 2 Mod. 2; 4 Com. Dig.
" 546, 548.  Where the thing granted is described, nothing else
" passes, as " those lands;" Hard. 225.  The grantee is restrained
" to the place, and shall have no lands out of it by the generality of
" the grant referring to it; as of land in A. in the tenure of B. the
" grant is void if it be not both in the place and tenure referred to.
" The pronoun " *illa*" refers to both necessarily, it is not satisfied till
" the sentence is ended, and governs it till the full stop; 2 Co. 33;
" S. P. 7 Mass. 8, 9; 15 J. R. 447; 6 Cr. 237; 7 Cr. 47, 48.  The
" application of this last rule to the words " *de illas*," in the eighth
" article, will settle the question whether its legal reference is to
" lands alone, or to " grants" of land.  The general words of a
" king's grant shall never be so construed as to deprive him of a
" greater amount of revenue than he intended to grant, or to be
" deemed to be to his or the prejudice of the commonwealth; 1 Co.
" 112, 13, b. " Judges will invent reasons and means to make acts
" according to the just intent of the parties, and to avoid wrong and
" injury which by rigid rules might be wrought out of the act;" Hob.
" 277.  The words of a grant are always construed according to the
" intention of the parties, as manifested in the grant by its terms or
" by the reasonable and necessary implication, to be deduced from the
" situation of the parties and of the thing granted, its nature and use;

" 6 Mass. 334, 5; S. & R. 110; 1 Taunton, 495, 500, 502; 7 Mass. 6:
" 1 B. & P. 375; 2 J. R. 321, 2; 6 J. R. 5, 10; 11 J. R. 498, 9; 3
" E. 15; Cro. Car. 17, 18, 57, 58, 168, 169; Plo. 170, b. 7; E. 621;
Cowper, 360, 363; 4 Yeates, 153." United States v. Arredondo,
6 Pet. 738, 40.

On these rules, principles, and cases, I formed my opinion in this
case, after the first argument, and now feel a perfect confidence that
they fully sustain it; willing to stand before the profession in this
attitude, I will not be forced into any other, by any omission of a
duty, however unpleasant. With this extract before them, the profession can now determine, whether the Court has impugned or affirmed the true principles of law, on the construction of public
grants by prerogative or legislative power, of any portion of public
property held as a trust for the benefit of all the people of a colony
or state.

The grant of the ferry is in these words, "The ferry between
Boston and Charlestown is granted to the college."

That there was but one ferry between those places is admitted; its
location had been previously fixed by the general court, at certain
points in the resolutions which they had passed from time to time;
those had been the only landings, to and from which passengers had
been taken, so that the term, "the ferry," was, in itself, a perfect
and complete description thereof. It had been leased to Converse,
and a clause was inserted in the case, that he was to have for three
years, "the sole transporting of cattle and passengers;" but this
right expired with the lease, when the ferry reverted to the colony
unincumbered with any condition whatever; so that they might
make such grant of it as they pleased. Had the grant to the college
been, "as fully as the same had been held by Converse," it would
have afforded some evidence of intention to have made it exclusive;
but no principle is better settled than that when the words "as fully
and entirely as it came to the hands of the king," are omitted,
nothing passes which is not specially described; vide 6 Pet. 739; and
cases cited.

The expired lease to Converse then can have no effect on the
grant as matter of law; so far as it indicates intention it is adverse
to the plaintiffs, for when an exclusive right was intended, it was
given in express terms; whereas this grant is, *the* ferry, *illa,* that
ferry, which had been established and kept up for ten years previously, at certain landings. This pronoun "the," or "illa," is necessarily descriptive of the place by direct reference to the ferry as
located in fact and long occupation. Ferry is a term of the law,
perfectly defined, and a grant of "the ferry," "that ferry," has the
same effect as a grant of "that land," "those lands," by which nothing else can pass but those which are referred to in words of description, by metes, bounds or occupation.

In ascertaining the meaning and effect of the grant of a ferry, we
must necessarily look to the ownership of the landing places, whether
it is in the grantee of the ferry or in the public. We must also look

to the ownership of the bed of the river, over which the right is granted. If the river is private property, a grant of a ferry to the owner of the bed and both sides thereof, is necessarily exclusive to the extent of his property; the public have no rights thereto, and no man has a right to land thereon without his permission. All that the owner acquires by the grant, is the franchise of exacting a toll, for the right of passing over his own property, the extent of which is limited thereby. The toll is for the use of his landing, his boats, and passing over his land to and from them, which excludes every construction of the grant, by which it would interfere with the right of another; 4 Burr. 2165. A grant of a ferry over a public river, " is a liberty by prescription, or the king's grant, to have a boat for passage upon a great stream for carrying of horses and men for a reasonable toll;" Terms of the Law, 223. It is to its extent a diminution of the public right, incumbering public property by the grant of a franchise of exacting toll for passing over it in his boats. If the landings on a public river, or an arm of the sea, are owned by the king, the grant of a ferry includes the right of landing on the shore, or in a public highway, as well as the franchise of toll. But the king cannot grant to A. a ferry between the landing places of another, for the ferry is in respect to the landings, which must be owned by the public or the grantee of the ferry; Sav. 11, 14; or he must have the consent of the owner to use them ; 1 Yeates, 167, 9; 9 S. & R. 32. This principle is said to have been overruled in two late cases; on examination, however, they affirm it, in 12 E. 336, 46; a question arose how a tax should be assessed on a ferry, on which the king's bench decided, that it should be assessed on the landings, as the local, visible, tangible evidence of the property in a ferry. In 6ʹB. & C. 703, the rule as laid down in Savil was considered, when so far from overruling it the two judges who gave an opinion, declared the rule to be, that it was sufficient if the grantee of the ferry had a right to use the landing places, though he did not own them, so that the only difference between the cases is, between the owning the landings in fee, and a right to use them under a lease or other consent of the owner. But if in these or any other modern cases, the doctrine laid down in Savil had been expressly overruled, it would not have had a retrospective effect to 1640, and changed the nature of the grant of this ferry. *Massachusetts* would, I think, not have recognised the power of English judges at this day to alter the rights of property, held by this ancient charter. A mere grant of a ferry by general terms, must, from its nature, be confined to the landing places and the route through the water between them; because if extended further, it must interfere with the rights of riparian owners, and the common right of every one to pass and repass on a public river or an arm of the sea. To extend the franchise by implication, to a place where the grantee has neither the right of landing or the franchise of exacting toll for passage, is also a restraint on the king, against granting a concurrent franchise to a riparian owner, on public landings or the ends of roads leading to public waters, as he may think necessary for the public good. Hence it has been an established principle of the common law, from magna charta to the present time, that the public right in and over all navigable rivers and arms of the sea, continues till an appropriation of some part is made by grant, on good consideration or reasonable recompense by the grantee; 1 Ruff. 8, Ch. 30; 2 Co. Inst. 58; 1 Mod. 104; Willes, 268; 1 Salk. 357. A general grant by the king of land in a royal haven, or which is covered by the sea, passes only the spot which is definitely granted, or which has been identified by a possession under the grant; and what is not described in the grant, or located by possession is presumed to have been abandoned. Though the grant was made in 1628, and its general terms were broad enough to embrace the place in controversy, the burthen of showing a title to the particular spot, was thrown on the claimant; 2 Anst. 614; 10 Price, 369, 410, 453; 1 Dow, P. C. 322.

The rule that public grants pass nothing by implication, has been most rigidly enforced as to all grants of toll for ferries, bridges, wharves, keys, on navigable rivers and arms of the sea, of which there cannot be stronger illustrations than in the cases which have arisen on the customs of London, and other places which impose tolls of various descriptions. By magna charta, the customs of London and other cities are confirmed, which has always been held to give to those customs the force of acts of parliament; yet these customs have always been held void, so far as they imposed a toll at any place where the city had not a right to demand them, or for a service or accommodation not performed or afforded, according to the precise terms of the custom; Hob. 175, 6; 1 Mod. 48; 1 Vent. 71; T. R. 233; 1 Mod. 104, 5.

So it is where a toll is demandable by an express grant, by custom or prescription on a public highway, in a public port, or for the use of public property, which is termed *toll throraugh*, because the party claiming it, is presumed to have had no original right to the place where he demands toll. He must therefore show not only his right to toll, by custom, prescription or grant, but must show some consideration for it, some burthen on himself, some benefit to the public, or that he or those under whom he claims, had once a right to the *locus in quo* which had been commuted for the toll, and this consideration must be applied to the precise spot where toll is claimed; Cro. El. 711; 2 Wils. 299; 3 Burr, 1406; 1 D. & E. 660; 4 Taunton, 137; 6 E. 458, 59; 4 D. & E. 667.

A claim of toll at a place where no toll has been granted, or where no consideration for it exists, is void by magna charta and the statute of Westminster, which prohibit all evil tolls; such as are exacted where none are due, exacting unreasonable toll where reasonable toll only is due, or claiming *toll through*, without fair consideration or reasonable recompence to the public; 2 Co. Inst. 219.

*Toll traverse*, or a toll demanded for passing on or over the private property of the claimant, or using it in any other way, is of a different description; being founded on the right which every man has to the exclusive enjoyment of what is exclusively his private property, its use by others is a sufficient consideration for the exaction of toll; Mo. 575; 2 Wils. 299; Cowp. 47, 8. But whenever toll is exacted for the passage over a public water, the nature of it changes; its foundation not being property, it rests on a grant or prescription, and if the toll is unreasonable the grant is void; 2 Co. Inst. 221, 2. The grantee must have the ownership or usufruct of the *locus in quo;* 1 Yeates, 167; 9 S. & R. 32, and within reasonable bounds; a prescription for a key half a mile in length is not good, unless the vessels unlade at the wharf; the Court say, "he may as well prescribe to the confines of France;" T. R. 223; 1 Mod. 104.

The right of ferry is a franchise which cannot be set up, without the license of the king; Harg. L. T. 10; or prescription; 5 D. C. D. 361, 7; Hard. 163; Willes, 512; 1 Nott and M'C. 394; 'rights of ferry on the waters of the public are not favoured;" they come too near a monopoly, and restrain trade; Hard. 163. "Courts are exceedingly careful and jealous of these claims of right, to levy money upon a subject; these tolls began and were established by the power of great men;" 2 Wils. 299. A legislative grant of a ferry, with a landing in a public road, the soil whereof is not owned by the grantee is void; 9 S. & R. 32; a charter to a turnpike corporation does not authorize them to erect a toll-gate on an old road, unless specially authorized, or it is necessary to give a reasonable effect to the statute; 2 Mass. 142, 6; 4 Mass. 145, 6; a town must show property in the land to low water mark, to authorize them to regulate its use under a law; 6 J. R. 135. The consideration of grants of ferries, is the obligation to provide and keep up proper accommodations for the public; 22 H. 6, 15; 6 E. 459; S. P. 1 V. jr. 114; the right is commensurate with the duty, and both must exist at the place where toll is exacted for passing; 4 D. & E. 667, 8; 1 Mass. 231.

As the right to the landings or their use is indispensable to the right to a ferry, a right to land at one place is not an incident, and cannot be made an appurtenance to a right to land at another place, even by the express words of the grant, according to the law of this Court, unless some other words are added by way of description, besides appurtenances. Land cannot be appurtenant to land, nor can one corporeal or incorporeal thing, be incident or appurtenant to another thing of the same nature; the incident must attach to the principal thing; 10 Pet. 54, and cases cited. The principal thing is that which is of the higher and most profitable service; the incident is something of a lower grade, which passes as appendant or appurtenant to the principal thing, without the words *cum pertinentibus;* Co. Lit. 307, a. The grant of a thing carries all things included, without which the thing granted cannot be had; that ground is to be understood of things incident and directly necessary; Hob. 234; so

20

that a man may always have the necessary circumstances, when he hath a title to the principal thing; Pl. 16; Pl. 317; Co. Lit. 56, a. A parcel severed from a manor, does not pass by a grant of the entire manor, unless where the severance is merely by a lease for years. An advowson appendant, does not pass by the word appurtenances as a part of the thing granted; it will pass where the grant is made with the additional words, " as fully and entirely as they came to the hands of the king, and with his certain knowledge," but not without these words; 10 Co. 65; Dy. 103, b; Pl. 6, 350, b; Pl. 18; 2 Mod. 2; 4 D. C. D. 546, 47, 8. When the word appurtenances is in the grant, there must be an intention manifested by other words, so that the court can be enabled to give them their intended effect, and hold them to pass what had been occupied, or used, with the thing directly granted; Pl. 170, 1; 11 Co. 52; Cro. Jac. 170, 189; Dy. 374; 7 E. 621; Cowp. 360; Cro. Car. 57, 8. This is the rule in cases of private grants of land, which are taken most strongly against the grantor, and in favour of the grantee, which has never been questioned; a fortiori, it must apply to public grants, and it follows conclusively, that where a grant by the king or a colony, omits even the word appurtenances, it will not pass a right which would not pass by that word alone. There is, however, another unquestioned rule, more directly applicable to the grant of a ferry, than the mere grant of land, or a substance to which a thing of the same substance cannot be appendant or appurtenant.

" But the grant of a franchise, a liberty, a particular right, on land or water, passes nothing more than the particular right; Co. Lit. 4, b; 4 D. C. D. 416, 542; 2 J. R. 322. The grant of a franchise carries nothing by implication; Harg. L. T. 33. Every port has a ville, and the grant of the franchise of a port shall not extend beyond the ville, because the court cannot notice it any further *ex officio*, though they will award an inquest in some cases, to ascertain the extent; Harg. L. T. 46, 47. Ancient grants and charters are construed according to the law at the time they were made; 2 Co. Inst. 282; 4 D. C. D. 546, 419; Co. Lit. 8, b, 94, b; 9 Co. 27, 8. The location of a patent 160 years old, shall not be extended beyond the actual *possessio pedis* under it; its boundaries must be ascertained by possession, and not the words; every doubt ought to be turned against the party who seeks to extend them; 7 J. R. 5, 10, 14. " It is undoubtedly essential to the validity of every grant, that there should be a thing granted, capable of being distinguished from other things of the same kind;" 7 Wh. 362.

A toll by prescription is better than by grant; 2 Co. Inst. 221; so is a franchise of a port, because the extent is according to the prescription; Harg. L. T. 33; but it must be confined to the subject matter and the ancient use; 1 Wils. 174; 6 E. 215; 7 E. 198; 2 Conn. R. 591; S. P. Wills. 268; 4 D. & E. 437; 2 H. Bl. 186. Under a charter for the erection of a road, canal, or bridge, the corporation must confine their action within the precise limits designated; any deviation from the route prescribed makes them trespassers; Coop. 77; 2 Dow. P. C. 519, 24. The law is the same though the road or canal is the property of the public, and constructed for general benefit; 20 J. R. 103, 739; 7 J. C. 332, 40; the definition of a road is, " the space over which the subject has a right to pass;" 2 D. & E. 234; beyond which there is no road; so of a canal, bridge, or ferry, with a grant of toll for passing: the nature and object of the grant in prescribing bounds is necessarily a limitation; nor does it make any difference, whether the toll is demanded in virtue of a direct grant, or one presumed by prescription, where there is no consideration existing at the precise point where toll is exacted, as is evident from the reason of the rule; " because it is to deprive the subject of his common right and inheritance to pass through the king's highway, which right of passage was before all prescription;" Mo. 574, 575; Pl. 793; 2 Wils. 299. If toll through is prescribed for, for passing through the streets of a town, the party must show the streets which he was bound to keep in repair, and that the passage was through such streets; 2 Wils. 299.

It would be easy to add references to other cases, but as the principles settled in those already cited, have for centuries been the established law of England, and the received law of all the states since their settlement, it is evident that no construction can be given to this grant, which will make it pass the exclusive right of ferriage between Boston and Charlestown. It can have no analogy to cases of donations to charities, unless it shall be held to be a charitable act to *roll out* the grant (in the words of Chief Justice Kent, 3 Caines, 306,) to the extent of some miles of the shores of a great river, so as to create a monopoly of the right of passage, and prevent the legislature from promoting the public welfare, by the grant of a concurrent ferry. On the first argument of this case it was contended that the grant extended one-third of an ancient day's travel, a *dieta*, or seven miles from the landings on each side of the river, which would be twenty-eight miles; this extravagant pretension was abandoned at the last argument, so that it is unnecessary to test its validity. But the plaintiffs still insist that their grant must be so extended as to prevent any injurious competition for the toll due for passage of boats between the places, at ferries contiguous, or so near as to diminish their profits, and also to secure to them the whole line of travel to the landings on each side of the river.

This is the ground on which they ask an injunction to prevent the nuisance by the erection of another bridge, and a decree of suppression if it should be erected; because, claiming under the ferry grant, the franchise thereby granted is imparted to the bridge to its full extent.

In considering this position I will first examine the authorities on which it is attempted to be supported.

In the year book 22 H. 6, 14, 15, Paston, J. said, "And the law is the same if I have from ancient time a ferry in a ville, and another should set up another ferry on the same river near to my ferry, so that the profits of my ferry are diminished, I may have against him an action on the case." That this has been the received law ever since is not to be questioned; but in its application to the present ferry grant, there are two important differences to be considered.

The rule applies only to *ancient* ferries; that is, ferries by prescription, or a presumed grant; next it applies to ferries in a *ville*, which is thus defined: " *Ville* is sometimes taken for a manor, and sometimes for a parish or a part of it;" Cow. L. Int.; "a tithing or town;" 1 Bl. Com. 114; "consisting of ten families at least;" 5 D. C. D. 249; 2 Str. 1004, 71; "the out part of a parish consisting of a few houses, as it were separate from it;" 3 Toml. L. Dict. 746, b; vide Co. Litt. 115, b.  From the nature of such a ferry, the rule applies only within these places; it never has been applied in England, to ferries on arms of the sea, between two places on its shores; the doctrine was expressly repudiated in Tripp v. Frank. 4 D. & E. 667, where there was an *exclusive* right of ferry *by prescription*, across the Humber, between Kingston and Barton, the profits of which were diminished by the defendant's ferry from Kingston to Barrow. It could not apply in this country, where the right of ferry exists only by legislative grant, and where we have no such subdivisions as correspond to a ville in England. Our towns, boroughs, and cities, are laid off by established lines, without regard to the regulations of Alfred, or the number of families or houses requisite to compose a hamlet, a ville, a part of a manor, or parish.

The inhabitants of these villes did not own the land they occupied; they held under the lord of the manor in whom the right of ferry was vested, as the owner of the soil and a grant of the franchise by prescription.

The tenant of that part to which it attached by prescription, being obliged to provide and maintain boats, &c., was protected against competition by the other tenants of the ville, who held under the same lord.  It was a part of the tenure by which the land was held, that the tenants should pass at the ferry; should grind the corn raised on the same land at the lord's mill, or that of his tenant, so that the profits of the ancient mill should not be impaired to their injury; 22 H. 6, 14, 15, by Paston, J.  The rule, of course, could have no application beyond the ville or manor, in which there existed such privity of tenure; the nature of the right is incompatible with the *jus publicum* in public waters, or private rights of property held independently of the lord of the manor.  Hence we find no case arising in England, in which this right has been sustained on any other ground than tenure, which is a conclusive reason against the application of the rule to any case in this country, where no such tenure exists, or can exist, as in English manors.

The plaintiffs have considered the grant of a ferry as analogous to that of a fair or market, and have relied on cases in which damages have been recovered for erecting rival fairs or markets; but these cases admit of the same answer as those of ferries by prescription within manors; they grow out of feudal tenures, are founded on feudal rights, and are wholly unknown in this country, either by grant or prescription.

Markets and fairs, however, differ from other franchises; the grant or prescription extends, ex vi termini, to seven miles or the dieta; F. N. B. 184, n.; 3 Bl. Com. 219; 2 Saund. 171, 2. The word "near" refers to the dieta in case of a rival fair or market; and to the ville in case of a ferry; if it is beyond, no action lies; 3 Bl. Com. 219. In cases where the action is sustained, it is not on the right of property; it must be an action on the case for consequential damages, arising from an unlawful act which injures another; if the act is lawful, no action lies; one may erect a mill near the ancient mill of another, because he is not bound to keep it in repair; 22 H. 6, 14; unless a special custom is alleged and found, as in 2 Vent. 291, 2.

Any man may keep a ferry for his own use, between his own landings within the limits of a ferry by prescription or the king's manor; Harg. L. T. 6, 73; but if he do it for toll, without license, he usurps a public franchise, and is finable on a presentment, or quo warranto; Harg. L. T. 73; he is not bound to keep up his boats, and as he does not share the burthens, he shall not have the benefit of the franchise; 3 Bl. Com. 219; and the act being illegal when done "without lawful authority or warrant," it is a nuisance, and case lies for damages consequent upon it; 1 Mod. 69; 2 Saund. 172, 4; Bull. N. P. 76; but the action does not lie, if the act, though unlawful, was not an interference with the right of the other, and within the limits of his prescription; Harg. 47. The king alone can prosecute for a purpresture or an usurpation on the jus publicum of a franchise, burthensome to the subjects generally; Harg. L. T. 85; 2 J. C. 283; 18 V. 217, 19; if it is outside the limits of an ancient ferry, a grant of the franchise if fairly made, gives a complete right to the enjoyment of the franchise which none can disturb; Wills. 508; because none but the king can interfere.

There is no case where the grant of a new ferry or other franchise has been held void on the sole ground of its interfering with the profits of an old one. Chapman v. Flaxmann was on a special custom laid and found, that all the inhabitants of the manor which belonged to the plaintiff, were bound to grind at his mills; the defendant occupied a messuage in the manor, and erected a mill to the plaintiff's injury, who recovered damages on the ground of the custom; 2 Vent. 291, 2. In Butler's case, the suit was to repeal a patent for a market at C., reciting that there was an ancient market within half a mile, and that the patent was obtained on an *ad quod damnum*, executed by surprise, and without notice, to the great damage of the former market, all of which was admitted by a demurrer, and the patent was repealed; 2 Vent. 344; 3 Ser. 220, 223. The suit was by the king, at the relation of the inhabitants of Rochester, and the patent avoided on the ground, that "the king has an undoubted right to repeal a patent wherein he is deceived, or his subjects prejudiced," that it was *jure regio* by the common law; 3 Lev. 221, 2; but it is not asserted in any part of the case, that the patent was repealable on the ground of the right of the relators to an exclusive market, or that they had any remedy otherwise than at the suit of the king.

In the report of the case, in Levins, it appears, that the city of Rochester was held of the king by a fee farm rent of twelve pound per annum, the effect of which was to make the citizens thereof the fee farm tenants of the king; as such they were privileged suitors, and entitled to redress when other tenants are not, which will explain the cases cited from Hardress, decided in the exchequer on bills in equity, to suppress rival ferries, mills, and markets.

In Churchman v. Tunstall, the plaintiff was the farmer of a common ferry time out of mind at a fee farm rent; the defendant owned the land on both sides of the Thames, and set up a ferry within three-fourths of a mile of plaintiff's ferry to his prejudice. The court dismissed the bill, " because it came too near a monopoly and restrained trade, and because no precedent was shown in point. The case of a beam that had been urged, was of a beam *in the king's own manor;*" Hard. 162, 3.

In Green v. Robinson and Wood, there was a custom in a manor held by the king in fee farm, that all the tenants and resiants thereof should grind at the lord's mill and not elsewhere; the defendant had erected another mill *outside of the manor*, near the old mill, by reason whereof many of the tenants left the lord's mill to his great prejudice; the bill was for the demolishing the new mill. The court, (Hale Athyns Turner,) said, that it was lawful for any tenant to set up a mill upon his own ground *out of the manor*, but not within the manor; they would prohibit him from persuading the tenants to grind at his mill, or fetching grist out of the manor thereto, but could not decree the mill to be destroyed, unless erected *within the king's manor*, to the prejudice of *his* mill. No precedents were shown, and the bill was dismissed, but without prejudice to the right of the lord of the manor; Hard. 174, 5.

In White and Snook v. Porter, one of the plaintiffs was a copyhold tenant for life, the other a purchaser of the inheritance of land in the king's manor held under a fee farm rent, who filed their bill for the suppression of a rival mill erected *within* the manor. It was decreed that the defendant should not take away or withdraw any grist from the old mill; but his mill was not decreed to be demolished, for that can be done *in the king's own case only*, or in the case of *his patentee*, who is entitled to the privilege of this court (of exchequer.) " And it was also held in this case, that to compel all the tenants within the king's manor, to grind at the king's mill, is a *personal prerogative* of the king's, which no other lord can have, without *tenure, custom*, or *prescription*. But it will extend to a fee farm, because it is for the king's advantage. And that the custom in this case does not go to the estate, but to the thing itself, and runs along with the mill into whose hands soever it comes, that the suit here must be *as debtor and accountant only*, because the copyholder for life is not liable to the fee farm.   And if two join as they do here, where one of them is, and the other is not, liable to the fee farm, that is irregular unless that other be a privileged person;" Hard. 177, 8.

In the Mayor, &c. v. Skelton, the bill was for demolishing a mill, *near* to a manor of the king's, which was granted to the plaintiffs in fee farm, whose mill was prejudiced by the one erected by the defendant.   A search was directed to be made for precedents, but none could be found, and the court held, that a mill *not within the king's manor*, could not be demolished where there was no tenure nor custom, whereby the inhabitants are bound to grind at the king's mill; Hard. 184, 5.

Two cases which involve the same principle, are reported by lord Hale, in his Treatise de Portibus Maris.   The town of New Castle on Tyne v. The Prior of Tinmouth, and The City of Bristol v. Morgan et al.   Both places were within the king's manors and were held by fee farm rent, the plaintiffs were therefore privileged suitors, and having made out their case, they obtained decrees for the demolishing the erections complained of, which were within the town and city, among which there was a ferry, upon which lord Hale remarks: " Upon these records these things are to be noted and collected, viz.

1. " In fact these places, (in which the erections were demolished,) were within the respective ports of Bristol and New Castle, and between the port town and the sea.

2. " That an erection of houses, or places of receipt for mariners, contiguous to, or near to the water of that port, between the port and the sea, is an injury to the port town, a forestalling of it, and a prejudice to the customs.

3. " That it may therefore be demolished by decree or judgment. But if it had not these circumstances it had been otherwise.

1. " If it had been built *contiguous* to the port town, it should not have been demolished; and upon that account the buildings *below* the town do continue, and are not within the reasons of these judgments.

2. " If it had been built *above* the port, it should not have been subject to such a judgment, for it is in that case no forestall between the port and the sea, and so no nuisance to the port town as a port town.

3. " If the building had been *out of the extent* of the port, as if it had been built three or four miles below the hill, it had not been within the reason of either of these judgments, nor might it have been demolished, for it could not be a nuisance to the port;" Harg. L. T. 79, 83.

In these and all other cases where rival ferries have been suppressed by decrees in the court of exchequer, they are suits by the king or his fee farm tenants, who by being his debtors and accountants, are entitled to the same privileges of personal prerogative as the king himself, and may sue in the exchequer as privileged persons. But no decree for a suppression will be rendered in any case, unless the erection is within the king's manor, and no restraint will be put upon the rival mill or ferry, if there is no tenure, custom, or prescription, which gives an exclusive right to the plaintiff, to compel the tenants of the manor to resort to his mill, &c.

It has been contended by the plaintiffs, that the case in Hard. 162, was overruled, and a contrary principle established afterwards, for which a reference is made to the argument of the attorney general, in 2 Anst. 608, and the opinion of the chief baron, in p. 416; but on a close examination of the cases, there will be found no discrepancy between the first and second decisions of the case of Churchman v. Tunstall. As reported in Hard. 162, the plaintiff sued in the exchequer, as "a farmer of a common ferry at Branford, in Middlesex, at a fee farm rent; the ferry was a common ferry, time out of mind, and he laid in his bill that no other person ought to erect any other ferry, to the prejudice of his, &c." He did not lay the ferry to be within the king's manor, or allege himself to be a fee farm tenant of the king; he was, therefore, not a privileged suitor in the exchequer, so as to be able to avail himself of the personal prerogative of the king. The ferry was also laid to be a common ferry.

In the case afterwards brought, the plaintiff sued "as tenant of an ancient ferry under the crown," Anst. 608; on which the chief baron, in referring to the decisions of lord Hale, remarks:—"But the cases cited, and those which lord Hale has given us in his Treatise de Portibus Maris, clearly prove, that where the king claims and proves a right to the soil, where a perpresture and nuisance have been committed, he may have a decree to abate it;" Anst. 616. Attorney General v. Richards.

This remark reconciles all the cases which have been referred to, showing that where the court of exchequer interferes to suppress any rival erection as a nuisance, it is where the locus in quo is the property of the crown, and the suit is brought by him, or his tenants, who sue in his right. Such was the case in Anstruther; the nuisance complained of was "the erection of a wharf in Portsmouth har-"bour, which prevented vessels from sailing over the spot, or moor-"ing there," &c.; it was abated on the ground of the property being in the king, and the erection being to the injury of the public. In such cases, the court of exchequer acts on an information by the attorney general, or at the suit of the king's patentee, or fee farm tenant; but this is a proceeding peculiar to that court. A court of equity never grants an injunction against a public nuisance, without a previous trial by jury, as it would, in effect, be tantamount to the conviction of a public offence; Harg. L. T. 85; 18 V. 217, 19; 19 V. 617, 20; 2 J. C. 283.

[Charles River Bridge v. Warren Bridge et al.]

Where a patent is repealed in chancery on a scire facias, it is at the suit of the king, on the ground that he was deceived, and his subjects thereby injured; but there is no case where a court of chancery has ever decreed the prostration of a mill, of a ferry, or other erection, on the sole ground of its diminishing the profits of an ancient one, or the want of power in the king to grant a concurrent franchise at any place not within the limits of one held by grant, custom, or prescription.

Taking, then, the cases relied on by the plaintiffs, as they are reported in the books, they not only fail to support their position, but directly overthrow it. The principles established, are equally fatal to their right to recover damages for the consequential injury by an action on the case, or to suppress any rival ferry by an assize of nuisance at law, or a bill for an injunction or suppression in equity. They must, in either case, show in themselves a right of property or possession in the place where a rival ferry is established, or a special custom, compelling the inhabitants of Boston and Charlestown to cross at their ferry, or they can have no standing in any court, even if they were *privileged* suitors in virtue of the *personal prerogative* of the king, as the fee farm tenants of a *royal* manor. As the plaintiffs do not sue in this, or any analogous character, by special privilege, it is unnecessary to show that they cannot be relieved in the character in which they sue, on any principle laid down in the case from Levins, or those cited from Hardress and Anstruther. An explanation of these cases was necessary, because they have been pressed with confidence as in point to the present, and for another reason; when explained, they show, that to bring the plaintiffs' case within them, it is requisite that they sue by the highest and most odious prerogative of the crown; that which is *personal* to the king for his *private advantage*, in his demesne lands. It was also proper as an *argumentum ad hominem*, to those who feel any sensibility in adopting the *royal* or *prerogative rule* of construing public grants so as to impair the public interest, by no constructive extension of them, to any public property not described expressly, or included by the necessary implication of its terms. With this explanation, it will not be difficult to ascertain which kind of *royal* prerogative is most congenial to our *republican* institutions; that which is personal within a royal manor, and enjoyed for private profit, or that which is a trust for the whole kingdom, and for the benefit of all its subjects; and whether the majority or minority of the court have properly applied the principle of the common law of ferries which was adopted in Massachusetts, as the law of the colony, in 1640, when the grant was made.

The case of Chadwicke v. The Haverhill Bridge has been pressed as evidence of the law of Massachusetts, not as the decision of any court, but as expressing the opinion of one eminent lawyer who brought the action, and of another who decided it as an arbitrator. Though I entertain the most profound respect for the professional

21

character of both the gentlemen alluded to, I cannot, as a judge, found my judgment on any opinion expressed by either, because not given under judicial responsibility. There can be but few cases, in which the mere opinion of counsel ought to be taken as authority in any court; but in this Court, testing the validity of a state law by the rules which are imperative upon us, I feel forbidden to defer my settled opinion on the law of the case, to that of any individual, however eminent.

There is no task more difficult or invidious, than to decide who were those eminent and distinguished members of the profession in former times, or who now are, to whose opinions a court of the last resort ought to pay judicial deference, and who were and are not deserving of such distinguished notice. Judges would incur great hazard in making the selection, and would form their opinions by very fallible standards, if they look beyond the state law on which the case arises, the provision of the constitution which applies to it, and the appropriate rules and principles which have been established by judicial authority. It is a risk which I will not incur, on any question involving the constitutionality of a state law; for if the case shall be so doubtful, that any man's opinions either way, which are not strictly judicial and authoritative, would turn the scale, I would overlook them, and decide according to the settled rule of this Court: that in every case the presumption is, that a state law is valid, and whoever alleges the contrary, is bound to show and prove it clearly. In obedience to this rule, I cannot recognise in any private opinions of any description, by whomsoever, or howsoever expressed or promulgated, any authority for rebutting such presumption. No more salutary rule was ever laid down by this Court, or impressed on its members in plainer language, than what is used by the late Chief Justice in the cases cited; nor can there be any rule in favour of the most strict observance of which, there can be any reasons which operate with such a weight of obligation on the Court as this ought.

There is no court in any country which is invested with such high powers as this; the constitution has made it the tribunal of the last resort, for the decision of all cases in law or equity arising under it. The twenty-fifth section of the judiciary act has made it our duty to take cognizance of writs of error from state courts, in cases of the most important and delicate nature. They are those only in which the highest court of a state has adjudged a state law to be valid, notwithstanding its alleged repugnance to the constitution, a law, or a treaty of the United States.

When this Court reverses the judgment, they overrule both the legislative and judicial authority of the state, without regard to the character or standing, political or judicial, of the individual members of either department; surely, then, it is our most solemn duty, not to found our judgment on the opinions of those who assume to decide on the validity of state laws, without any official power, sanction, or responsibility. If we defer to political authority, there can be none higher than the three branches of the legislative power; if to judicial authority, the highest is the solemn judgment of the members of that court, in which is vested the supreme judicial power of the state.

There is another still higher consideration, which arises from the effect of a final judgment of this Court under the twenty-fifth section; it is irreversible; it is capable of no correction or modification, save by an amendment to the constitution; it must be enforced by the executive power of the Union, and the state must submit to the prostration of its law, and its consequences, however severe the operation may be. That the case ought to be clear of any reasonable doubt in the mind of the Court, either as to the law, or its application, is a proposition self-evident; and there are no cases to which the rule applies with more force, than to those which turn on the obligation of contracts.

If we steadily adhere to it as a fundamental rule, that the judgment of the supreme court of a state on the validity of its statutes, shall stand affirmed, until it is proved to be erroneous, the effect would be most important on constitutional questions, and lead to a course of professional and judicial opinion, which would soon assign to all the now doubtful parts of the constitution, a definite and established meaning.

The plaintiffs have also relied on the opinion of the late learned chancellor of New York, in 4 J. C. 160; and 5 J. C. 111, 12; in which he puts the case of a rival ferry set up so near an old one as to diminish its profits, and refers to the rule laid down in F. N. B. 184; Bro. Ab. Action on the Case, pl. 57, tit. Nuisance, pl. 12, 2 R. A. 140; 3 Bl. Com. 219; 2 Saund. 172; and which is taken from the 22 H. 6, 14, 15. In putting this case as an illustration of those then before him, this great jurist stated the proposition in general terms merely, without that precision which he adopts as to the points directly presented, and he has deduced a rule much broader than the cases warrant, when closely examined. For the purposes of the cases then under consideration, the broad rule laid down might well be applied to the grants contained in the laws of the state on which the cases turned, as a safe guide to their construction. But when a question depends on the law, as established by the adjudged cases and old writers of standard and adopted authority, we must take it from the books themselves. Having already reviewed the cases in detail from the 22 H. 6, and stated my conclusions from them, I submit their correctness, without further remarking upon the rules prescribed, in relation to the extent of the rights of ferry.

I would have remained satisfied with what has been already said, if there had not been these expressions in the opinion in 4 J. C. 160, 1. "It would be like granting an exclusive right of ferriage between two given points, and then setting up a rival ferry within a few rods of those very points, and within the same course and line of travel. The common law contained principles applicable to this

[Charles River Bridge v. Warren Bridge et al.]

very case, dictated by a sounder judgment, and a more enlightened morality."

After a reference to the rule laid down from the books which are cited, the opinion proceeds: " The same rule applies, in its spirit and substance, to all exclusive grants and monopolies. The grant must be so construed as to give it due effect, by excluding all *contiguous* and *injurious competition.*" As these propositions are supported by an authority which cannot be too highly respected, and is difficult to oppose with success; I feel bound to support the negation of them, by a reference to cases and books which would have been deemed unnecessary, but for this opinion.

In Harg. L. T. 83, it has been seen that lord Hale uses the word *contiguous* to a port town, in contradistinction to *within it,* and most distinctly negatives the idea, that a contiguous ferry or other erection would be demolished, however injurious it might be. In his opinions as chief baron of the exchequer, in the cases cited, he decided upon the same principle. The authority of his treatise de Portibus Maris is universally admitted, as the best evidence of the law as it was understood in his time, in which he says, " It is part of the *jus regale* to erect public ports; so in special manner are the ports and the franchises thereof;" Harg. L. T. 53, 4. " A port hath a *ville*, or city, or borough," keys, wharves, cranes, warehouses and other privileges and franchises; Harg. 46, 77. "If a man hath *portum maris*, by prescription or custom, it is as a manor; he hath not only the franchise but the very water and soil within the port;" Harg. 33. "Every port is a franchise, or liberty, as a market or a fair and much more." It has of necessity a market, and tolls incident; it cannot be erected without a charter or prescription; Harg. 50, 1; or if it is restrained, it cannot be extended or enlarged in any other way; ib. 52. Where it is by a custom or prescription, the consideration is the interest of the soil both of the shore and town, and of the haven wherein the ships ride, and the consequent interest of the franchise or liberty, which constitute the port in a legal signification; which are acquirable by a subject by prescription without any formality; ib. 54; and in ordinary usage and presumption they go together; ib. 33. The extent of the port depends on the prescription or usage; the court cannot take notice of its extent, further than the ville or town at its head, that gives it its denomination; if any further extension is alleged it is ascertained by the *venire facias de vicineto portus*, ib. 47, 70. The difference between a port by charter, and by custom or prescription, is thus illustrated:

" If the king at this day grant *portum maris de S.* the king having the port in point of interest, as well as in point of franchise, it may be doubtful whether at this day it carries the soil or only the franchise, *because it is not to be taken by implication.*" "But surely if it were an ancient grant, and usage had gone along with it, that the grantor had also the soil; this grant might be effectual to pass both, for both are included in it;" Harg. 33; S. P. Cowp. 106.

The difference between an ancient grant, and one made at this day, is this: If made beyond legal memory, and in terms so general and obscure, as not to be any record pleadable, but ought to have the aid of some other matter of record within time of memory, or some act of allowance or of confirmation; they shall now be allowed only to the extent of such allowance or confirmation, and shall be construed according to the law when it was made, and the ancient allowance on record; 9 Co. 28, a; or prescription will be taken as evidence of the existence of a grant, and to supply its presumed loss by the lapse of time; 1 Bl. Com. 274; 2 Bl. Com. 265; though the record is not produced, or proof adduced of its being lost, a jury will presume the grant; Cowp. 110, 11; but if the grant is within time of memory, and wants no allowance, confirmation, or presumption, to give it effect, it is pleadable without showing either; 9 Co. 28. This is called a grant at the present day; an ancient grant is by prescription. When a grant of the franchise of a port by prescription, or an ancient grant of an ancient port, is thus made out, it imports the incident franchises of markets, fairs, ferries, keys, wharves, landings, &c., and the toll for each; and the franchise is supposed to have been founded on the right of soil in fee simple, for no prescription can be founded on any less estate; 2 Bl. Com. 265. As tenant in fee of soil and franchise to the extent of the port, no right of property can be of a higher grade, or be entitled to a higher degree of protection by the law; the fee of the soil is a greater right than a mere liberty or franchise in or over it; the principal franchise of a port is higher and more important than any of the incidental franchises. When once established, the king cannot resume them, narrow, or confine their limits; 1 Bl. Com. 264; for the crown hath not the power of doing wrong, but merely of preventing wrong from being done; 1 Bl. Com. 154. But however high and sacred these ancient grants of soil and franchise are, they are not protected from grants by the king, which may diminish their profits by injurious and contiguous competition; the contrary doctrine is laid down by lord Hale, and there cannot be found in the common law, a case or dictum to the contrary.

"If A hath a port in B, and the king is pleased to erect a new port *hard by that*, which it may be is more convenient for merchants, though it be *a damage to the first port*, so that there be no obstruction of the water, or otherwise, but that ships may, if they will, arrive at the former port, this, it seems, may be done. But then this new port must not be erected *within the precincts of the former*;" "he may erect a *concurrent port, though near another*, so it be not within the *proper limits* of the former, as shall be shown in the case of Hull and Yarmouth, hereafter;" Harg. 60, 61, to 66, 71.

"But it cannot be erected within *the peculiar limits* by charter or prescription, belonging to the former port, because that is part of the interest of the lord of the former port. Neither can the first port be obstructed, or wholly defaced, or excluded for arrival of ships, but by act of parliament, or the consent of the owners of the ancient port;" Ib. 60, 61. "If a subject, or the king's fee farmer has a port at R, by prescription or charter, and the king grants that no ships shall arrive within five miles, he cannot, within that precinct, erect, de novo, a port to the prejudice of the former, though he might have done it without this restrictive clause; but by this inhibition, this precinct is become, as it were, parcel of the precinct of the port;" Ib. 61; S. P. 66, 7.

Both of the ferries of Yarmouth and Hull, were held under the crown, at a fee farm rent; Ib. 61, 68. So that they united the highest rights of property, with all the privileges which devolved on them, in virtue of the personal prerogative of the king, and by the force of his grant. Yet neither availed them to prevent injurious and contiguous competition, by the erection of a concurrent and rival port; ib. 70. If the king own the port, he may license the erection of a new wharf, "whereof there are a thousand instances;" Ib. 85. The king's tenants cannot set up a port; Ib 51, 73. A subject who claims a port by prescription, must own the shores of the creek or haven, and the soil; "but he hath not thereby the franchise of a port, neither can he so use or employ it, unless he hath had that liberty time out of mind, or by the king's charter;" "he cannot take toll or anchorage there, for that is fineable by presentment, or quo warranto ;" Ib. 54, 73.

In these unquestioned principles of law, we find its rules which define the nature and extent of all franchises on the shores or waters of public rivers, havens, or arms of the sea, which can be enjoyed by an individual or a corporation. If it is by prescription, or an ancient grant, it is founded on an existing right of property in fee, the consideration for the presumed grant of toll is for passing over or using private property, and the franchise is of a toll traverse, which from its nature is exclusive to the extent of the private ownership, which is defined by the possession and usage, which constitute the title by prescription. If the right of *property* is prescriptive, but the *franchise* is granted by a charter within legal memory, which is in existence, is pleadable, and is or can be produced, then, as nothing passes by implication, the court *ex officio*, can look only to the charter for the extent of the franchise; if it is alleged that it has had a greater extent by usage, an inquest goes to ascertain the fact. In this case too, the franchise being a toll traverse, the jury may find it to the extent of the usage under the charter, and the right of property by prescription, so far as they unite. But when there is no existing right of property, except that which is the *jus publicum*, a grant of toll for its use, or passage over it to any subject, is the franchise of *toll thorough*, or toll on a public highway, which is void whether by prescription or the king's charter, unless for good consideration or reasonable recompense, which must be made to appear to have existed at the time of the grant, and to have been continued so long as toll is exacted. In such case the franchise is never extended by any implication or construction, but is confined to the precise place where the consideration exists; and so far from the usage of exacting toll at any other spot being evidence of a right, it is fineable on indictment or quo warranto. The customs of London to the contrary, though by their confirmation by magna charta, they have the force of acts of parliament, are illegal and void, as usurpations on the public right, and injurious to the people at large; and even the king's fee farm tenants in his own manors are not exempted from the rule. An evident consequence of these principles is, that the king may grant a concurrent franchise, contiguous, or near to the place where a former one exists, either by charter or prescription, if it is not within its precise limits. Whenever he shall deem it necessary for the public good, it is his right by prerogative, his power is discretionary, which the law will not control, unless it is so exercised as to prejudice the right of property existing previously. So long as its possession and use is left to the proprietor, the law does not notice the mere diminution of profits of an existing franchise on a public river, or an arm of the sea, by the erection of a rival franchise beyond its limits; the competition is beneficial to the public by the increased accommodation afforded, and a diminution of toll exacted.

In deciding on prerogative or legislative grants, the court can look only to the power and right by which they are made; questions of policy, expediency, or discretion, are not judicial ones; if necessity or public good brings a power into action, the court cannot judge of its degree or extent; 4 Wh. 413. It "would be to pass the line which circumscribes the judicial department, and to tread on legislative ground. This Court disclaims all pretensions to such a power;" ib. 423. The same rule applies to all officers or tribunals in whom a discretionary power is vested by law, without any appeal or supervisory power in any other tribunal being provided; their acts done in the exercise of an honest and sound discretion, can be invalidated only by fraud in the party who claims under them, or an abuse or excess of authority in the depository of the power; 6 Pet. 729; 1 Cr. 170, 1; 2 Pet. 412; 4 Pet. 563; 2 Pet. 167; 20 J. R. 739, 40; 2 Dan. P. C. 521, &c.; 10 Pet. 477, 8.

That the power of the king over navigable rivers and arms of the sea is plenary, is undoubted; the power is vested in him for the public good, and it is his duty to so exercise it; he may make an exclusive grant of a franchise, or may make concurrent grants at his discretion, subject to the qualifications stated. He may grant a monopoly on proper consideration, but his grant of a franchise is not an exclusive one per se; it must be so in terms, or it is limited to the precise place and object; and the king is at liberty to make concurrent grants at his pleasure. The power of the king is thus declared by lord Thurlow: "The king may, if he pleases, grant licenses to twenty new play houses, and may give liberty to erect them in Covent Garden and Drury Lane, close to those which are established;"

1 V. Jr. 114; but he adds, "but would it be right to do so." This is matter of discretion, which is referred to the chancellor as the keeper of the king's conscience, who, after hearing the case, advises the granting or refusing the patent as he may think just, as may be seen in the case Ex parte O'Reilly; 1 V. Jr. 113, 30. The ancient mode on an application for a grant, was to sue out a writ of *ad quod damnum*, on which an inquest was held, and on the return of the inquisition the grant was made or denied; but it may be dispensed with by a clause of *non obstante* in the patent; F. N. B. 226. The grant is therefore valid without the writ, but is *voidable* by the king on a scire facias, if it is injurious to another on the ground of the king having been deceived; 3 Lev. 222. But the grant could not be annulled in a collateral action between A and B, otherwise there would be no necessity of resorting to chancery, to repeal it by a scire facias at the suit of the king; this is always issued on the application of a party by petition, setting forth the injury he sustains by the grant.

It only remains to apply the foregoing principles to the case of an ancient ferry in a ville, as a test of the rights of the owner by the common law. Such a ferry is by prescription; the franchise is founded on the property in the landings, it can rest on no other right; the right of property is in the lord of the fee, and the franchise is in him as a toll traverse, to the extent of the local custom or prescription, but no further, even in the king's manors, or in favour of his fee farm tenants. The position in the year book, 22 H. 6, goes no farther; no writer of authority has asserted that the owner of such a ferry has any right beyond the ville, or manor, which is the line and boundary of the right of soil, and no adjudged case has sanctioned such doctrine. There is no case or principle in the common law, which gives any colour for the assertion, that the franchise of an ancient ferry is more protected against injurious and contiguous competition, than the higher franchise of a port; the doctrine of lord Hale, and the cases in Hard. 163, &c., are to the point, that contiguous competition, by the diminution of the profits of an ancient ferry, is a *damnum absque injuriæ*. Nor in the whole body of the law, is there expressed a doubt that the king may grant a concurrent franchise of any description, which does not extend within the limits of an existing one. Let these principles be applied to the present case.

Charles river is an arm of the sea, the colony owned a ferry over it, together with the landing places, till 1640, and held possession of it by their tenants; the soil of the adjacent shores of the river was owned by the colony, or its grantees; the rights of riparian owners extended to low water mark, or one hundred rods on the flats, on each side. All pretence, therefore, of any right in the college by prescription, or the presumption of an ancient grant which had been lost, is wholly out of the question; the grant made in 1640, is "a grant made at this day;" it is pleadable, it is produced from the record, and the Court can notice it *ex officio.*

It is the grant of a ferry on a public highway; the franchise is of a *toll thorough,* the very nature whereof precludes any extension of it by implication or construction, beyond its precise limits, and the very spots at which the consideration for the grant exists; any exaction of toll at any other points, is the usurpation of a franchise, which, so far from giving a right, subjects the grantee to a fine.

Taking the common law to have been, from its first settlement, the law of Massachussetts, its oldest and best settled rules are, in my mind, conclusive against the pretensions of the plaintiffs, in virtue of the ferry grant. That they ought to be applied in their utmost strictness, against any construction of colonial grants which tend to create monopolies by implication, is, I think, the policy and spirit of all our institutions, and called for by every consideration of public interest. The proposition that a grant within legal memory, of toll thorough on an arm of the sea, over a public highway, of a ferry which had been occupied by the public at defined and described landings, would make it unlawful for the king to grant a concurrent ferry at other landings, would shock the sense of the profession in England, as subversive of the law. Such a proposition, as to the grant of such a franchise in these states, would be still more monstrous; because, if sustained, it would not only subvert its common and statute law, but, by infusing such a grant into the constitution, all legislative discretion would be annihilated forever, and a monopoly created by implication and mere construction, which no power in the state or federal government could limit.

I have confined my opinion in this case to the grant of the ferry by the colony, thinking it important that the principles which apply to such grants, should be more fully explained than they had been. As to the grants to the plaintiffs by the acts of the legislature, in 1785, and 1792, I can have nothing to add; the view taken by the Court, in their opinion, is, to my mind, most lucid and conclusive; supported alike by argument and authority, it has my unqualified concurrence in all the results which are declared.

### POOLE AND OTHERS v. FLEEGER AND OTHERS.

So far as my general views of the origin and nature of the federal constitution and government may be peculiar, that peculiarity will be carried of course into my opinions on constitutional questions. There are none which can arise, in which it is more important to attend carefully to the reasons of one's judgment, than in those where the prohibitions on the states come under consideration; those which have arisen have been found the most difficult to settle, because they involve not only the question of the powers granted to congress, and those reserved to the states, but on account of the nature and variety of the prohibitions and exceptions. In the case of Briscoe v. The Bank of Kentucky, ante 116, 117, I gave my views of the three classes of prohibitions, in the first clause of the tenth section of the first article of the constitution, which in their terms are absolute, operating without any exception, to annul all state power over the prohibited subjects.

The next clause of the same section contains prohibitions of a different kind. "No state shall, without the consent of congress, lay imposts or duties on imports or exports, except what may be absolutely necessary for executing its inspection laws; and the nett proceeds of all duties and imposts, laid by any state on imports or exports, shall be for the use of the treasury of the United States, and all such laws shall be subject to the revision and control of the congress. No state shall, without the consent of congress, lay any duty of tonnage, keep troops or ships of war in time of peace, enter into any agreement or compact with another state or with a foreign power, or engage in war, unless actually invaded, or in such imminent danger as will not admit of delay."

It will be perceived that these prohibitions apply to two distinct classes of cases; in those embraced in the first sentence, it is not only requisite that congress should consent to state laws laying duties and imposts on imports and exports, but they are made subject to its revision and control. In the second class, nothing more is required than the consent of congress to the specified acts or laws of a state, giving no power whatever over them, after such consent has been given. There is also one particular in which compacts and agreements between one state and another, or with a foreign power, stand on a peculiar footing; all the other cases to which the prohibition applies, embrace those subjects on which there is a grant of power to congress to legislate, or which have a bearing on those powers; as to lay duties and imposts, regulate commerce, declare war, &c. Whereas the sole power of congress in relation to such agreements or compacts, is to assent or dissent, which is the only limitation or restriction which the constitution has imposed, provided they are not treaties, alliances, or confederations, which are absolutely prohibited by the first clause of the section, and cannot be validated by any consent of congress.

As the compact between Kentucky and Tennessee does not come within this prohibition, and is one merely of boundary between the two states, the subject matter is not within the jurisdiction of congress, any farther than that it is subject to its consent, which, once given, the constitution is *functus officio* in relation to its controlling power over its terms or validity. The effect of such consent is, that thenceforth the compact has the same force as if it had been made between states who are not confederated, or between the United States and a foreign state, by a treaty of boundary: or as if there had been no restraining provision in the constitution. Its validity does not depend on any recognition or admission in or by the constitution, that states may make such compacts with the consent of congress; the power existed in the states, in the plenitude of their sovereignty, by original inherent right; they imposed a single restraint upon it, but did not make any surrender of their right, or consent to impair it to any greater extent. Like all other powers not granted to the United States, or prohibited to the states by the constitution, it is reserved to them, subject only to such restraints as it imposes, leaving its exercise free and unlimited in all other respects, without any auxiliary by any implied recognition or admission of the existence of the general power, consequent upon the particular limitation.

Herein consists the peculiarity of my reasons for affirming the judgment of the circuit court in this case; fully concurring with the opinion delivered, as to the original power of the states to make compacts of boundary, as well as to the effect of the prohibition, being "a single limitation or restriction" upon the power. Vide 11 Pet. 209. I can give it no other effect by implication, without impairing the great principle on which the reserved powers of the states rest. Though the result, in this case, would be the same, whether the right of making compacts of boundary is original in the states, or exists by the admissions of the constitution, it might have an important bearing on other questions and cases, depending on the same general principle, as to the granting and restraining power which established that instrument. If it is considered as the source of the powers which are reserved to the states, it necessarily admits that its origin is from a power paramount to theirs, and limits them to the exercise of such as it recognises or tacitly admits, by imposing limited restraints. This is a principle which, once conceded, will destroy all harmony between the state and federal governments, by resorting to implication and construction to ascertain their respective powers, instead of adopting the definite rule furnished by the tenth amendment. That refers to the constitution for the ascertainment of the specific powers granted to the United States, or prohibited to the states, as the certain and fixed standard by which to measure them; and then, by express declaration, reserves all other powers to the states, or the people thereof. The grant in the one case, or the prohibition in the other, must therefore be shown, or the given power remains with the state, in its original plenitude, not only independent of any power of the constitution, but paramount to it, as a portion of sovereignty attached to the soil and territory, in its original integrity.

By adhering to this rule, there is found a marked line of separation between the powers of the two governments, the metes and bounds of which are visible; so that the portion of power separated from the state by its cession, can be as easily defined as its cession of a portion of its territory by known boundaries, a reference to which will bring every constitutional question to an unerring test. I have therefore considered those which have arisen in this case, as involving a general principle applicable to all restrictions on states. Though a narrower view would suffice to settle the questions presented upon this compact, or any compact between the states of this Union: yet, when we consider that the power of a state to make an agreement or compact, with *a foreign power*, is put on the same footing as one between two or more states, the necessity of an adherence to principle is the more apparent.

It is a settled principle of this Court, that the boundaries of the United States, as fixed by the treaty of peace in 1783, were the boundaries of the several states, 12 Wh. 524; from which it follows, that on a contest between a state and a foreign power respecting the boundary between them, the state has the same power over the subject matter, as if the contest was with another state. It must then be ascertained, what is the source of that power, its extent by original right, how far it is restricted by the constitution; and when a compact of boundary is made with the consent of congress, whether their legislative power can be exercised over it to any extent. When this is done, it must then be inquired, how far the judicial power has been extended over such compacts by the constitution, and in controversies arising under them, what are judicial questions on which courts can act, as distinguished from political questions, which must be referred to the parties to the compact.

In this view of the subject, I am disposed to take broader ground than is done in the opinion of the Court, and think it necessary to examine whether the powers of a state depend in any degree on the recognition or admission in the constitution, as the construction put upon it by those who framed or adopted it.

This is a sound principle, when applied to grants of power by paramount authority, to a body subordinate to it, which can act only under the authority of the grant; and fairly applies to the powers of the federal government, which is a mere creature of the constitution. Such is the established rule of this Court, where there is an express exception of a particular case, in which any given power shall not be exercised, that it may be exercised in cases not within the exception; otherwise the exception would be useless, and the words of the constitution become unmeaning.

But the principle is radically different, when it is applied to a provision of the constitution, excepting a particular case from the exercise of state legislation, or containing a prohibition that a state law shall not be passed on any given subject, or shall not have the effect of doing what is prohibited; in such cases, there results no implication of power in other cases, for a most obvious reason:—That states do not derive their powers from the constitution, but by their own inherent reserved right can act on all subjects which have not been delegated to the federal government, or prohibited to states. This distinction necessarily arises from the whole language of the constitution and amendments, and is expressly recognised in the most solemn adjudications of this Court. "The government, then, of the United States, can claim no powers which are not granted to it by the constitution; and the powers, actually granted, must be such as are expressly given, or given by necessary implication;" 1 Wh. 326; Hunter v. Martin. "The powers retained by the states, proceed from the people of the several states, and remain, after the adoption of the constitution, what they were before, except so far as they may be abridged by that instrument;" 4 Wh. 193. So where there is an exception to the exercise of the power of congress, as in the first clause of the ninth section of the first article of the constitution. "The migration or importation of such persons as any of the states, now existing, shall think proper to admit, shall not be prohibited by congress prior to the year 1808. The whole object of the exception is to preserve the power to those states which might be disposed to exercise it, and its language seems to convey this idea to the Court unequivocally. It is an exception to the power to regulate commerce, and manifests, clearly, the intention to continue the pre-existing right of the state to admit or exclude for a limited period;" 9 Wh. 206, 7, 216. So when a state is prohibited from imposing duties on imports, except what may be absolutely necessary for executing its inspection laws. "This tax is an exception to the prohibition on the states to lay duties on imports and exports. The exception was made, because the tax would otherwise have been within the prohibition;" 12 Wh. 436. "If it be a rule of interpretation to which all assent, that the exception of a particular thing, from general words, proves, that in the opinion of the lawgiver, the thing excepted would be within the general clause, had the exception not been made, we know no reason why this general rule should not be as applicable to the constitution as other instruments;" 12 Wh. 438. In applying this rule to deeds, the language of this Court is strong and clear. "It is observable that the granting part of this deed begins by excepting, from its operation, all the lots, &c., which are within the exception. The words are, doth grant, &c., except as is hereinafter excepted, all those hereafter mentioned and described lots, &c. In order, therefore, to ascertain what is granted, we must first ascertain what is within the exception; for whatever is included in the exception, is excluded from the grant, according to the maxim laid down in Co. Litt. 47, a. *Si quis rem dat et portem retinet illa pars quam retinet semper cum eo est et semper fuit;"* 6 Pet. 310.

In a subsequent case, at the same term, the same rule and maxim was adopted, and applied to a treaty with a foreign nation. "It became, then, all-important to ascertain what was granted, by what was excepted. The king of Spain was the grantor, the treaty was his deed, the exception was made by him, and its nature and effect depended on his intention, expressed by his words, in reference to the thing granted, and the thing reserved and excepted, in and by the grant;" 6 Pet. 741. As this was a treaty of cession, granting soil and sovereignty, it is, in the latter respect, precisely analogous to the grant of power, by the constitution, to the federal government; so that its exceptions, prohibitions, and reservations, as well as grants, must be interpreted as all other instruments, grants, treaties, and cessions, taking the words as the words of the grantor, referred to the subject matter granted or excepted, &c.

Assuming, on the reasons and authority referred to in the preceding general views, that the constitution is a *grant* made by the *people of the several states,* by their separate ratifications, and that the prohibition on their pre-existing powers are their separate voluntary covenants, restraining the exercise of those which are reserved, over the subjects prohibited, these conclusions necessarily follow:— That a prohibition upon a state, as to any given subject, can, by no just reasoning, enlarge or vary the powers delegated to congress, so as to bring, within its jurisdiction, any matters not within the enumerations of the powers granted. That where the assent of congress is made necessary to validate any law of a state, congress can only assent or dissent thereto or therefrom, but can exercise no legislative power over the subject matter, without some express authority to *revise* and *control* such state law, by regulations of its own. And that in the absence of any power in congress, to do more than simply assent or dissent, the assent is a condition; and when once given to an act of a state, it has the same validity as if no prohibition had been made in the constitution against the exercise of any right of the state, to do the act in virtue of its reserved powers, or any condition in any way imposed, to affect its original inherent sovereignty. The assent of congress is made an exception to the prohibition, and when given, takes the case out of the prohibition, and leaves the power of the state uncontrolled, on the common law rule, that "an exception out of an exception leaves the thing unexcepted;" 4 D. C. D. 290.

"No state shall, without the consent of congress, enter into any *agreement* or *compact* with another state, or a foreign power."

By the terms, then, of this clause, whenever the consent of congress is given to any such agreement or compact, the prohibition is fully satisfied and ceases to operate; the states stand towards each other, and foreign powers, as they did before the adoption of the constitution, so far as this sentence abridged their reserved powers. But as the consent of congress cannot dispense with the prohibition in the first sentence of this section, it becomes, by necessary implication, a proviso or limitation to the second. That such agreement or compact shall not be a *treaty, alliance,* or *confederation; if* it does not come within the constitutional meaning of these terms, the agreement or compact is valid, if made with the consent of congress; if it does, it is void by the first part of the prohibition, which annuls whatever is done in opposition to it.

A reference to the articles of confederation will show the sense in which these terms are used in the constitution, in their bearing on this case.

Article 6. " No state, without the consent of the United States, in congress assembled, shall *send any embassy to,* or *receive any embassy from,* or *enter into any conference, agreement, alliance, or treaty,* with, any king, prince, or state. No two or more states shall enter into any *treaty, confederation,* or *alliance* whatever, between them, without the consent of the United States in congress assembled, *specifying accurately* the *purposes* for which the same is to be entered into, and *how long it shall continue;"* 1 Vol. Laws, 15.

Article 9. " The United States, in congress assembled, shall have the sole and exclusive right and power of *sending and receiving ambassadors,* entering into *treaties* and *alliances,"* &c. " The United States," &c. " shall also be the last resort on appeal, in all disputes and differences, now subsisting, or that may hereafter arise, between two or more states, concerning boundary, jurisdiction, or any cause whatever, which authority shall always be exercised in the manner following," &c., 1 Vol. 16.

" All controversies respecting the private right of soil, claimed under different grants of two or more states, whose jurisdiction as they may respect such lands, and the states which passed such grants, are adjusted, the said grants or either of them being, at the same time, claimed to have originated antecedent to such settlement of jurisdiction, shall, on petition of either party to the congress of the United States, be finally determined as near as may be, in the same manner as is before prescribed for deciding disputes respecting territorial jurisdiction between different states;" 1 Laws, 17.

From these provisions it is most manifest, that the framers of the constitution had the whole subject matter directly before them, and substituted the prohibitions in the tenth section of the first article, for those in the sixth article of confederation, with two important changes.

1. In the discrimination between the prohibition on states, in relation to foreign powers, and between themselves, apparent in the two first sentences of the sixth article of confederation. All *embassies to or from,* and all *conferences or agreements* with foreign powers, are

prohibited by the first sentence; while the second sentence prohibits only *treaties, alliances, and confederations,* between two or more states. In each sentence the consent of congress is made a condition; but in the second there is a further condition, that the *purposes and duration* of the treaty shall be specified, and the words *conference* or *agreement* are omitted, so that it prohibited only such as were treaties, &c., and left the states free to make agreements or compacts, touching their boundaries, without the consent of congress.

Hence we find, that after these articles were ratified, the states made agreements, compacts, or conventions with each other, settling their boundaries, or confirming those previously made, of which the following are instances: Pennsylvania with New Jersey, in 1783; 2 Smith's L. 77; with Virginia in 1784; ib. 261; with New York in 1786, confirmed in 1789; ib. 510; Georgia with South Carolina in 1787; Laws of Georgia, App. 752; none of which refer to any consent of congress.

But in the constitution, agreements and compacts between the states and with foreign powers, are put on the same footing, being prohibited if congress does not consent, and valid if consent is given, and the condition of specifying the purposes and duration thereof, wholly omitted; thus leaving the power of the states subject only to the condition of consent.

2. The constitution gives congress no power to act on the boundaries of states, or on controversies about the titles to lands claimed under grants from different states; its whole jurisdiction consists in the power of assenting or dissenting to an agreement or compact of boundary. The only part of the constitution which grants any power on this subject to the federal government, is in the third article, which declares, "That the judicial power of the United States shall extend, &c., to controversies between two or more states, between citizens of the same state, claiming land under grants of different states," &c. These are the two cases which were defined in the two sentences of the ninth article of confederation, on which congress could act, but which the constitution has authorized no other than the judicial power to take within its cognizance.

From this view of the constitution, in its application to the agreements and compacts between states respecting their boundaries, the results are, to my mind, most clear and satisfactory; that when congress has exercised the only power confided to them over this subject, by consenting to the compact, their whole jurisdiction is completely *functus officio.* Such compacts are, thenceforth, the acts of sovereign states, which, interfering with no power granted to the United States by the constitution, or prohibited by it to the states, must be deemed to be an exercise of their reserved powers, neither given, or in any way abridged by that instrument, and by the thirty-fourth section of the judiciary act, are binding as rules of decision by this and all other courts of the United States, "in suits at common law." The consent of congress has been given to this compact, and the present suit is one at common law; there can be then no doubt, that the compact must be taken as made by competent authority, and as prescribing the rules by which the rights of the contending parties must be ascertained.

This suit does not present for the action of the judicial power, "*a controversy between two or more states,*" or "between citizens of the same state, claiming lands under grants of different states," but a controversy "between citizens of different states," in which the circuit court was bound to decide precisely as the state courts were; 2 Pet. 656; 5 Pet. 401; in whom the title to the premises in dispute is vested, which lie south of Walker's line, and north of latitude 36° 30' north.

It is admitted that the northern charter boundary of North Carolina is 36° 30' of north latitude, which is so declared in the constitution of that state and Tennessee; neither state therefore had any right to lands north of that line; having no original title thereto, any grants from either state would be on that ground merely void, according to the settled doctrine of this Court; 9 Cr. 99; 5 Wh. 303; 11 Wh. 384; 6 Pet. 730. It is clear then, that as the lands in dispute are situated without this boundary, those states had no title which could pass by their grants to the defendants, and that the plaintiff must recover under their title by warrant under Virginia, consummated by a patent from Kentucky, unless the defendants have, in some way, acquired a better title than the state under whom they claim, had by original right. As Virginia had the oldest charter, no part of her territory could be taken from her without her consent, or an express grant by the king, by his prerogative right of disposing of all the vacant lands in the colonies before the revolution, except within the provinces granted to proprietaries. Such grant or consent is not pretended, but the defendants rely on the implied consent of Virginia and Kentucky, in laws recognising Walker's line as the boundary between them and North Carolina and Tennessee, and acts of ownership and possession, long exercised by these states, over lands between that line and 36° 30' north latitude, as giving to them and the grantees under them, a title by prescription. These grounds of defence present very important points for consideration, and in my opinion are of a political, rather than a judicial nature.

The consent of congress to the compact, strips the case of every provision of the constitution which can affect it, saving the grant of the judicial power over "controversies between two or more states," which I take to be suits between states, touching matters in controversy between them. But here there is no controversy between states, nor can a suit be sustained in the circuit court, where a state is a party, this Court alone having original jurisdiction of such cases; this is the ordinary action of ejectment, in which each party rests upon his own title. The plaintiff on a grant from a state, whose original title and jurisdiction confessedly embraced the land in question; the

[Poole et al. v. The Lessee of Fleeger et al.]

defendant under grants from states, who as confessedly had no original right of soil or jurisdiction to the lands they granted; so that
every question affecting the rights of other states, arises collaterally
in a suit between two individuals. The states have adjusted all
matters heretofore in controversy between them, by a solemn compact, the sixth article of which places the grant to the plaintiff on its
original validity under the laws of the states from which it emanated
and was perfected, and within whose acknowledged rightful boundary the lands granted are situated. If this compact is valid, the defendant has no standing in court; if it can be declared invalid in a
collateral action, on the grounds contended for, it follows as a necessary consequence, that any judicial power, state or federal, is competent to annul it, though it is consistent with the constitution of the
state, and ratified according to that of the United States; S. P. 10
Pet. 474. The exigencies of the defendants' case require them to
go to this extent, for the terms of the sixth article are neither ambi-
guous or admit of any construction which can give the defendants
any protection, unless they can show the plaintiffs' " grant to be invalid and of no effect, or that they have paramount and superior
titles to the land covered by such Virginia warrants;" to do which
they must break through the constitution of the states under whose
grants they claim, as well as the compact assented to by congress.
There could be no title *paramount* to a Virginia warrant, duly
taken out, entered, surveyed, and patented, unless that state had in
some way lost her original right of soil and jurisdiction north of latitude 36° 30'; or Kentucky had encroached on the *superior* title of
Tennessee, who had no pretensions to the territory north of that
line by charter, who renounced them in her constitution, and by
solemn compact stipulated expressly that Virginia warrants should
be considered as rightfully entered for this land.

This leaves the defendant but one position to assume, in which he
can invoke the action of the judicial power, which is, that before the
compact was made, the state of Tennessee had for the reasons set
forth in the argument, or on some other ground, became incompetent to make a compact with Kentucky, by which the boundary
between them should be any other than Walker's line. In other
words, that the state was by her grants to the defendants, or those
under whom they claimed, estopped from so settling her boundaries,
as to exclude the lands she had granted; that Virginia and Kentucky
were also estopped from making grants of land within the disputed
territory by their adoption of Walker's line, and because North Carolina and Tennessee had acquired a right by prescription; of consequence, that though these states had granted lands to which they
had no title originally, yet when their title by prescription attached,
their grants became valid, and no compact between Tennessee and
Kentucky could divest them, or impair their legal effect.

So far as the argument rests on the prohibition of the constitution
against impairing the obligation of the contract of grant, it is a suf-

[Poole et al. v. The Lessee of Fleeger et al.]

ficient answer, that : s a grant by a state of land to which she has no title is void, there .s no obligation in the contract, no right of property to impair or violate. Whether the state will refund the purchase money, or grant an equivalent out of what she does own, (as was done by Pennsylvania, as to lands granted to her soldiers which were within the state of New York,) is optional with the state, but such grant cannot estop her from making a compact of boundary, or impose on her any obligation to confirm a void title. The other points raised in the argument, present the question of how far judicial power can be exercised in settling the boundaries of states.

In a controversy between states as to their boundaries, the constitution has given original jurisdiction to this Court; whether it can be exercised by the inherent authority of the Court, or requires an act of congress to prescribe and regulate the mode of its exercise, need not be now examined; but it will be assumed *ex gratia*, that it is by a bill in equity, according to the practice of this Court, and the mode of proceedings in chancery.

In the great case of Penn v. Lord Baltimore, Lord Hardwicke laid it down as an established rule, that the court of chancery had no original jurisdiction of a question relating to the boundaries between the two proprietary provinces of Pennsylvania and Maryland, in any other case than where there was an agreement between the two proprietaries for settling their boundaries. In such case chancery would enforce the agreement by a decree for a specific performance; but without an agreement the question was not one within the jurisdiction of the courts of the kingdom, and was only cognizable in council before the king, as the lord paramount under whom the provinces were held in soccage, by the tenure of fealty and some nominal reservation. "The subordinate proprietors may agree how they may hold their rights between themselves;" "if a settlement of boundaries is fairly made without collusion, the boundaries so made are to be presumed to be the true and ancient limits," made between parties in an adversary interest, each concerned to preserve his own limits, and no other or pecuniary compensation pretended; 1 V. Sr. 447 to 454.

It is then the *agreement*, or *compact*, which alone gives jurisdiction to a court of equity, to decree on the boundaries of provinces owned by proprietaries subordinate to the king; otherwise, it is a political question, to be settled in council, and not a judicial one for any court. It cannot be doubted, that the king in council was competent, by an order of council, to settle any question of disputed boundary between those colonies which had royal governments by their charters, or in those provinces which were under proprietary governments, as he was equally the lord paramount of all. When the colonies and provinces became states by the revolution, they adopted this principle in the article of confederation; by delegating to congress, as the then only power which was paramount over contending states, the power to appoint a tribunal to settle their disputed boundaries. On the same principle, the constitution made congress paramount over the states, by making their agreements and compacts touching their boundaries, subject to its approbation; and by assigning to this Court, the cognizance of "controversies between states," which includes those relating to boundaries, made it so. Thus the line is most distinctly defined, which separates the political and judicial questions which arise touching the boundaries of provinces; where there is an agreement, it is matter of judicial cognizance, to decree what and where the agreed boundary is; where there is none, it was a matter cognizable only before the king in council before the revolution. But even then, proprietaries were competent to settle the boundaries of their respective provinces, by an agreement without the license of the king; and chancery would enforce its execution by a decree *in personam* on the delinquent proprietary, without any reference to the rights of the king, other than adding to the decree a clause of *salvo jure coronæ*; 1 V. Sr. 449, 454; which was more form than substance, as those rights continued, be the boundary where it might.

When the prerogative of the king, and the transcendent powers of parliament devolved on the several states by the revolution, 4 Wh. 651, there could be no paramount power competent to prescribe the boundaries of states, which were sovereign by inherent right, until they should appoint some common arbiter, to whose decree they would submit. By the confederation, congress appointed the tribunal, and by the constitution this Court was authorized to decide these questions; but in both cases, the subject matters referred were "*controversies*," not "*compacts* or *agreements*;" controversies open and existing, which states could not settle; not those which they had settled by solemn compacts, about which there was no difference in construction, and which both states had faithfully executed. If a controversy did exist, either as to the terms or the execution of the compact, or in the absence of a compact, the question of boundary depended on the line of original right, or the joint or separate acts of the contending states, the tribunal thus appointed could settle it as the umpire between them. But it could exercise no authority which exceeded the submission; it could not establish a boundary different from what both states had made, or from that which resulted from their antecedent rights and relations with each other, when they could not adjust them amicably. The umpire must base his award on the compact, if one exists; if not, on the right of the states, as adverse claimants to the same territory; he cannot look through or over the compact, and make an award on grounds which would annul any of its provisions, by giving to either state any thing which she had renounced, or stipulated that it should be held by the other state, its citizens or grantees, "as rightfully granted." No arbiter between nations ever assumed such power; no nation would submit to its exercise; no such power is granted to this Court, and any construction of the constitution which should so torture its plain language, and most manifest intention, would shake the Union to its centre.

If these views are correct, their application to this case is decisive. It comes up on a writ of error from a circuit court, in a suit at common law between citizens of Pennsylvania, claiming under Virginia and Kentucky, and citizens of Tennessee, claiming under that state and North Carolina, in which the circuit court, and the courts of the state, have, by the 11th section of the judiciary act, a concurrent jurisdiction, and on which this Court acts by its appellate power. The plaintiff claims to recover the land in virtue of a title confirmed by the compact. The defendant does not attempt to show that the plaintiff's title is invalid, or of no effect on any construction of the compact, or any doubt as to what or where the agreed boundary is; but rests his whole case on showing that Walker's line had been so definitely established, before the compact, as to annul those provisions which confirm the plaintiff's title. As the effect of so adjudicating on the rights of the parties, would be an assumption by the ordinary judicial power of a state, or an inferior court of the United States, of an authority to force upon two states, a boundary which both disclaim, a power which this Court, as the constitutional arbiter between them, could not exercise, in virtue of its original jurisdiction, it is clear that it cannot so act by appellate power. In deciding suits between individuals claiming lands by grants of different states, between whom there was a compact of boundary, this Court looks only to the compact, its terms and construction, to ascertain the relative rights of the parties, without looking beyond it in order to find out what the boundary ought to have been; Vide Sims' Lessee v. Irvine, 3 Dall. 425, 456, &c.; Lessee of Marlatt v. M'Donald, at the present term, arising under the compact between Pennsylvania and Virginia. Adopting the principles of the common law laid down in Penn v. Baltimore, that where boundaries are doubtful, it is a proper case for an agreement, which being entered into, the parties could not resort back to the original rights between them; 1 V. Sr. 452, and those of the law of nations, laid down in the opinion of the Court in this case, it follows:—That the only questions for our judicial cognizance by appellate power, are those which arise on the construction of the compact, and the locality of the boundary as agreed and declared by a compact ratified by congress, to be decided by the same principles as a question arising on a cession by a state of territory to the United States, of which the case of Handly's Lessee v. Anthony, is an illustration.

That case arose on the cession by Virginia to the United States, of the North Western Territory; one party claimed under Kentucky, the other under the United States, by a grant of land in Indiana; the question of the boundary between these states, came up collaterally, and was decided on the terms and construction of the act of cession and the compact between Virginia and Kentucky; 5 Wh. 375. But in the case of Foster & Elam v. Neilson, where

[Poole et al. v. The Lessee of Fleeger et al.]

the title to the land in dispute turned upon the boundaries of the cession of Louisiana by Spain to France, and by France to the United States, it was otherwise. The land was situated south of lat. 31° N., west of the Perdido, east of the Mississippi, and north of the Iberville; being part of what the United States had long contended was ceded as part of Louisiana, and which Spain insisted was retained by her as part of West Florida; one party claimed by a Spanish grant made after the cession, the other by mere possession, on the ground that the Spanish grant was void.

This Court held, that the question of boundary was one which must be acted on by the political department of the government, and "that it was the province of the Court to conform its decision to the will of the legislature, if that will has been clearly expressed;" 2 Peters, 307. That case presented the precise question on which this turns. "To whom did the country between the Iberville and Perdido rightfully belong, when the title now asserted by the plaintiffs was acquired;" 2 Pet. 300. Had there been a compact by the two governments, declaring that the land belonged to one of them or its grantees, or the boundary not contested, it would have been purely a judicial question between individuals, as to which had the title; but as it depended on a boundary contested by both nations, the Court was not competent to settle it. This principle was affirmed in The United States v. Arredondo, which turned on the construction of the treaty with Spain, ceding the Floridas to the United States; and this Court held, that without an act of congress, submitting the question to the decision of the Court as a judicial one, it would have been a political question, on which congress must act, before it was cognizable by the Court; 6 Pet. 710, 735, 743.

Now as the necessary consequence of over-riding the compact, is to throw the parties back to the original right of the different states, to revive an old controversy between them about their boundaries, and to make the title of the parties depend on the very question which, in the case of Foster & Elam v. Neilson, this Court declared itself incompetent to decide—"To whom did the country between latitude 36° 30' and Walker's line, belong rightfully, when the title, now asserted by the plaintiffs, was acquired," my answer is—That was a political question between the two states, who have settled it by a compact, in virtue of the requisite sanction of the constitution, to the exercise of a power reserved to the states; and that compact declares that the grants of lands in this territory, made in virtue of Virginia warrants, "shall be considered as rightfully entered or granted." And being fully convinced that I am bound to take this compact as the rule for my judgment, the law of this case, the test by which the rights of parties are to be settled, and finding in it abundant authority for affirming the judgment of the circuit court, I should feel, that by any further consideration of the points made in the argument of the plaintiffs in error, it might be inferred that I entertained doubts of the soundness of the principles on which my opinion is founded. These principles are, in my judgment, as unquestionable as they are fundamental, and cannot be impaired without great danger to the harmony, if not the permanency of the Union.

---

## The Mayor and Aldermen of the City of New York v. Miln.

The direct question on which this case turns is, whether a law of New York, directing the commanders of passenger vessels, arriving from foreign ports, to make a report of their numbers, &c., and to give security that they shall not become chargeable to the city as paupers, before they shall be permitted to land, is repugnant to that provision of the constitution of the United States, which gives to congress power "to regulate commerce with foreign nations," &c. In considering this question, I shall not inquire whether this power is exclusive in congress, or may be, to a certain extent, concurrent in the states, but shall confine myself to an inquiry as to its extent and objects. That the regulation of commerce, in all its branches, was exclusively in the several colonies and states, from April, 1776, has been shown in the preceding general view, pages 70, 71; and that it remained so subject to the ninth article of confederation, till the adoption of the constitution; one great object of which was to confer on congress such portion of this power as was necessary for federal purposes, is most apparent from the political history of the country, from the peace of 1782 till 1787; Vide 1 Laws U. S. 28 to 58. It was indispensable to the efficiency of any federal government, that it should have the power of regulating foreign commerce, and between the states, by laws of uniform operation throughout the United States; but it was one of the most delicate subjects which could be touched, on account of the difficulty of imposing restraints upon the extension of the power, to matters not directly appertaining to commercial regulation.

"The idea that the same measure might, according to circumstances, be arranged with different classes of powers, was no novelty to the framers of the constitution. Those illustrious patriots and statesmen had been, many of them, deeply engaged in the discussions which preceded the war of our revolution, and all of them were well read in those discussions. The right to regulate commerce, even by the imposition of duties, was not controverted; but the right to impose a duty, for the purpose of revenue, produced a war, perhaps as important, in its consequences, to the human race, as any the world has ever witnessed;" 9 Wheat. 202; Gibbons v. Ogden.

In the declaration of rights, in 1774, congress expressly admitted the authority of such acts of parliament " as are bona fide restrained to the regulation of our *external* commerce, for the purpose of securing the commercial advantages of the whole empire to the mother country, and the commercial benefits of its respective members; excluding every idea of taxation, internal or external, for raising a revenue on the subject in America, without their consent." But in admitting this right, they asserted the free and exclusive power of " legislation in their several provincial legislatures, in all cases of *taxation and internal polity*, subject only to the negative of their sovereign, as has been heretofore used and accustomed;" Ante, p. 69. Taxation was not the only fear of the colonies, as an incident or means of regulating external commerce; it was the practical consequences of making it the pretext of assuming the power of interfering with their "internal polity," changing their "internal police," the "regulation thereof," " of intermeddling with our provisions for the support of civil government, or the administration of justice;" Vide Journ. Cong. 28, 98, 147, 177.

The states were equally afraid of entrusting their delegates in congress with any powers which should be so extended by implication or construction, of which the instructions of Rhode Island, in May, 1776, are a specimen. " Taking the greatest care to secure to this colony, in the strongest and most perfect manner, its present form and all the powers of government, so far as it relates to *its internal police*, and conduct of our own officers, civil and religious;" 2 Journ. 163. In consenting to a declaration of independence, the convention of Pennsylvania added this proviso: that " the forming the government, and regulating the *internal police* of the colony, be always reserved to the people of the colony;" Ante, p. 71. In the 3d article of confederation, the states guaranty to each other their freedom, &c., and against all attacks on their sovereignty and trade; in the treaty of alliance with France, the latter guaranties to the states their sovereignty "*in matters of commerce*," absolute and unlimited. In the 9th article of confederation, the same feeling is manifest in the restriction on the treaty making power, by reserving the legislative power of the states over commerce with foreign nations. It also appears in the cautious and guarded language of the constitution, in the grant of the power of taxation, and the regulation of commerce, which give them in the most express terms, yet in such as admit of no extension to other subjects of legislation, which are not included in the enumeration of powers. In giving power to congress "to lay and collect taxes, duties, imposts, and excises," the objects are defined; " to pay the debts, and provide for the common defence and general welfare of the United States." This does not interfere with the power of the states to tax for the support of their own government, nor is the exercise of that power by the states, an exercise of any portion of the power that is granted to the United States; 9 Wh. 199. " That the power of taxation is retained by the states, is not abridged by the grant to congress, and may be exercised concurrently, are truths which have never been denied;" 4 Wh. 425. It results from the nature and objects of taxation, that it must be con-

[New York v. Miln.]

current, as the power of raising revenue for the purposes of each government, is equally indispensable, though the extent of taxation is a matter which must depend on their discretion; Ib. 428; 4 Pet. 561, 3. The objects of taxation depend, of course, on those to which the proceeds are to be applied. Congress is limited to those which are defined in the terms of the grant, but the states have no other limitations imposed on them than are found in their constitutions, and such as necessarily result from the powers of congress, which states cannot annul or obstruct by taxation; 4 Wh. 400, &c.; 9 Wh. 816, &c.; 2 Pet. 463. In other respects, the taxing power of congress leads to no collision with the laws of the states; but the power to regulate commerce has been a subject of more difficulty from the time the constitution was framed, owing to the peculiar situation of the country. In other nations, commerce is only of two descriptions, foreign and domestic; in a confederated government, there is necessarily a third; "commerce between the constituent members of the confederacy;" in the United States, there was a fourth kind, which was carried on with the numerous Indian tribes, which occupied a vast portion of the territory. Each description of commerce was in its nature distinct from the other, in the mode of conducting it, the subjects of operation, and its regulation; from its nature, there was only one kind which could be regulated by state laws; that commerce which was confined to its own boundaries, between its own citizens, or between them and the Indians. All objects of uniformity would have been defeated, if any state had been left at liberty to make their own laws, on any of the other subjects of commerce; but the people of the states would never surrender their own control of that portion of their commerce which was purely internal. Hence the grant is confined "to regulate commerce with foreign nations, and among the several states, and with the Indian tribes;" which restricts the term commerce to that which concerns more states than one, and the enumeration of the particular classes to which the power was to be extended, presupposes something to which it does not extend. "The completely internal commerce of a state, then, may be considered as reserved for the state itself;" 9 Wh. 194, 5.

This government is acknowledged by all to be one of enumerated powers. The principle that it can exercise only the powers granted to it, would seem too apparent to have required to be enforced by all those arguments which its enlightened friends, while it was depending before the people, found it necessary to urge. This principle is now universally admitted; 4 Wh. 405. Another principle is equally so. That all powers not granted to the United States, or prohibited to the states, remain as they were before the adoption of the constitution, by the express reservation of the 10th amendment; 1 Wh. 325; 4 Wh. 193; and that an exception presupposes the existence of the power excepted; 12 Wh. 438. Though these principles have been universally adopted, their application presents questions which perpetually arise, as to the extent of the powers which are granted or prohibited, "and will probably continue to arise as long as our system shall exist;" 4 Wh. 405. It would seem that the term commerce, in its ordinary sense, and as defined by this Court, would by this time have become intelligible; it has been held to embrace every species of commercial intercourse, trade, traffic, and navigation; "all foreign commerce," and "all commerce among the states;" 9 Wh. 193; 12 Wh. 446; the regulation of which has been surrendered. But it has been at the same time held, that as to those subjects of legislation "which are not surrendered to the general government," inspection, quarantine, health laws of every description, the internal commerce and police of a state, turnpike roads, ferries, &c., "no direct general power over these objects is granted to congress, consequently they remain subject to state legislation;" 9 Wh. 203; and "ought to remain with the states;" 12 Wh. 443. In the broad definition given in these two cases, "to commerce with foreign nations, and among the several states," it has been applied in the most cautious and guarded language, to three kinds of commerce which are placed under the jurisdiction of congress, expressly excluding the fourth kind, the internal commerce of a state. The Court very properly call these branches of commerce, units; 9 Wh. 194; each a distinct subject matter of regulation, which the states might delegate or reserve. It would contradict every principle laid down by the Court, to contend that a grant of the power "to regulate commerce with foreign nations," would carry with it the power to regulate commerce "among the several states, or with the Indian tribes," either by implication, construction, or as a means of carrying the first power into execution. It would be equally so, to contend that the grant of the three powers could embrace the fourth, which is as distinct from all the others as they are from each other; as units, they cannot be blended, but must remain as distinct as any other powers over other subjects which have not been surrendered by the states. If, then, the power of regulating internal commerce has not been granted to congress, it remains with the states as fully as if the constitution had not been adopted; and every reason which leads to this result, applies with still greater force to the internal polity of a state, over which there is no pretence of any jurisdiction by congress. No subtlety of reasoning, no refinement of construction, or ingenuity of supposition, can make commerce embrace police or pauperism, which would not, by parity of reasoning, include the whole code of state legislation. Quarantine, health, and inspection laws, come much nearer to regulations of commerce, than those which relate to paupers only; if the latter are prohibited by the constitution, the former are certainly so, for they operate directly on the subjects of commerce; the ship, the cargo, crew, and passengers; whereas poor laws operate only on passengers who come within their purview.

On the same principle by which a state may prevent the introduction of infected persons, or goods, and articles dangerous to the persons or property of its citizens, it may exclude paupers who will add to the burdens of taxation, or convicts who will corrupt the morals of the people, threatening them with more evils than gunpowder or disease. The whole subject is necessarily connected with the internal police of a state, no item of which has to any extent been delegated to congress, every branch of which has been excepted from the prohibitions on the states, and is of course included among their reserved powers.

If there is any one case to which the following remark of this Court is peculiarly applicable, it is this: " It does not appear to be a violent construction of the constitution, and is certainly a convenient one, to consider the power of the states as existing over such cases as the laws of the Union may not reach;" 4 Wh. 195. Let this case be tested by this rule, and let it be shown that any clause in the constitution empowers congress to pass a law which can reach the subject of pauperism, or the case of a pauper imported from a foreign nation or another state. They are not articles of merchandise or traffic, imports, or exports. Congress cannot compel the states to receive and maintain them, nor establish a system of poor laws for their benefit or support; and there can be found in no decision of this Court any colour for the proposition that they are in any respect placed under the regulation of the laws of the Union, or that the states have not plenary power over them. The utmost extent to which they have held the power of regulating commerce by congress to operate as a prohibition on states, has been in the cases of Gibbons and Ogden, to the *vessel* in which goods or passengers were transported from one state to another, and in Brown v. Maryland, to the *importation of goods* from foreign ports to the United States.

In the former case, the only question was whether a state law was valid, which prohibited a vessel propelled with steam from navigating the waters of New York, though she had a coasting license; in the latter, the question was whether a state law " could compel an importer of foreign articles to take out a license from the state before he shall be permitted to sell a bale or package so imported." Both laws were held void, on account of their direct repugnance to the constitution and existing laws of congress; the Court holding that they comprehended vessels of all descriptions, however propelled, and whether employed in the transportation of goods or passengers; and that an importer of goods, on which he had paid or secured the duties, could not be prevented from selling them as he pleased, before the packages were broken up. In the New York case, the whole reasoning of the Court was to show, that " a coasting vessel, employed in the transportation of passengers, is as much a portion of the American marine as one employed in the transportation of a cargo;" and they referred to the provisions of the law regulating the coasting trade, to the constitution respecting the migration or importation of certain persons, to the duty acts contain-

24

ing provisions respecting passengers, and the act of 1819, for regulating passenger ships for the same purpose; 9 Wh. 215 to 219, &c. Nothing more was decided, or was intended to be decided, than that the power to regulate commerce, including navigation, comprehended all vessels, and "the language of the laws excluding none, none can be excluded by construction." "The question then, whether the conveyance of passengers be a part of the coasting trade, and whether a vessel can be protected in that occupation, by a coasting license, are not and cannot be raised in this case. The real and sole question seems to be, whether a steam machine in actual use, deprives a vessel of the privilege conferred by a license;" 9 Wh. 219. It is evident, therefore, that there is nothing in the cases then before the Court, in their reasoning or judgment, which can operate unfavourably on the present law; on the contrary, there is much, (in my opinion,) which directly affirms its validity, not merely negatively, but positively, as the necessary result of the principles declared in these and other cases.

Taking it as a settled principle, that those subjects of legislation which are not enumerated in the surrender to the general government, remain subject to state regulation, it follows, that the sovereignty of the states over them, not having been abridged, impaired, or altered by the constitution, is as perfect as if it had not been adopted. Having referred to the cases in which this Court has defined the nature and extent of state sovereignty, "in all cases where its action is not restrained by the constitution," (ante, page 13, 14, 15, 87, 91, 95, 98,) it is unnecessary to make a second quotation from their opinions, the inevitable conclusion from which is, that independently of the grants and prohibitions of the constitution, each state was and is "a single sovereign power," a nation over whom no external power can operate, whose jurisdiction is necessarily exclusive and absolute within its own boundaries, and susceptible of no limitation not imposed by itself, by a grant or cession to the government of the Union. The same conclusion results from the nature of an exception or reservation in a grant; the thing excepted or reserved always is in the grantor, and always was, vide ante, 64, 65; of consequence, the reserved powers of a state remain as stated in the treaty of alliance with France, and the confederation.

The states severally bound themselves to assist each other against all attacks on account of *sovereignty, trade,* or any other pretext whatever. France guarantied to them their liberty, sovereignty, and independence, absolute and unlimited, as well in matters of government as commerce. (Ante, 79, 80.) So the states remain in all respects where the constitution has not abridged their powers; the original jurisdiction of the state adheres to its territory as a portion of sovereignty not yet given away, and subject to the grant of power, the residuary powers of legislation remain in the state. "If the power of regulating trade had not been given to the general government, each state would have yet had the power of regulating the trade within its territory; 3 Wh. 386, 389; and this power yet adheres to it, subject to the grant; the only question then is, to what trade or commerce that grant extends. This Court has held that it does not extend to the internal commerce of a state, to its system of police, to the subjects of inspection, quarantine, health, roads, ferries, &c., which is a direct negation of any power in congress. They have also held that, "consequently, they remain subject to state legislation," which is a direct affirmation that those subjects are within the powers reserved, and not those granted or prohibited. We must then ascertain what is commerce, and what is police, so that when there arises a collision between an act of congress regulating commerce, or imposing a duty on goods, and a state law which prohibits, or subjects the landing of such goods to state regulations, we may know which shall give way to the other; which is supreme and which is subordinate, the law of the Union, or the law of the state. On this subject this Court seems to me to have been very explicit. In Brown v. Maryland they held, that an importer of foreign goods may land them, and hold them free from any state taxation, till he sells them or mixes them with the general property of the state, by breaking up his packages, &c. Up to this point then, the goods remained under the protection of the power to regulate foreign commerce, to the exclusion of any state power to tax them as articles of domestic commerce. This drew a definite line between the powers of the two governments, as to the regulation of what was commerce or trade, and it cannot be questioned that it was the true one; the power of congress was held supreme, and that of the state subordinate. But the conclusion of the Court was very different, when they contemplated a conflict between the laws which authorized the importation and landing of ordinary articles of merchandise, and the police laws of a state, which imposed restrictions on the importation of gunpowder, or articles injurious to the public health. In considering the extent of the prohibition on states against imposing a tax on imports or exports, the Court use this language:

"The power to direct the removal of gunpowder, is a branch of the police power which unquestionably remains, and ought to remain with the states. If the possessor stores it himself out of town, the removal cannot be a duty on imports, because it contributes nothing to the revenue. If he prefers placing it in a public magazine, it is because he stores it there, in his own opinion, more advantageously than elsewhere. We are not sure that this may not be classed among inspection laws. The removal or destruction of infectious or unsound articles, is undoubtedly an exercise of that power, and forms an express exception to the prohibition we are considering. Indeed, the laws of the United States expressly sanction the health laws of a state."

"The principle then, that the importer acquires a right, not only to bring the articles into the country, but to mix them with the common mass of property, does not interfere with the necessary power of taxation, which is acknowledged to reside in the states, to that dangerous extent which is apprehended. It carries the prohibition in the constitution no further, than to prevent the states from doing that which it was the great object of the constitution to prevent;" 12 Wheat. 442, 444. Now, as it is acknowledged that the right of the importer, so secured by the constitution and acts of congress, is subject to the restraints and limitations of the police laws of a state, and the removal and destruction of dangerous, infectious, and unsound articles, is an undoubted exercise of the power of a state to pass inspection laws, the consequence is obvious. The power of congress is, and must be, subordinate to that of the states, whenever commerce reaches that point at which the vessel, the cargo, the crew, or the passengers on board, become subject to the police laws of a state; the importer must submit to inspection, health, and quarantine laws, and can land nothing contrary to their provisions. For such purposes, they are an express exception to the prohibitions on the states against imposing duties on exports and imports, which power might have been exercised by the states, had it not been forbidden; 9 Wh. 200; the restriction presupposes the existence of the power restrained, and the constitution certainly recognises inspection laws as the exercise of a power remaining in the state; ib. 203; 12 Wh. 438, 42. The constitution thus has made such laws an exception to the prohibition. The prohibition was a restriction on the pre-existing power of the state, and being removed as to all police laws and those of inspection, the effect thereof is, by all the principles of this Court, as to exceptions, the same as by the rules of the common law. "An exception out of an exception, leaves the thing unexcepted;" 4 D. C. D. 290. (Ante 65.)

It may, therefore, be taken as an established rule of constitutional law, that whenever any thing which is the subject of foreign commerce, is brought within the jurisdiction of a state, it becomes subject to taxation and regulation by the laws of a state, so far as is necessary for enforcing the inspection and all analogous laws, which are a part of its internal police. And as these laws are passed, in virtue of an original inherent right in the people of each state, to an exclusive and absolute jurisdiction and legislative power, which the constitution has neither granted to the general government, or prohibited to the states, the authority of these laws is supreme, and incapable of any limitation or control by congress. In the emphatic language of this Court, this power " *adheres* to the territory of the state as a portion of sovereignty not yet given away." It is a part of its soil, of both of which the state is tenant in fee, till she makes an alienation.

No opinions could be in more perfect conformity with the spirit and words of the constitution, than those delivered in the two cases. They assert and maintain the power of congress over the three kinds of commerce which are committed to their regulation; extend it to all its ramifications, so as to meet the objects of the grant to their fullest extent, and prevent the states from interposing any obstructions to its legitimate exercise within their jurisdiction. But having done this; having vindicated the supremacy of the laws of the Union over foreign commerce, wherever it exists, and for all the purposes of the constitution; the Court most strictly adhered to that line, which separated the powers of congress from those of the states, and is drawn too plainly to be mistaken, when there is a desire to find it.

By the constitution, "The congress shall have power," " to regulate commerce with foreign nations, and to pass all laws which may be necessary and proper for carrying into execution the foregoing power," " as to regulate commerce," &c.

By inherent original right, as a single sovereign power, each state has the exclusive and absolute power of regulating its internal police, and of passing inspection, health and quarantine laws; and by the constitution, as construed by this Court, may lay any imposts and duties on imports and exports, which may be absolutely necessary for executing its inspection laws, and those which relate to analogous subjects.

Here are two powers in congress, by a grant from states; one to regulate, the other to enforce, execute, or carry its regulations into effect: there are also two powers in a state, one to pass inspection laws, the other to lay duties and imposts on exports and imports, for the purpose of executing such laws. The power of the state is original, that of congress is derivative by the grant of the state; both powers are brought to bear on an article imported, after it has been brought within the state, so that each government has jurisdiction over the article, for different purposes; and there is no constitutional objection to the exercise of the powers of either, by their respective laws. The framers of the constitution foresaw and guarded against the conflict, by first providing against the imposition of taxes, by a state, on the articles of commerce, for the purposes of revenue, and next securing to the states the execution of their inspection laws, by this provision—"No state shall,. without the consent of the congress, lay any imposts or duties on imports or exports, except what may be absolutely necessary for executing its inspection laws; and the nett produce of all duties and imposts laid by any state on imports or exports, shall be for the use of the treasury of the United States; and all such laws shall be subject to the revision and control of the congress."

There can be no plainer or better defined line of power; a state can, by its reserved power, tax imports and exports to execute its inspection laws; it can tax them for no other purpose, without the consent of congress, and if it is even by an inspection law, it is subject to two restrictions; the United States are to receive the nett produce, and congress may revise and control the law. If the inspection law imposes no duty or impost, congress has no power of revision or control over it, and their regulations of commerce must be subject to its provisions; no restraints were imposed on this reserved power in the states, because its exercise would neither defeat nor obstruct any of the powers of congress, and these are the reasons of the Court for the construction of the constitution which they have given.

"It carries the prohibition in the constitution no farther, than to prevent the states from doing that which it was the great object of the constitution to prevent."

This object is clearly pointed out in the clause above quoted, by the nature of the prohibition, with its qualifications; it was not to wholly deny to the states the power of taxing imports or exports, it only imposed, as a condition, the consent of congress. In this respect, it left to the states a greater power over exports than congress had; for, by the ninth section of the first article, they were prohibited from taxing exports, without any qualification, even by the consent of the states; whereas, with the consent of congress, any state can impose such a tax by a law, subject to the conditions prescribed. But if the state law imposes no tax on imports or exports, the prohibition does not touch it, either by requiring the consent of congress, or making the law subject to its revision or control; consequently, an inspection law, which consists merely of regulations as to matters appropriate to such subjects, is no more subject to any control, than any other law relating to police. If the law imposes a tax, it then becomes so far subject to revision; but this power to revise and control extends only to the tax; and as to that, congress cannot go so far as to prevent a state from imposing such as "may be absolutely necessary for executing its inspection laws." Thus far the power of the state is incapable of control; and as this Court has declared that health, police, and quarantine laws, come within the same principle as inspection laws, the same rule must apply to them: the powers of the states over these subjects are absolute, if they impose no tax or duty on imports or exports. If they impose such a tax, the law is valid by the original authority of the state, and if not altered by congress, by its supervisory power, is as binding as it would have been before the constitution, because it has conferred no original jurisdiction over such subjects to congress.

Taken in this view, the object of this prohibition is apparent, and when carefully examined, will be found materially different from the prohibitions in the next sentence, which relate to matters wholly distinct, and are as different in their nature as their object. Among them is a prohibition on the states, against laying a duty on tonnage, without the consent of congress, but it imposes no other condition; so that if this consent is once given, no revision or control over the law exists. This provision would apply to a law regulating pilots, which has never been considered by congress as a regulation of commerce, and has been left to the states, whose laws have been adopted from the beginning of the government: such adoption being the consent required by the constitution.

When the constitution thus gives congress a revising and controlling power over state laws, which impose a tax or duty on imports or exports, or in any case makes their consent necessary to give validity to any law or act of a state; the meaning, object, and intention is, to declare that no other restriction exists. Any case, therefore, which does not come within the prohibition, or in which the prohibition is removed by the performance of the condition, can be no more reached by any act of congress, than if no jurisdiction over it had been granted. The reserved power of the state, when thus disencumbered of all restraints, embraces the case as one appropriate to its exclusive power of regulation, which congress cannot interfere with; though they may tax or regulate the same thing for federal purposes, they cannot impair the power of the states to do either, for such purposes and objects as are recognised or authorized by the constitution. Thus the states, by inspection and analogous laws, may regulate the importation and exportation of the subjects of foreign commerce, so far as is necessary for the execution of such laws; for all other purposes, the power of congress over them is exclusive, until they are mixed with the common mass of the property in a state, by a package sale. Thus, all the objects of the constitution having been effected, the state has the same power over the articles imported, as over those which had never been subject to the regulation of congress.

In applying these plain deductions from the provisions of the constitution, as expounded by this Court, to the present case, it comes within none of the prohibitions. The law in question encroaches on no power of congress, it imposes no tax for any purpose; it is a measure necessary for the protection of the people of a state against taxation, for the support of paupers from abroad, or from other states, which congress have no power to impose by direct assessment, or as a consequence of their power over commerce. The constitutional restraints on state laws, which bear on imports, exports, or tonnage, were intended, and are applicable only to cases where they would injuriously affect the regulations of commerce prescribed by congress; not the execution of inspection or analogous laws, with which the constitution interferes no further, than to prevent them from being perverted to the raising money for the use of the state, and subjecting them to the revision and control of congress. In this view of the respective powers of the general and state governments, they operate without any collision. Commerce is unrestricted by any state laws, which assume the obstruction of navigation by any vessels authorized by law to navigate from state to state, or from foreign ports to those of a state, whether to transport goods or passengers. Imported articles remain undisturbed under the protection of congress, after they are landed, until by a package sale they become incorporated into the common mass of property within a state, subject to its powers of taxation and general jurisdiction. But neither vessels or goods are protected from the operation of those laws and regulations of internal police, over which the states have an acknowledged power, unaffected by any grant or prohibition which impairs its plenitude; the consequence of which is, congress have no jurisdiction of the subject matter, can pass no laws for its regulation, or make any exemption from their provisions.

In any other view, collisions between the laws of the states and congress would be as inevitable as interminable. The powers of a state to execute its inspection laws, is as constitutional as that of congress to carry into execution its regulations of commerce; if congress can exercise police powers as a means of regulating commerce, a state can, by the same parity of reasoning, assume the regulation of commerce with foreign nations, as the means of executing and enforcing its police and inspection laws. There is no warrant in the constitution to authorize congress to encroach upon the reserved rights of the states, by the assumption that it is necessary and proper for carrying their enumerated powers into execution; or to authorize a state, under colour of their reserved powers, or the power of executing its inspection or police regulations, to touch upon the powers granted to congress, or prohibited to the states. Implied or constructive powers of either description, are as wholly unknown to the constitution, as they are utterly incompatible with its spirit and provisions.

"The constitution unavoidably deals in general language;" 1 Wh. 326; "it marks only its great outlines and designates its important objects;" 4 Wh. 407; but these outlines and objects are all enumerated; none can be added or taken away; what is so marked and designated in general terms, comprehends the subject matter in its detail. A grant of legislative power over any given subject, comprehends the whole subject; the *corpus*, the body, and all its constituent parts; so does a prohibition to legislate; yet the framers of the constitution could not have intended to leave it in the power of congress to so extend the details of a granted power, as to embrace any part of the corpus of a reserved power. A power reserved or excepted in general terms, as *internal police*, is reserved as much in detail and in all its ramifications, as the granted power to regulate commerce with foreign nations; the parts or subdivisions of the one, cannot be carried into the other, by any assumed necessity of carrying the given power in one case into execution, which could not be done in the other. Necessary is but another word for discretionary, when there is a desire to assume power: let it once be admitted as a constitutional apology, for the assumption by a state of any portion of a granted power, or by congress of any portion of a reserved power, the same reasoning will authorize the assumption of the entire power. States have the same right of deciding when a necessity exists, and legislating on its assumption, as congress has. The constitution has put them on the same footing in this respect; but its framers have not left their great work subject to be mangled and mutilated by any construction or implication, which depends on discretion, or actual or assumed necessity. Its grants, exceptions, and reservations, are of entire powers, unless there are some expressed qualifications or limitations; if either are extended or contracted by mere implication, there are no limits which can be assigned, and there can be no certainty in any provision in the constitution or its amendments. If one power can be incorporated into and amalgamated with another distinct power, or if substantive and distinct powers which are vested in one legislative body, can be infused by construction into another legislature, as the means of carrying into execution some other power, the consequences are obvious.

Any enumeration or specification of legislative powers is useless, if those which are omitted are inserted on the ground of necessity; this would be supplying the defects of the constitution by assuming the organic powers of conventions of the people in the several states; so it would be, if constructive restrictions on the states were made in cases where none had been imposed, or none resulted from the granted powers which were enumerated. When an implied power or restriction would thus be added as a constructive provision of the constitution, it would have the same force and effect as if it was expressed in words, or was apparent on inspection; as a power which was necessary and proper, it must also be construed to carry with it the proper means of carrying it into effect, by a still farther absorption by congress of specific powers reserved to the states, or by the states of those enumerated in the grant to congress. Let then this principle be once incorporated in the constitution, the federal government becomes one of consolidated powers, or its enumerated powers will be usurped by the states. When the line of power between them is drawn by construction, and substantive powers are used as necessary means to enforce other distinct powers, the powers, the nature, and character of the federal and state governments must necessarily depend on the mere opinions of the constituent members of the tribunal which expounds the constitution from time to time, according to their views of an existing necessity. No case can arise in which the doctrine of construction has been attempted to be carried farther than in this; the law of New York, on which this case turns, has but one object, the prevention of foreign paupers from becoming chargeable on the city or other parts of the state; it is a part of the system of internal police, prescribing laws in relation to paupers. The state asserts as a right of self-protection, the exclusion of foreigners who are attempted to be forced upon them, under the power of the laws for the regulation of commerce, which the defendant contends protects all passengers from foreign countries till they are landed, and puts it out of the power of a state to prevent it. On the same principle, convicts from abroad may be forced into the states without limitation; so of paupers from other states, if once put in a vessel with a coasting license; so that all police regulations on these subjects by states must be held unconstitutional. One of two consequences must follow. There can

25

be no poor laws applicable to foreigners; they must be admitted into the state, and be supported by a tax on its citizens, or congress must take the subject into their own hands, as a means of carrying into execution their power to regulate commerce. Their laws must not be confined to the sea-ports in the states into which foreign paupers are introduced, they must extend to every part of the state to which paupers from other states can be brought; for the power to regulate commerce among the several states is as broad in all respects as to do it with foreign nations. " It has been truly said, that commerce, as the word is used in the constitution, is a unit, every part of which 'is indicated by the term." " If this be the admitted meaning of the word in its application to foreign nations, it must carry the same meaning throughout the sentence, and remain an unit, unless there be some plain intelligible cause which alters it;" 9 Wh. 194. To my mind there can be no such cause for discriminating between an imported and a domestic pauper; one is as much an article of commerce as another, and the same power which can force them into a state from a vessel, can do it from a wagon, and regulate their conveyance on the roads or canals of a state, as well as on its rivers, havens, or arms of the sea. In following out these principles to their consequences, congress may, and to be consistent ought to go further. Poor laws are analogous to health, quarantine, and inspection laws, all being parts of a system of internal police, to prevent the introduction of what is dangerous to the safety or health of the people; and health and quarantine laws extend to the vessel, the cargo, and passengers. Laws excluding convicts and paupers are as necessary to preserve the morals of the people from corruption, and their property from taxation, as any laws of the other description can be; nor do they interfere any further with the regulations of commerce; as laws in *pari materia*, they must stand or fall together, or some arbitrary unintelligible distinction must be made between them, which is neither to be found in the constitution, or decisions of this Court. If the principle on which health and quarantine laws are sustained is applied to this case, the validity of the law in question is not to be doubted; if this principle is not so applied, then it is an unsound one which must be abandoned, whereby the reserved powers of the states over their internal police, must devolve on congress, as an incident to, or the means of regulating " commerce with foreign nations," and " among the several states." There is no middle ground on which health and quarantine laws can be supported, which will not equally support poor laws; nor can poor laws be declared void on any ground that will not prostrate the others; all must be included within, or excepted from the prohibition.

When we recur to the political history of the country from 1774, to the adoption of the constitution, we find the people and the states uniformly opposing any interference with their internal polity, by parliament or congress; it is not a little strange that they should have adopted a constitution which has taken from the states the power of regulating pauperism within their territory. They little thought that in the grant of a power to regulate commerce with foreign nations and among the states, they also granted as a means, the regulation of internal police; they little feared that the powers which were cautiously reserved to themselves by an amendment, could be taken from them by construction, or that any reasoning would prevail by which the grant would be so stretched as to embrace them. We should never have had a federal government if there had been a declaration in its frame that congress could pass poor laws, or interfere to revise or control those passed by the states; or that congress could legislate on any subject of legislation over which no jurisdiction was granted to them, and which was reserved to the states or people in the same plenitude as they held it before they surrendered any portion of their power. The constitution gives no colour for such doctrines, nor can they be infused into it by any just rule of interpretation; the tenth amendment becomes a dead letter if the constitution does not point to the powers which are " delegated to the United States," or " prohibited to the states," and reserve all other powers " to the states respectively or the people." Any enumeration of powers granted, any specific prohibitions on the states, will not only become wholly unmeaning, if new subjects may be brought within their scope, as means of enforcing the given powers, or the prohibitions on the states extended beyond those which are specified, but the implied powers and implied prohibitions must be more illimitable than those which are express.

When the constitution grants a power, it makes exceptions to such as were not intended to be absolute; but from the nature of those which are assumed, they are not included in the enumeration, and cannot be controlled by the exceptions, which apply only to what is granted. When prohibitions are imposed on the states the constitution uses terms which denote their character, whether they are intended to be absolute or qualified. In the first clause of the tenth section of the first article, the prohibitions are positive and absolute; no power can dispense with them: those in the second are qualified; " no state shall, without the consent of congress," is merely a conditional prohibition; when the consent is given, the condition is performed; and the power of the state remains as if no condition had ever been exacted; Vide ante, Poole and Wife v. Fleeger. But if a state lays a tax on imports or exports, then two other conditions are imposed, the produce goes to the United States, and congress may revise and control the state law; congress can, however, do no more than consent or dissent, or revise or control the law of the state, they have no power to pass a distinct law, embracing the same subject in detail. The original primary power is in the state, and subject to the consent and supervision of congress, it admits of no other restriction.

Now, when a law which imposes no tax on imports, exports, or tonnage, is brought within a prohibition by construction, it cannot be validated by the consent of congress; and if they can take jurisdiction of the subject, they cannot be confined to mere revision or control, the power must be co-extensive with their opinion of the necessity of using it, as the means of effecting the object. This seems to me utterly inconsistent with the constitution, which has imposed only a qualified prohibition on the power of states to tax the direct subjects of·foreign commerce, imports and exports. I cannot think that it intended, or can be construed, to impose an unqualified prohibition on a state to prevent the introduction of convicts or paupers, who are entitled to no higher protection than the vessel or goods on board, which are subject to state taxation with the assent of congress, and to health, inspection, and quarantine laws, without their consent. I can discriminate no line of power between the different subjects of internal police, nor find any principle in the constitution, or rule of construing it by this Court, that places any part of a police system within any jurisdiction except that of a state, or which can revise or in any way control its exercise, except as specified. Police regulations are not within any grant of powers to the federal government for federal purposes; congress may make them in the territories, this district, and other places where they have exclusive powers of legislation, but cannot interfere with the police of any part of a state. As a power excepted and reserved by the states, it remains in them in full and unimpaired sovereignty, as absolutely as their soil, which has not been granted to individuals or ceded to the United States; as a right of jurisdiction over the land and waters of a state, it adheres to both so as to be incapable of exercise by any other power, without cession or usurpation. Congress had the same power of exclusive legislation in this district, without a cession from Maryland and Virginia; they have the same power over the sites of forts, arsenals, and navy yards, without a cession from a state, or purchase with its consent, as they have to interfere with its internal police. It is the highest and most sovereign jurisdiction, indispensable to the separate existence of a state; it is a power vested by original inherent right, existing before the constitution, remaining in its plenitude, incapable of any abridgment by any of its provisions. The law in question is confined to matters of police, it affects no regulations of commerce, it impairs no rights of any persons engaged in its pursuits; and while such laws are not extended beyond the legitimate objects of police, there is, in my opinion, no power under the constitution which can impair its force, or by which congress can assume any portion or part of this power under any pretext whatever. By every sound rule of constitutional and common law a power excepted or reserved by a grantor, "always is with him and always was," and whatever is a part of it is the thing reserved, which must remain with the grantor.

If it is doubtful whether the power is granted, prohibited, or reserved, then, by the settled rules and course of this Court, its decision must be in favour of the validity of the state law; 6 Cr. 128; 4 Pet. 625; 12 Wh. 436; ante, 147. That such a course of decision is called for by the highest considerations, no one can doubt; in a complicated system of government like ours, in which the powers of legislation by state and federal government are defined by written constitutions ordained by the same people, the great object to be effected in their exposition, is harmony in their movements. If a plain collision arises, the subordinate law must yield to that which is paramount; but this collision must not be sought by the exercise of ingenuity or refinement of reasoning; it ought to be avoided whenever reason or authority will authorize such a construction of a law, " *ut magis valeat quam pereat.*" While this remains, as it has been, the governing rule of this Court, its opinions will be respected, its judgments will control public opinion, and tend to give perpetuity to the institutions of the country. But if state laws are adjudged void on slight or doubtful grounds, when they are not manifestly repugnant to the constitution, there is great reason to fear that the people or the legislatures of the states, may feel it necessary to provide some additional protection to their reserved powers, remove some of the restrictions on their exercise, and abridge those delegated to congress.

www.ingramcontent.com/pod-product-compliance
Lightning Source LLC
Chambersburg PA
CBHW031547260326
41914CB00002B/303